comeback

comeback

a mother and daughter's journey through hell and back

Claire Fontaine | Mia Fontaine

HARPER PERENNIAL

NEW YORK • LONDON • TORONTO • SYDNEY

A hardcover edition of this book was published in 2006 by HarperCollins Publishers.

Designed by Kris Tobiassen

First paperback edition published 2007

The Library of Congress has catalogued the hardcover edition as follows:

Fontaine, Claire.
    Come back : a mother and daughter's journey through hell and back / Claire and Mia
    Fontaine.—1st ed.
        p.   cm.
    ISBN-13: 978-0-06-079216-9
    ISBN-10: 0-06-079216-7
    1. Mothers and daughters.   2. Runaway teenagers—United States—Biography.
    I. Fontaine, Mia.   II. Title.

    HQ798.F66 2006
    306.874087'4—dc22
    [B]   2005058455

ISBN: 978-0-06-085971-8 (pbk.)
ISBN: 0-06-085971-7 (pbk.)

07 08 09 10 11 WBC/QWF 10 9 8 7 6 5 4 3

For my mother

—CLAIRE

For my Morava sisters and for all lost children, of any age, who are trying to find their way home

—MIA

partone

1.

It is its own religion, this love. Uncontainable, savage, and without end, it is what I feel for my child.

She signs everything she gives me, "Your one and only daughter, Mia," or, "Your One True Child, Mia." Curled into my lap, she reads about the baby bird that fell from the nest and can't find her mommy. Mia squishes into my chest, "I'm glad I came out of your egg, Mudder."

From the moment I take her out into the world, we hear it, every day— *those eyes*! Mia has huge, pale eyes, with pale blue whites, framed by a mass of amber curls. But the brows leap out above them—they're thick, wide, shiny dark swoops. Like the brows of ancient Persian women, painted in profile. "My God, where did she get those eyes—is she adopted?" "Are those brows real?" "She's not yours, is she?" This we hear often; it frightens her. She has no idea we look nothing alike. She thinks we are identical.

My fear that the constant ogling will make her vain seems confirmed when I overhear her, at age four, at the bathroom mirror, murmuring, "Those fabayous eyes! She is so gordzuss." I wince, moving to the door to have a little talk on the importance of inner beauty, then stop, still unseen by her. She's referring to Betty Ann, the doll that was once mine, smiling down at her. She then scowls at the imaginary idiot who'd dare question their relationship, "Of course, she's mine! Mine, all mine!"

I step back in silent mirth, happy that what she takes from those encounters is how much I love her. Before I had Mia, I had never loved deeply, nor felt deeply loved. I was unshared.

Mia is fifteen now, and she and I are in the clouds above Austria. The sun has not risen and she is spread across her seat and mine, asleep. I watch her sleep, as I have done nearly every night of her life. We are on our way to eastern Europe. Not to see castles or rivers or onion-domed villas. Not to see long-lost family. Not even to see each other. I am leaving her there.

Mia will be locked up. She is broken now. Thin, pink scars beribbon her thighs and stomach, her ankles are bruised by a felon's leg shackles, her wrists by handcuffs. She is medically malnourished and made up like a whore. Inside, she is dark and damaged and gone. I don't know when I'll see her again. I don't know if I'll ever see *her* again, my one true child. My desperate hope is that she can be repaired, even badly patched. Mostly, though, I simply hope they can keep her, that she does not escape, as she has done again and again and again and again. Each time to do worse things with worse people, criminals finally. The only thing left would be death, hers or someone else's.

I look down at her, both of us just skin and bone and thin, little breaths. What's left of me staring at what's left of her.

January 30, six months ago to the day, I am absurdly happy. I'm adapting a book I love into a screenplay for an Oscar-winning producer; my husband, Paul (Mia's stepfather), is my best friend, and tomorrow we're putting in a bid to buy our first home. Most of all, I'm Mia's mom. The wise, funny, sparkling Mia who still wants lullabies and butterfly kisses each night. My mother is flying in tomorrow to visit; Mia hasn't seen her Bubbie in two years.

It's a cold, gray day. Mia woke early with a sore throat and fever. I made her favorite soup before I left because I know I'll be working past her bedtime tonight for the first time in her life. The story outline of the screenplay is due tomorrow.

The book I'm adapting is beautifully written but has no dramatic structure, no story to film. Creating one has been my task. It tells of a woman who has lost a child and found herself in another world, foreign and hostile.

Mia calls my office twice to tell me she loves me. There's something in her voice, subtle. It's not her usual, comfort-me sick voice. This voice is tender, as if I am the one in need of comfort. She calls again at nine in the evening to ask for a lullaby. I've sung them to her across the nation. Hushabye, my little darling and I'll see you in the morning.

I have no idea.

I drive home after midnight, feeling such a sense of good fortune. I'm pleased with what I've written, I'm buying a house tomorrow, I have the weekend free to spend with my family. The rain has cleaned LA's dirty sky and the moon and stars are brilliant.

As I walk to my back door, I see that Mia's bedroom window is open, the one by her bed. It's freezing outside. I come in asking Paul about her. He's still at his drafting table. He's a graphic designer and has a deadline tomorrow, too.

"I checked her twenty minutes ago, she's sound asleep."

"With the window open?"

He looks up from his drawing, puzzled. "Of course not."

We walk back to check on her, wondering if she opened it because of her fever. Her room is dark, ice cold, the curtains billow softly at the open window. Paul goes to shut the window as I go to her bed to check her forehead—but she's not there.

"Paul, where's Mia?"

Paul checks her bathroom.

"She's not in here—"

We're suddenly a tornado of fear and sound, hollering Mia!Mia! Mia!, slapping on lights, whipping through rooms and closets— ohmyGodohmyGod, she's gone, someone's taken her—someone's kidnapped my daughter, my baby girl!

The laws of physics and biology change. Air thickens, has substance, like oil. Light is suddenly crystalline, astringent; my pupils screw down. Paul falters and sits on the bed like a dropped marionette. I run to call the police but nothing cooperates. Bowels and knees collapse, lungs shrink, lips move but my tongue is sand, useless. I can't stand up or walk, but suddenly I can float.

From above I see this: a Polaroid by Hieronymus Bosch, a tableau with two figures agonized and contorted, reduced to an animal state.

We see it at the same time, on her desk. In her tiny writing. My call to the police will be different. No one has taken Mia. She has taken herself. I can't breathe.

Dear Mommy and Paul,

    Please read this with an open mind and don't freak out or worry. I need to experience real life . . . People out there are more real, they'll take care of me. I'll be okay, I have a Swiss army knife and mace . . . Please don't feel guilty, I couldn't have asked for better parents . . .

I'm not freaking out, I'm *wild*. I am dancing with shock. I'm terrified. What *people*, what *life*, out *where*?! This is madness, delusion, it's the fever, she's lost her mind! My precious child is alone on the streets with a Swiss army knife and no mind. Back off rapist with HIV, go away drifter with a blunt object, I have a retractable corkscrew and nail file!

I want to holler, pound, smash. I have sprung back to life, my synapses are on fire, my legs feel bionic, my lungs could amplify her name across Los Angeles. I want to fly over the city with infrared Mia-seeking vision.

The police officer in my kitchen stares at the letter, saying, "She doesn't seem angry, she seems to love you very much."

Of course she loves us, we're great parents, she's a great kid, why do you think we're in such shock! I want to grab him and shake him, I'm already doing the math: Time = Distance! Every minute we stand here, she gets farther away!

He looks at her photo and we know what he's thinking. Girl like that on the street. She is striking, exotic. She's a target is what she is.

. . . I'm sick of life, everything seems so pointless . . . I've been pretty screwed up for a while, this will solve stuff.

"Solve what?" the officer asks.

We don't know! She saw a therapist last year, struggled through some issues, but nothing that would even *hint* at anything like this, nothing. She doesn't do drugs, she doesn't disobey us, she's a good kid, a great student.

"Can you get some officers to help you look for her?" Paul asks softly.

Can you be less polite right now, Paul?

"Oh, she's long out of Beverly Hills," the officer says matter-of-factly. I want to vomit.

He asks about her friends. They're great kids, too, no drugs, good families. Wait. There's one. Someone new.

Paul grabs the phone first, then hands it to me. He can't bear to ask the father who answers. I can. I'd said all along. Go check your daughter's bed, I tell him. Check for your weirdo witch girl. It's *wicca*, Mom, Mia said. She found Talia unique; she felt badly for her because she had few friends at school.

When he returns his voice has shrunk. I can hear his wife crying.

By sunrise our friends start arriving. Favors are called in, a DA says use his name or the police won't do anything, they don't look for runaways, LA's crawling with them. Paul throws together full-color missing posters. We argue about putting REWARD on them. Will it make people more alert, make someone call us? What if it gives someone the idea to kidnap her for the reward? The police won't touch the question.

All the while, "This can't be happening, this can't be happening" is hammering inside my skull. I start calling every kid she knows, every parent.

Mia told her best friend Hilary and swore her to secrecy. But she didn't tell her where she was going. Hilary's a mess, inconsolable; she never thought Mia would actually do it. She's furious at Talia. All her friends are. She didn't fit in, with her, like, valley-speak and wicca crap; she corrupted Mia.

One of Mia's classmates is lying, I can tell. I demand to speak to her mother. She calls back in five minutes with the first information I get, a name, some suggestions. I am so grateful. But I hope she beat it out of her.

I begin a succession of cagey phone conversations, maneuvering between threats and cajoling. I've never heard of most of these people. This one says call that one, that one says she may be here, another one says she may be there. Finally, someone says, someone said, they said, she said, something about Venice on Saturday. Maybe.

That's tomorrow. She could be dead by tomorrow.

My friend Karin helps me dress, she practically shoves food in my mouth. It tastes like wood chips. She's a writer as well. She reads through my work, puts it together for me. I can't miss this meeting, can't let the producer know anything, can't lose this job. Because I know instinctively that whatever has happened to Mia is going to cost a lot of money to fix.

Forget the new house—call the broker.

* * *

I drive to the producer's house in the hills overlooking this huge city where Mia is doing godknowswhat. Or being done to—no, no, stop thinking, just knock on the door.

I know this book so intimately, I can respond to questions with some intelligence, even in this wretched state. But my skin is twitching, I feel like packaged panic trying to sit still and say the right things, like, "The character's awareness of the savagery beneath the surface," and, "This society is a dead organism." Instead of things like, "My child is missing, I'm terrified."

"Claire, it's very important the audience knows that she wanted to go."

He actually says this. Of all the art my life could imitate, not this book. Just keep writing, make your head nod.

The sun breaks through and his hillside patio blazes with light-flickered leaves. We've covered everything, I'm dying to dash out of here. But he's feeling relaxed, sociable. He says, "Let's enjoy the sun before it goes away," as he motions me to follow him to the patio. It's something he knows I enjoy and I don't want to do anything to make him suspect anything's wrong.

"Sounds lovely," I hear myself say as my body somehow locomotes itself outside. The sunlight sears my eyes, they're so raw from tears and no sleep. He sinks back into his chaise, I sit bolt upright in mine. He closes his eyes, smiles a Buddha smile. And breathes.

He's meditating.

After fifteen minutes, the time it takes to strangle a girl, to rape a girl, to push her into a dented blue van, he sighs and purrs:

"God, life is beautiful, Claire—isn't it?"

I've driven home from Coldwater Canyon a thousand times, but I can't find my way home. I'm crying and driving from one street to another like a drunken tourist. Nothing is familiar, someone switched worlds on me. The giant red circle I keep passing finally makes the trip from retina to brain and registers. The Zen Grill, we eat there all the time. I've been driving in the same one mile around my home for two hours.

My mother's waiting for me when I get home. She knew immediately something was wrong when she saw our friend waiting for her at the airport instead of Paul. She's a Holocaust survivor, she has a nose for disaster.

She hugs me but doesn't say much. She's in shock but she insists on helping. She wants to help me look, this tired woman who has already suffered the unspeakable.

I take her with me to Hollywood Boulevard. Tonight, the neon, fog, and drizzle have draped this world in a pearlescent, dreamy light, like a fine tulle veil over a hard-favored bride. We cruise slowly, me looking left, her looking right, like johns looking for action through the buzz and glow. My God, all the kids. A city full of baby addicts and hookers. I had never noticed. I never had to.

We go into police stations with my posters and questions. Police here are buried in scum and vice and angry humanity. Ranting crazies in dreadlocks, pouting whores in leather bras and purple boas, seething pimps—I've never seen so many burgundy warm-up suits. I plead with the officers for their help. They look at me like I'm nuts, like take a look around, lady, do I look like I can help you?

Please, I insist, she's not a street kid, she's a good girl, something's snapped, she's a Hopkins Academy student. This last one raises brows. It is a conservative prep school, one whose girls do *not* end up on missing posters.

When I post them, my skin crawls. The looks on the faces of sleazy bastards when they see her picture. A mother could kill them with slender, manicured hands.

I have a gut feeling she's not here. I race home to drop off my mother, then drive to Santa Monica's Third Street Promenade. It's an outdoor mall, blocks long, a favorite haunt of Mia and her friends. A subculture of street kids is always camped there around a fountain. Dirty, loud, addicted, faces full of steel rings, missing teeth. They've no money to buy food, but they buy hair dye, sporting cockscombs and plumages of every color. Some are smart, some drug-fried, some just "not regular" as we West Side moms say, we respectable families who cut this cobbled family a wide berth without interrupting our conversation, like stepping around dog shit. They're just part of the urban landscape, as if the fountain spawned them, as if they'd swum upstream through the sewers and came spouting out while we slept. Now, I realize there are weeping mothers from here to the Atlantic.

I push through the Friday night crowd, looking, looking, looking. I give posters to store owners, pleading have you seen her, can you watch for her? It is so easy to know which ones have children.

I give posters to the street kids, I say the reward is big, no questions asked. One girl says she's seen Mia around, a week ago maybe. She gives me nothing useful, but she cares, they all do, one actually pets me and says don't worry. These kids I've avoided and pitied are pitying me. Many won't live past twenty, twenty-five. A girl with fat, shiny cheeks and a shaved head hugs me and says she wishes her mom was nice like me. She can't be more than thirteen.

Paul and I lie in bed for a couple of hours, not like people resting, like felled trees. We don't hug or cling. One touch and I will fall apart. My heart hasn't stopped beating like a chased rabbit since I saw her empty bed.

I go over the last time I saw her, Thursday morning. She followed me to the door, shivering with fever, hugging me with her little stick arms. She already knew then. She said, I'm glad Bubbie is coming. Why, Mia, so Bubbie can comfort me, provide minor distraction?

> Don't let this disrupt your lives, just think of me like when I was on my student trip in Thailand.

Right, I'll take Bubbie to Las Vegas as planned, see the Cirque du Soleil and pretend you're hailing a tuktuk in Chiang Mai. Mia left before my mother came because she knew Bubbie would see through her charade. She knew her grandmother would have seen what her mother was blind to.

Paul and I have gone through a thousand possible scenarios, explanations. We have no more guesses left. We lie on our backs, whispering into the darkness.

"It's so cold tonight." "She must be soaking wet—her raincoat is here." "Her fever will get worse."

Neither of us says, "Don't worry, we'll find her tomorrow."

Before sunrise, I raise a glass of water to my lips and find that all of my teeth have loosened.

We meet early to strategize, five teams, each taking part of Venice. My brother Henry will search on foot. The Beverly Hills police have sent two off-duty officers on bicycles. By now, I know how rare this is. Even more so because it's raining and cold.

Venice is Hollywood Boulevard on the beach. Every slimeball who made their way west seems to end up there hawking something— string bikinis, incense, drugs, sex. I'd corner every one of them but the rain's cleared the streets. I'd follow them into whatever holes they crawled into, if I knew where they were. I'd follow them and figure out what they want more than they might want my daughter. Shop owners here shrug off my pleas and posters. They earn their livings off kids like Mia.

My girlfriend drives me through the tourist areas. It's hard to see behind Dumpsters or into doorways, the skies are so dark with rain.

"Maybe she's inside somewhere," she says hopefully, trying to cheer me.

"Inside is bad."

I don't speak much, I can't manage whole sentences. My brain's looping images with short captions: defense wounds, dental records, kitchen knife, coroner.

I search the rooms in Venice's skuzzy youth hostel. I walk into a dank room with a picnic table and fake trellis. A scruffy, pony-tailed guy in leather pants sits there smoking. European for sure. I show him my poster, asking if he's seen her. He waves me closer with the cigarette, his eyes narrow as he scrutinizes Mia's face, nodding slightly, as if she looks familiar. My heart starts thumping with hope.

"She's only fifteen, she's sick, we'll pay anything!"

He looks up at me for a moment and then because he thinks I don't understand him, he says in French that she would make a nice little fuck.

Henry has been walking for hours in the rain. He's tall and massive, a bodybuilder with a deep, booming voice. His sheer size and sound are frightening, thank God, because when he turns out of an alley to go to home for a rest, he frightens a grubby guy named Rain when they practically walk into each other.

Rain is walking arm in arm with Mia and Talia.

"Mia!"

It takes but a second for Henry to recover his surprise, Rain to backpedal, and Talia to take off running. Mia is so stunned to see her uncle, she hesitates long enough for him to grab her. He yells for Talia but she's already down the block.

They were walking to the old school bus Rain lives in. He was about to drive the girls to Haight-Ashbury. His bus-house was parked a block beyond Henry's car. If Henry had turned that corner a minute earlier or later, we may never have seen her again.

Henry has taken Mia to his fiancée Margaret's apartment. I call him on the way there, breathless with questions, bright with happiness! He's evasive, just saying that Mia's not, uh, happy. That's okay, we've found her, she's safe, I can fix whatever's wrong, I'm her mother!

Henry and Margaret hug me as soon as I come in, a little too tightly. The look in their eyes makes my stomach sink. His manner on the phone only now kicks in. Mia's in the bedroom. They don't accompany me.

Mia's hunched over on the bed, turned away from the door. Her honey-colored curls are lank and matted, her feet are bare and muddy, she's got on wet clothes I don't recognize.

"Mia?" I say softly as I start to put my arms around her.

She twists away and darts to the bathroom.

"Mia!" I rush after her and jam my body into the doorway to keep it open.

"Leave me alone," she hisses hoarsely.

"Mia, what's wrong, tell me what's going on!"

"I didn't want to be found! Fuck off!"

I am too dumbstruck even to cry. In this speechless moment, I get my first real look at her. She's higher than a kite, she has a strange reek, her creamy olive skin is streaked with grime, her nose and cheeks are bright red. Mia's eyes are big and clear. These eyes are slitty, dark and puffed, they're glassy and bloodshot. But, the animal look in them—what drugs can do this? I can't reconcile who I'm seeing with my daughter. It's like she spent the night in Frankenstein's lab next to a savage little beast and someone hit the switch.

I didn't think anything could ever be worse than seeing her empty bed. I was wrong—this is. And a cold fear is setting in that after this, there might be another worse, that this worse might just be the frost on the grass before winter falls.

* * *

I drive to the Venice police station with Mia to report her found. Paul's waiting in the parking lot. He looks so small and hapless against the lead gray ocean behind him.

Mia gets out of the car sullen and nasty, sidestepping the stepfather she adores. I stare at the ground to avoid seeing the look on his face when he sees her. He says Talia's father was upset that Henry only caught Mia. I feel sick for her parents, though there was nothing Henry could have done, unless he let go of Mia. He had to choose.

Officer Carol handles our case, a no-nonsense blonde who is harsh with Mia. Mia denies knowing anything about Talia's whereabouts. She looks sharply at Mia.

"You don't know how lucky you are, young lady. Very few parents look for their kids and even fewer ever find them."

She takes me aside to show me 8 × 10 glossies she shows runaways to scare them. Crime scene shots of girls who weren't so lucky, photos the tourist bureau doesn't show. I've seen enough of them doing research to know those images never leave you. Facedown, twisted-legged girls behind garages with their panties in their mouths, rat-eaten girls in Dumpsters, charred girls in bathtubs, in the pugilist position, as if they stood a chance. Because I still think Mia's too sensitive, that this won't happen again, I tell her not to show her.

Paul stays to help Talia's father look for her while I drive Mia home. I realize how stupid it was to drive alone with her. She could jump out at any stop. I'm careful and sweet, talking about little things, something the cat did, the hat Bubbie knitted her. I don't know what else to say, I'm so scared and bewildered.

Mia just stares out the window, then suddenly demands to use a pay phone on the way home. Because I'm afraid to make her mad, I find one and obey her command to stand far away. But not so far I can't catch her if she bolts. Whoever she calls isn't there, thank God, because I don't want any Venetians showing up outside her bedroom window. For all I know she was trying to call Rain's brother, Thunder, to come spring her.

I'm so wasted and shaky, I can hardly pull the car in straight. I rake it along the carport wall. Getting Mia in the back door proves just as difficult, because whatever drugs she took in Venice must be time-release. She suddenly switches from surly and mean to grinning and unsteady. I help her stumble to her bedroom, drop her backpack, sit with her on the bed.

"I like sleeping on the floor," she rasps and slides to the carpet.

This is creepy, but I just stroke her hair and say cheerfully, "Okay, I'll make you a bed there."

"No, it's cool just like this. It's just for tonight, anyway."

"What? Mia, you're home, you live here, you're not going anywhere."

She lets out a squeak of a laugh, "Yes, I am! I belong out there, Mom. They're waiting for me."

"Out where, Mia, what are you talking about, who's waiting?"

She tucks her knees up under her chin and looks up at me. I cup her little face in my hands. And then her face goes slack, her milky-pink, swimmy eyes pop open wide and she looks right through me as if she's just been possessed.

"Mia?"

She starts a trance-like croaking, "I have to go, I have to go, I have to go . . ."

This isn't Mia, this is science fiction, this is a pod. I'm in Kafka's *Metamorphosis*, gaping at a giant roach-Mia chanting, "I have to go, have to go, have to go . . ."

I grab her and shake her, yelling at my child who is here and not here. I sink to the floor in front of her, crying like a broken animal, howling like only a mother can howl.

"Don't cry, Mommy, don't cry," she coos back in her ragged voice, wrapping herself around me. "It's okay, Mommy, don't cry."

But she doesn't say, "Don't cry, Mommy, I won't leave again." She comforts me with, "Don't cry, Mommy, I'll be okay out there, they'll take care of me."

Winter is burying us already.

Paul comes home to find Mia asleep on the floor curled around me. He lifts her into her bed. I don't tell him what happened, I don't have the words yet to describe it. We drag ourselves to the living room, two dazed parents who have no idea what they're fighting or how to fight it. But we better learn fast, because we suspect the battle's just beginning.

First, we shove the piano in front of the front door. Then, Paul starts screwing her bedroom windows shut while I get her backpack and empty it on the dining table. I scour every corner of it, I even smell the lint. I'm treasure hunting for Mia, for clues to whatever is "out there."

I find three packs of cold medicine capsules and a journal, one I haven't seen before. It's obvious why she kept it hidden. It seems our bouncy, bright Mia, the A student who never said a disrespectful word to us, who laughed and cuddled with us, has led a double life for nearly a year. She kept another Mia hidden from us, one several shades darker.

Paul sits beside me as we read poems and entries about whips and chains, broken glass, gutters and blow jobs. Phone numbers of homeless shelters, of people we've never heard of. Are these the people who will "take care of her"? Out there where she has to go, has to go, has to go?

There are quotes by street kids doing revolting things with revolting people. I remember a library book she brought home last year for her photography class. A photo essay of LA and San Francisco runaways and addicts, *Raised by Wolves*, by Larry Clark. Apparently, she thought it was a guide book.

I cannot comprehend a Mia who wanted this. We close the journal. We'll have to read the rest in small doses. The pages themselves feel slimy, repulsive. How could she possibly hide this so well?

"She's either very smart or very sick," Paul says.

The word we've been avoiding. Sick. Like the TV commercial—"This is your brain on drugs." She's scrambled her eggs permanently. Or maybe the chicken came first—she felt "pretty screwed up" first, then took drugs to feel better.

Enough shock and horror, Claire, *think*, think of what to do. Okay, right, yes. Detox. Get the drugs out of her system. Get us all into counseling. Take her on a trip, make new house rules, have family meetings. Of course, she'll come to her senses, we're a resilient bunch! Who knows, this may even lead to better communication!

But. That journal. What if we detox her and when she comes down she isn't the same girl that went up? What if she's the journal Mia? What if Mr. Hyde never returns home to become Dr. Jekyll again?

Ooowww. Too bright. And too early. I stuff my face under my pillow to block out the sun. Now I can't breathe. Fuuck! I go to get up but I feel like my muscles have turned to gum. I pull the covers back over my head. The sun lights up the pattern on the blanket and it's actually kinda pretty. Those big blue flowers, they're somehow comforting. And, somehow, strangely familiar. I'm awake in an instant.

Shit! I can't be back here. How did this happen?! I'm not supposed to be here!

I make a mad dash across my bed to the window. I shove it up but it won't go higher than four inches. This is impossible! I crawled out this same window four days ago. Then I see the screws. Motherfuckers!

Wait! There's a screwdriver in the utility room. I creep down the hallway, skipping the creakier floorboards. I slip into the utility room, slide out the drawer, lift out the screwdriver and tiptoe back to my room.

I hear Mia creeping around and jump up, "Paul, she's gone for the screwdriver!"

But Paul's not the least alarmed. I stop, suddenly realizing—

"You hid the Phillips."

He nods. I know why he did it, but it seems cruel to trick her. I don't want to do anything to anger her. Too late.

"Mooooommmmmmmmmm!!" comes Mia screaming down the hallway.

We run to block the back door, she stops us in the kitchen, clutching the screwdriver.

"You can't keep me here! Let me out of here!"

"Mia, calm down, we'll—," Paul starts to say.

"No! I'm not staying here," she spits, "I hate you!"

I touch her arm softly to calm her, which only enrages her.

She raises the screwdriver over me. "You better let me go!"

Paul grabs her arms and she fights him like a biker chick. He wrestles her to the floor, uncurls her fingers from the screwdriver. She wriggles and yells as he yanks the screwdriver out of reach and stands up quickly.

Mia lies on her back with Paul standing over her. They stare at each other and time seems to stop. For an eerie moment, we're all frozen in place.

Then Mia's face crumples as she starts to cry.

"Eat, Mia, eat. Just one little slice of pear," she says. I have no appetite. I just want to curl up into nothingness.

"Come on, honey, just one piece. Mia, you're probably just depressed, that's all. We'll pull through this."

I stare at her through a fog. "We?" **I** *was about to fix everything, not we. All her so-called help did was ruin everything. She still doesn't get it, doesn't realize I'm beyond her now.*

I walk behind Paul and Mia to the car. We've gotten her a bed in a hospital psych unit for teenagers with problems. Somewhere she can't escape until she's better, whatever "better" means now.

I walk behind them as I did a few days ago, on the way to school. I held her lunch bag. Her uniform hung crooked from the way she rolled the waistband like all the girls did. She took Paul's hand, swinging it as she joked with him. Now, Paul's holding her hand to make sure she doesn't get away.

I remember the first time Mia took Paul's hand, when she was four. I suddenly stop, because I remember something else. Another memory surfaces from the deep end of our history.

I have borne witness to another metamorphosis just as surreal as Mia's. In another lifetime, one I thought was long behind us.

2.

Chicago, early 1980s. I reached twenty utterly unprepared for life in general and life in the late seventies in particular. As a thick-lensed nerd, my character was shaped by the Brontés, Carolyn Keene, John Wayne, and the Girl Scout Handbook. When I looked up from my beloved books, I never got over the shock.

I expected a world where good guys won, integrity was considered a virtue, and a good heart and a fine mind would take a woman far. What I got was the era of "the evil that lurked within," of the flawed protagonist, of Transformer action figure heroes that concealed monsters—just a twist of the appendages! Nancy Drew had left the building. There was no right or wrong, no black or white, because the gray area was where the hip hung out. Sans moi, because I never got it—"it" being whatever got you "in," a condition involving drugs, sex, and a sangfroid I didn't possess.

On the rocky climb to adulthood, between a sash full of Scout badges and glitter rock, I could find no purchase. When I hit twenty, I had so little sense of who I was that I was often caught off guard by my reflection in a mirror. I'd stop and look at the girl closely, hoping the image would reveal the essence. I was afraid that there just wasn't a lot of *me* to me.

Oh, I knew it was out there somewhere, the rest of me, and it walked and talked and smelled like starched shirts and shaving cream. He was going to tell me who I really was. His love would be as rain on a seedling; he would water me and, lo, I would blossom. I wanted to be loved like Elizabeth Browning, I wanted Heathcliff, Dr. Zhivago, Atticus Finch, such a mensch. If my inner child was a seventh-grader who would never be one of The Cool, my outer adult would find happiness in being one of A Pair. And once I was, My Real Life would finally begin.

* * *

The man who would become Mia's father was soft-spoken, cultured. Nick P. was a successful city planner, about six-foot-four, lanky and pale, with soft brown eyes and thick, silky blond hair that fell over his forehead. The real clincher was that there was mystery to him. Sudden black moods, silences for no reason. It was so Rochester. He was *cool*. I felt like Cinderella at the ball, I was full of happiness and hope. My Real Life was about to begin.

I don't know which surprised me more—that he tended his lush garden *au naturel* or that it was full of marijuana. We had just gotten engaged after a year of dating and I'd moved into his place near downtown Chicago. I guess that explained the sudden mood shifts. He was relieved I finally knew. He'd been smoking pot, he said, twice a day for seven years.

"Twice a day? For seven YEARS?" I managed, shocked you could do that and still live. I knew next to nothing about drugs. I didn't even drink.

"No wonder you're so moody. And what's with the naked thing?"

He rolled his eyes at me as if to say what a dummy, what a nerd. "A, you're assuming I'd be different if I didn't smoke it, and B, don't be such a prude. Europeans don't have a problem with it, the body is just part of nature."

Thus began his pattern of justifying anything he did by making me the prude, the unsophisticated. He intimidated me with the threat of being *uncool*, a social death sentence.

I was afraid of losing him, but more afraid, however, of being arrested. I told him I wouldn't marry a drug user and he promised he'd stop. It didn't occur to me to question his integrity. Worse, it didn't occur to me to question why someone had to anesthetize himself twice a day in the first place.

I met his family shortly before we married. They were worldly, well-connected, Mayflower stock, and Nick was their Golden Child. But, there was a tension and weirdness I simply couldn't make sense of. His sister flaunted promiscuity like a virtue. I watched her sit in her dad's lap by the pool. In a bikini. His father began his first conversation with me with a joke about a frog performing oral sex on a woman.

Nick seemed to age backward around his father, to shrink. His mom was nice if a bit odd. She was constantly trying to cheer up what was un-questionably the unhappiest clan I'd ever met. A family full of sarcasm and resentment.

On the one hand, I found them strangely fascinating—jaded, complex—there was almost a glamour to their misery. On the other hand, when I was with them, it felt like one of those *Highlights* magazine drawings with the caption, "What's wrong with this picture?" Only I couldn't see what it was because, now, I was *in* the picture.

It will be obvious later that what was most wrong with the image, the vulture in the teacup, was my unconscious capacity for denial. I would come to have an outright talent for it. Of all that would go horribly wrong with our marriage, this of all things would buy me a first-class ticket to hell. Each turning away, each bright smile and reconfigured reality an-other coin for the conductor. And I'd swear the view was beautiful all the way down.

The first time his mother visited after we were married, she forgot her robe. Declining one of mine, she breezed into Nick's closet and emerged wearing one of his crisp white dress shirts over only her underclothes. Like a young woman who's just spent the night at her boyfriend's. She asked, "How do I look?" My new-daughter-in-law mouth said "Fine," but my brain was zipping through its image inventory of American family life, to find a match, to make this normal.

Nick had been cold to her since she arrived. She said she thought his foul temper was because he wasn't ready for marriage. Once she left, he told me it was because she rubbed his hand the whole way from the air-port. You mean she held it? I asked.

"No, she stroked it for a really long time. It felt sexual. It really pissed me off."

I had no idea what to make of this, so I stored it in the "How the grown-up world works" file, thought of it as one more lesson in sophisti-cation. Though I did mention it to my mother.

"I think his mother has funny ideas about that kind of thing," she said.

"What do you mean funny—funny how?"

"Well, she said something very weird on the phone to me last sum-mer. We were talking about the Old Testament and incest came up, and she said, 'You know, when you think about it, what could be more beautiful than a father making love to his daughter?' I was floored. Maybe she thinks it's beautiful to rub her son's hand, too."

Okay, so his mom's weird, I thought, they're all weird. He didn't get to pick his family.

Nick was never the same after that visit. A bitterness arose in him; the family sarcasm emerged like an activated gene. I didn't make the connection, see the significance. I brushed it aside like I would so many other things in the next few years, odd isolated things I shrugged off, cast aside like unmatched beads. Ones that didn't match the shiny bauble I was making called My New Happy Family.

One day I would look down at them, all those beads, I would look carefully and notice that they *did* match, they *did* fit together. Perfectly. They made a necklace that would one day hang us both, Mia and me.

"I don't think he's ready to be a father, do you?"

I'd just told his mother I was pregnant. I'd gotten used to such comments, because whatever the family's game plan for Nick's life was, I didn't seem to be following it.

I'd never been so excited in my life. I loved everything about pregnancy, about children. I didn't understand the fear pregnant women had of the baby having something wrong. I wasn't afraid of anything! And I was so sure it was a she that I hardly bothered with boys' names. I read the latest research on what made babies happy and curious, I made colorful crib mobiles, sewed ruffle-edged flannel sleepers. I crawled on the floor to see what her view would be like and decorated a mini-world down at baseboard level for her.

I loved when she got hiccups in my belly, when she rolled around and kicked. As big as I grew, I never waddled, I was gliding, flying. I was running toward her arrival with my arms open, laughing. When I caught my reflection in the mirror then, I was smiling.

Mia's birth was unbearable. I'd refused any medication so it wouldn't contaminate my milk. The pain was so severe that when the nurses bore down to squeeze out the afterbirth, I bit one of them to make her stop. I was yelping like a speared beast when suddenly in front of me appeared a tiny, bewildered little face. The nurses stopped torturing me long enough to let me hold her.

I cooed and laughed. She was bobbing her little head in search of me. Then she clamped down on my breast and it was like lightning.

"Owwww, why is she biting, she's not supposed to have teeth! Owww! This is killing me! I'm scaring her!" She hung on for life, would simply not let go.

"Bet you wish you had those meds, now, honey," purred the nurse I had bitten. She pried Mia away from me and Mia opened her little mouth and started to wail, too. We were upsetting the whole ward with our hollering. We were operatic, the two of us.

We met each other crying, my baby girl and I.

Mia came home with me to cry some more. Sleep, nurse, shriek. She pulled her skinny little legs up and cried and cried and cried. Nothing I did helped.

Then one gorgeous, sunny morning at three weeks, she pulled away from my breast and smiled big enough to crinkle her eyes, waving her little arms as she grinned up at me.

It was the first time I thought she loved me. I held her before me and we stayed like that for a long time, staring and smiling ourselves into each other.

That moment was the beginning of the forgetting. Of no longer knowing where I ended and she began.

Nick's mother, as it turned out, was right. He wasn't ready for fatherhood. He was coming unglued. Screwing up at work, crying when reprimanded for it. Saying hateful things about his family but drawn to them more and more. He would be foul one moment and giggling the next. I never knew which husband was coming home from work.

He began sleeping all the time and eating obscene amounts. I watched him eat an entire head of cauliflower, raw, holding it in his hand like an apple. After dinner. He works so hard, I thought, no wonder he's so hungry. When he ate an entire sheet cake my mother made for a party, with his fingers, she finally blurted, "Wake up, Claire, nobody eats or sleeps that much unless they're on drugs."

So, there it was. Again. Only this time he made no promises; he didn't even try to hide it. I had no choice but to acknowledge that whatever had made Nick need drugs every day when I first met him hadn't gone away. The haunted, hungry part of him had never stopped hungering, he just grew better at hiding it. My Jekyll of a husband had been using everything at his disposal, including his considerable intellect, to keep his Hyde stoppered like a genie. Until the very thing that once shushed and petted it—seven years, twice a day—had now bit down hard and set him howling into our lives.

The next two years of my life were a dichotomy between the sheer joy of mothering Mia and the sheer madness of marriage to a man who sucked up more pot than air, along with who knows what else. But he wasn't just a drug addict—he was a spoiled, narcissistic one. Nothing he ever did was wrong.

I had to argue with a grown man that you didn't take your baby up on the roof with you to fix it while your wife was at the market (the neighbor almost called the police). That you didn't put a baby to sleep beside a vaporizer (she got third-degree burns). That you didn't walk around a toddling daughter naked, whether or not the Europeans did, or the Japanese, the Finns—he was running out of happy nations.

But, *no*, he'd say shrilly, drugs have nothing to do with my behavior! It's you, you're going to make her scared of heights, she loves helping Daddy! Who asked you to turn the vaporizer on before you went to bed! You're going to teach her to be ashamed of her body! Sometimes, he'd use his soft, scholarly voice, explaining, rationalizing, trying in all sincerity to get me *to see*.

The only thing more pathetic than a druggie arguing the benefits of drugs is someone trying to convince them otherwise. It's like arguing with the Mad Hatter, except you're married to him.

Had I known, I would have spent my youth reading Thomas de Quincy and William Burroughs. As it was, I was armed only with self-blame, with *I'm sorry*, with *Calm down, I'm worried*, as if *I* had to apologize for his behavior. It's understandable, I told myself, he's worked to death. If I could just get him to stop the drugs, if I could just not let it bother me, or just let him get high at home. If-I-could-just had become the theme song of my marriage. The refrain of the Good Wife.

* * *

When I caught him getting high while driving Mia, I threatened to call his boss and tell him where the petty cash was going. He shot off the sofa and grabbed my purse. He screamed as he whipped everything in it across two rooms like a major league pitcher. He shrieked as he embedded lipstick in my cheerful yellow drywall, he can't take it! he's going to kill me! kill me!

Mia started to cry. I ran to her crib as he stormed to his car and sped away. He stayed gone for three days. Came back with no explanation and I didn't ask, didn't care. I had three whole days with no screaming, no pot stink, no flying objects.

If Mia was registering any of it, even that last screaming episode, you could hardly tell. She just wanted me to carry her through the world telling her the name of everything, telling her stories. She wanted me to make the stoplights change, make frozen bananas, sandcastles, and seashell queens named Mia. I called her my little monkey, the nickname I had as a little girl.

The sandy beach on Lake Michigan was our favorite place. All that splashy brightness. She loved to run across the sand, squealing and laughing as she looked back to make sure I was chasing her. I'd pretend I was running as fast as I could and still couldn't catch her and she'd just giggle like mad and take off again. Running was only fun if I chased her.

Nothing ruined what it felt like to mother Mia, nothing sullied it. Every time I looked at Mia, I felt a jumping happiness in my chest that no fear or crazy husband could dim.

"I'll kill you! I'll kill us both!" Nick screamed as he jerked the wheel left and sent the car flying across the opposite lanes. We'd just left marriage counseling. It wasn't his cup of tea.

"I hate you, bitch! I hate this marriage!" He slammed the car up a curb and into an empty lot. It was like the wide prairie before us. He hit the gas.

I heard a hoarse, "Stop, please stop," as if some other woman were saying it. Terror had disembodied my voice from me, made me my own ventriloquist.

"I want you both gone! Take the baby and go!" He spun the car around, floored it, and we screeched back to the street, barely missing two cars.

And then the car sputtered. And died.

Oh, sweet miracle, we'd run out of gas. I gaped in amazement as the car rolled toward miracle number two—a gas station right in front of us.

One of lunacy's virtues being instant mood change, Nick simply sighed and coasted to self-service as if nothing had happened. The second he screwed the gas cap on, I shot into the driver's seat, started the car, and left him there.

The next day, he strolled in as serene as a Buddha, saying in his soft, stoned voice that we don't need therapy anymore, "Therapy's the problem, it just stirs things up."

Therapy's the problem? Stirs things up? That he could say that right after trying to kill me was stupefying. I, on the other hand, had sat up all night realizing that it wasn't the fighting, the "stirring up," that was the problem. It was the things being stirred up, the very things themselves. Like Alice in Wonderland, I'd been away from the real world so long, the one inhabited by sane people, that I'd forgotten that one shouldn't *have* to argue about things like taking babies on roofs, naked gardening, or parenting on drugs. I'd fallen down a rabbit hole where miserable, intimidating creatures argued the ridiculous, the dangerous, and the perverse.

It was time to crawl out of the hole, which was going to take some doing. Like learning to bite my tongue at his screwy ideas. To smile and be agreeable. Because I wasn't going to be as clueless getting out of this mess as going in. I would bide my time while I got a degree so I could support Mia. Then I'd take her and get out. Before he did kill me.

"See," he said of the return of his sweet, accommodating wife, "what did I tell you? Therapy, schmerapy."

Now that Mia spoke and walked, he spent more time playing with her. He'd giggle on the floor with her, pulling on a curly blonde wig from her dress-up box. I'll wish later I'd never bought that wig. For years, she'd have nightmares of him wearing it.

While Nick was at work, I'd scour college catalogs at the library. Then I'd go home and pretend. This retreat from the battlefield was a relief for both of us. I was worn out from fighting him. He must have been worn out from fighting him, too. Because he mistook my new acquiescence for approval, permission. For freedom to be who he really was, at last.

Which would end up being so much worse.

3.

"What's wrong with relaxing in my own home, Claire? There's no one here but us." One of *us* was an already walking, talking little girl. He'd started going around naked again. "You're going to teach her to be ashamed of her body," he clucked. He'd wait a week or two, then do it again.

One morning, I found him sitting in bed with her, reading the comics. He always slept nude, almost always woke up with an erection. I picked her up and walked out as I threw him his underwear.

"What's your problem, she doesn't know what it is."

He reminded me that it was a natural thing, a normal part of life. Nothing is normal about you, I wanted to say.

"I can't believe you did that without asking me first!" Nick yelled as he walked in the door from work.

"Asking you what?" I had no idea what he was talking about. Mia was helping me set the table. She grabbed onto my legs, scared.

"I hate bangs on women! I like to see her whole face!"

The Hatter was back. Later, when he'd calmed down, he decided to expound in earnest his theories on raising happy children. This should be interesting, I thought. He announced that henceforth Mia herself would decide on her haircut.

"You'd let a two-year-old make that choice? What if she wants to shave it off?"

"Of course," he said, "it's her body."

"What if she wants to shave her legs and dye her hair when she's three?"

"Of course, once she's able," he replied, encouraged by my calm responses.

"So, it's sheer ability that sets a child's limits, not parental guidance?"

He decided to reveal at last how he saw Mia's unfolding future: "Children should be able to do whatever adults do once they're able to."

The possibilities chilled me. "Really? A ten-year-old has the *literal* ability to drink or smoke marijuana or have sex, that's okay?"

"Why not? How will they learn about themselves, about life? And why shouldn't they feel the pleasure of their God-given bodies? Other cultures allow it."

Other cultures allow cannibalism. I was recalculating our departure date with each answer.

"Sex isn't something children should be protected from, Claire. It's like protecting them from good food or music."

I practically sprang from my chair and strode off to clean, cook, anything to get away from his satisfied face, his folded hands.

Because the air in my house felt deadly. From the stink of animal breath. There is a wolf outside our door, I thought. Watching with glittering eyes and waiting. Till Mia was older, to do what wolves do with girls, ravish them. After they've lost their bowlegged, baby-fat bodies and grown slim hips and tender breasts.

Forget the degree, get any job and then a divorce. I have time for that, I thought, she's not yet three, she's still safe. What on earth could anyone even *do* with a toddler's squirmy little piglet body? An absurdity, an impossibility.

Sexual abuse wasn't in the media then. I'd never even heard the word pedophile.

Or I'd have remembered that wolves liked little pigs.

It was the tears.

It was Sunday morning and Mia was in the laundry basket, handing me things to fold. He was reading the Sunday paper. On the front page was a story of the children who were molested in a home care center. He was reading what the kids said the owners did to them after their parents dropped them off. When the owners were done, they would bring in the bird. Sometimes a cat. Mostly birds. Their necks were easier to twist.

At night, in their beds at home, I thought it was not between their legs nor their soft lips that those children touched, to comfort. I thought it was their necks.

I thought they were older kids, school age.

Mia tumbled from the basket and I picked her up to fly her around the room. She giggled and gasped in flight as I dipped her high and low.

He stopped reading to ask softly, "Why is what they did so bad? Why do people hate them so much?" With genuine, sad puzzlement. I stopped dead in my tracks. Mia was aloft in my hands, in midflight. A twitchy disgust tied my tongue.

"Not the bird part," he said, without looking up.

"Because they're sick, *sick*," I said, bringing Mia down, walking to the door.

"But what makes them sick?" His voice was tight, pleading. I hadn't heard that voice before. I held Mia close and turned in the doorway. And I saw that it wasn't me he was asking. He was staring out the window, with tears in his eyes.

Something in me contracted, I felt shrink-wrapped, suffocated. My body was sending up an alarm, saying *leave now*. Only years later, I would look back and know that what my body was also trying to tell me was this: that the wolf had already come in the door, unzipped his husband-suit, and stepped out with his hungry hands.

He was very quiet when I told him. We can do it amicably, split everything down the middle. He just nodded and left. I sat up waiting. Because quiet scared me. He was back at 3 a.m., surprised to find me awake and telling him to pack some things and leave. He didn't pack, he didn't speak. He exploded.

He roared, picked up a glass-topped coffee table and smashed it to slivers at my feet. Then he flew through the house like a crazed beast, grabbing everything in his path and smashing it, hollering and screaming gibberish.

He threw chairs, demolished shelves, pulled down pictures and whizzed them at me like Frisbees. I played dodgeball with books, shoes, and records. He blocked exits, ripped the phone from the wall.

He wasn't going to kill me tonight, he bellowed. Noooo! He'd do that when I wasn't expecting it. When I was leeeeast expecting it.

"THIS IS JUST" as a wall clock smashed into me—
"TO SCARE" as my sewing box sailed into a window beside me—
"THE SHIT" as knives and silverware whistled through the air—
"OUT OF YOU!" as he stomped a lampshade to death.

Mia's screaming sent me bolting down the hall. I grabbed her out of her crib and kept dodging him, trying to get to the door, a window, any escape. The madness continued as long as there was anything to demolish. Food, plants, furniture. Mia dug her fingernails so far into my neck she drew blood.

He yelled *"Give me the baby!"* at the same time he was throwing our house at us. Until there was almost nothing left to destroy, until he'd worn himself out. Until he stood, spent, amid the splinters and shards, cried, and left.

Mia and I stayed with my mother for only a few days. It made her nervous, all the drama, my bruised ribs, gouged neck. Mia, however, acted as if nothing had happened at all. When we returned home, she marched about the wreckage, singing, making forests and islands of the debris. She imitated me taking photos of the carnage.

I didn't know if this was a child's remarkable resilience or if she thought she'd dreamt it or if she'd simply buried and forgotten it. I called her doctor, who assured me that if she was distressed, she would show it.

A neighbor came by to ask how I was, said they were afraid he might have hurt me. "They" turned out to be half my block, who stood in my front yard in their jammies at 4 a.m. listening to "all that screamin' and bangin' goin' on." Ringside seats to the show. No one wanted to knock or call the police. It "wasn't really our business."

Nick didn't call, which unnerved me. The thing about being told "when you least expect it," is that then you *always* expect it. I spent nights in her room, sitting up, listening. Jerking my head up when I nodded off.

I was half-dead with exhaustion. I finally took a cab to the lake, too sleep deprived to drive. I staggered across the beach to a wide-open spot, jammed our umbrella in the sand, and waited for Mia to take her nap. I tied her to my waist with a jump rope, lest she wake up and toddle away from me, then passed out cold beside her.

It was almost dark when I woke. Mia was sitting beside me, patting me and muttering to herself. She burst into a smile when my eyes opened. "Thee, mudder, I patected you! Did you have a good thleep?"

"The husband shall have the right to decide how and where the child has her hair cut for each alternate haircut until the child is old enough to decide on her own." He insisted on the clause in the divorce papers we were having drawn up.

I insisted on sole custody and no overnights, but I had no choice but to allow visitation. All I could do was demand he see her with his family present. I began making plans to move as far away as possible. I assumed he'd go on with his life and leave us alone. I assumed wrong.

Mia and I moved into a depressing orange shag, slimy pool, popcorn-ceiling apartment. Nowhere else would take a child. I took a sales job I hated near my mother so she could watch Mia.

Mia was an easy child, happy but not boisterous. Her laughter was light, her movements delicate, considered. She was intensely curious, quietly exploring the world like a little scientist. She was not chatty, she spoke carefully. When she giggled, "You're a mean mommy!" in the tub one night, I was surprised. I knew all of her small vocabulary and "mean" wasn't in it.

"What's a mean mommy?" I asked her, playing along. "Uh-oh, I'm gonna be in biiiig trouble!" she laughed giddily.

Her behavior had been jittery and odd since I'd picked her up from a visit earlier that day. I asked Nick why he told her she'd be in big trouble. Fuck you, he screamed, you're poisoning her! She's already calling someone else daddy, I can tell! Which was ludicrous. Mia wouldn't want to call anyone "daddy" again for the rest of her life.

A week later, I picked Mia up at my mom's after work. She'd been playing there with my sister's baby, Rosie. After I took her home and put her to bed, the phone rang.

"Now stay calm," my sister said to me.

I sat down and suspected that whatever calm I still had was about to vanish altogether.

When my sister was changing Rosie's diaper, she said, Mia scooted in front of her, spread the baby's legs, and demonstrated on her "what my daddy do to me." Mom saw it, too, she added.

All I could hear after that was my own voice saying he did it he did it he did it he didn't wait till she was older he did it to her little piglet body to her little self.

I sat up all night, trying to "stay calm." I wanted to yell, I wanted to cry, I wanted to wring his neck. I wanted to watch her sleep. But it made my heart break.

I took her to her pediatrician in the morning to see if she was hurt in some way, to ask him what to do. She didn't seem hurt, just hyper, clingy.

When I told the doctor what she demonstrated on her cousin, he didn't say much. Just looked her over, checked her chart, then had her go play in the waiting room. He closed her file, smiled at me and said, "So, I hear you want to take Mia out of state?"

Bastard.

Nick must have figured where my first stop would be if he got caught. He'd already started damage control, called on the boys to close ranks. Oh, that vindictive wife, that mean mommy.

"You know, Nick is a good man. Are you sure you want to do this?"

I was sure I wanted to slap his splotchy, grinning face, yank out his sparse fluffs of hair. Gritting my teeth around men was becoming something of a skill by now.

"This is about Mia, not me. What do I do about what he did to her?"

"I wouldn't make much of it, she's okay. If it happens again, bring her in. I'm sure once you tell Nick what she said, it won't happen again." He smiled and left.

I was frustrated, angry, confused—he's a jerk, but he's still a doctor, he must know what he's talking about. Should I not make much of it, not reinforce the event in her mind? The one thing I did know was not to make Mia feel she'd done something wrong. But I would make damn sure Nick knew he did.

"Mia told what you did to her, you pervert," I told him. "She tells on you, she demonstrates! You're worse than a rapist, it's your own child!"

He didn't hang up, didn't argue. He just listened. I was shaking.

"You touch her again and you will rot in jail. You know what they do to molesters in jail, don't you? Even murderers can't stand a child molester!"

He was silent, then quietly said thank you, and hung up. Of course, he didn't argue, I thought, he knows he's been caught. That ought to stop him, he isn't about to get himself thrown in jail, oh my the family name. He won't dare touch her again. The doctor said so. And the mother listened.

Nick had made the earlier mistake of thinking that my agreeableness was acquiescence. My mistake was worse. I mistook his for fear. I thought big, scary me, the Powerful Mother, I locked the evil wolf out for good.

"I'm not fat, pink, and ugly!" Mia blurted in the tub after a visit with Nick.

She started to cry, jumped out of the tub, and went streaking about naked and wet. Her behavior began changing. Some days she'd grow suddenly somber and clingy. Others, she'd laugh out of the blue. She started wetting her pants. Her nursery school told me she'd become withdrawn, twice they found her with her panties off.

She began to lick everything, to put everything in her mouth. I thought she was regressing to baby behavior, probably from the separation caused by my working. I had no idea that what she was doing was not regressing, it was *advancing*. To adult behavior.

One rainy night, she stopped talking as I ran her bath. She refused to go into the bathroom. She clenched her fists and turned red with a kind of contained rage. I picked her up and she screamed. She went rigid and said, "Daddy hurt me down there."

Life changed forever. I talked listened moved ate slept but in a reality filtered through this. The world thrummed with the strange, sick tone of a nightmare. One I couldn't shake, because it wasn't mine. It was as if the devil himself was dreaming, he was asleep and dreaming of our lives, Mia and I.

We would be a long time waking him.

4.

My days of suburban isolation were over. This time, her doctor's partner reported it to The Authorities. Mia and I were about to enter the city's labyrinthine mechanism for the protection of its youth, Child Protection Services. Once you step over that threshold, your life is no longer yours. You spend months and years waiting, in endless freezing hallways, in dingy offices, on dirty plastic chairs, waiting to hear your fate for that week. You get scrutinized, ignored, supported, vilified, validated, admired, scorned, pitied. You can't ask, you get asked, you can't tell, you get told.

THE AUTHORITIES, STEP ONE:
A POLICE REPORT

The big Officer sat in my pink velvet chair asking me but what did you *yourself* actually see, I don't wanna know what your sister saw. I tell him again about what Mia said to me that night, about Nick's lap, the erections, about finding him sleeping naked on her floor by her crib, about what he said about kids and sex.

The Officer sighed impatiently, repeating, "Okay, so he read the Sunday paper with her, that's it?"

"No. He didn't just read the paper the way you would. Unless you put your kid against your erect penis to read the paper, too. Why won't you write what I'm saying?"

Writing "Child stated and demonstrated sexual molestation by father" was simply not a possibility for this Officer. This was before wives had much credibility with the law in domestic matters, children even less. It was also before I knew anything about relevant statistics. If one in three or four women have been molested as children, the percentage of men doing the deed can't be too far behind. If you were a gambler, the odds on Mr. Officer weren't too bad. Maybe I'd hit the jackpot.

THE AUTHORITIES, STEP TWO:
CHILD PROTECTION SERVICES INTERVIEW #1

Carrie H was a beautiful woman with big, sad eyes who took Mia into a room full of dolls and toys. To find out who did what, who didn't, and if the who didn't could be trusted to protect Mia. She couldn't share anything Mia said with me. But, can you tell me how can I help her, I pleaded, I don't know what to do, my baby girl's stopped smiling. She yells at the daddy ducks to get dead, she wants to kill the daddy gorilla at the zoo, she wets her pants again. What does this mean, is she damaged emotionally? What do I do about her sadness, her anger, her little slumped shoulders? She had no answers, none of them would.

Carrie interviewed me, too, but I remembered little of it. I could hardly remember my own address. I moved slowly, comprehended slowly. I felt trapped in a dark, cottony silence. And yet I was astounded when Carrie noted in her report that I appeared depressed. I didn't say anything about being depressed. It never occurred to me that she could see on my face what I saw on Mia's.

THE AUTHORITIES, STEP THREE:
CHILD PROTECTION SERVICES INTERVIEW #2

A perky Intake Counselor bounced into Mia's bedroom to assess her, using her toys and stuffed animals. To find out more of who did what and make recommendations. She didn't interview me and wouldn't tell me anything Mia said either, though she did tell me that until further notice I must not allow her father to see her.

THE AUTHORITIES, STEP FOUR:
DR. FLYNN

All I wanted to do was give Mia a treat afterward, something sweet to balance the exam, like at the pediatrician.

Dr. Flynn snatched it from me. "You want her to associate having someone touch her genitals with a treat? You're supposed to be teaching her never to let anyone touch her there!"

I had no idea, I had no training for this. She looked at me as if I were an accomplice, as if I let it happen.

I buckled Mia into her car seat, went around the back of the car, and sat on the bumper, where Mia couldn't see her mother fall apart, in the street between two cars. Maybe Dr. Flynn was right, maybe I *was* to blame. Maybe I should have smelled the coffee and left him after his mother's first visit.

THE AUTHORITIES, STEP FIVE:
THE STATE'S TWO CENTS

Mia played in yet another room full of toys for a state attorney behind two-way glass. Again, little was said to me. Mia rarely told me much, either. Our time together was almost free of him, she didn't speak of what he'd done and I never asked. We did what we always did, played at the beach, spent days at the zoo. She just did it more sadly.

While I waited during her interview, I picked up a doll from a basket in the waiting room. A girl ragdoll with pigtails. I tossed her back and her dress flipped up. Someone had taken off her panties and she wasn't like any of the dolls I used to play with. She had genitals, openings. I picked up the other dolls, children and adults with private parts, and was pierced with a sudden despair.

I crawled about the floor searching for the girl doll's panties, I fixed all their clothes, zipped up zippers, buttoned shirts. I laid them in their basket home. Then I noticed that their mouths were holes, too. I looked at the children on their backs with their open pink mouths and felt like I couldn't take another breath on this earth. I curled up on the floor and wept.

Nick was busy, too, either crying to my mother, all I did was love my daughter, I don't want to go to jail. Or continuing to discredit me. Our accountant greeted me with how can you do this to him, to such a good Catholic boy. I'd gone from vindictive wife to vindictive *Jewish* wife.

He called people snarling he'd find the person who did this to Mia!

Too stupid to realize that he'd just acknowledged that a "this" had happened at all, a day after telling a detective nothing happened, that his wife had made it all up.

He'd end up implicating himself in all kinds of ways. Most pedophiles don't see their transparency. Because keeping your actions a secret isn't that difficult. Concealing your very nature is almost impossible.

He would make a career of threatening "to get" people—me, my mother, his therapist, his therapist's children, Mia's psychologist, oh, they'll all be very sorry.

THE AUTHORITIES STEP SIX:
THE CHILD PROTECTION TEAM REPORT

Recommendation: Protection of Child from Father until he is under treatment, further evaluation of the Child, mothers-of-abused-children therapy for Mother.

Treatment? For what, a sexual preference? As far as I was concerned, the only treatment that would work was measured in miles.

I applied to a college in another state. We would get counseling there. Not so fast, said the authorities, your divorce is now a matter before the court. You're not going anywhere. I had to start the application process all over again, to a local university.

For the next two years, our fate lay in the hands of the Honorable Judge Percy Moran. He was handsome, curt, easily angered. I was alternately afraid of him and furious at him. For two years, the judge ignored what I said about Nick's violence, threats, or bizarre behavior.

Nick denied touching Mia. The judge knew there was evidence to the contrary. The judge didn't care. He wanted more proof, more reports.

He initiated Round Two of the system: The Experts. Court-appointed psychiatrists and psychologists, experts in sex abuse, psychological testing. We endured two years of smaller hoops with bigger fires, so the honorable judge could get at The Truth. Of course, all he needed to do was talk to Mia. She was the keeper of Nick's secrets. But why listen to a small girl? Courts then didn't listen to big girls, ask rape victims, ask black-eyed wives.

Anything Mia or I said was invalid until one of the experts said it, too. And I never got over the fear of the consequences if they didn't. It was ever present, my fear that he could hurt her again.

I was reduced to two emotions, love and fear. I felt them so intensely, it must have altered my DNA. I'd mutated into a Mia-protecting machine. Equipped with heightened receptivity to every nuance of her behavior and mood. To the judge's. To knowing when to least expect something. To everything, everywhere, every day. I lost the ability to think one thought at a time. No thought was unaccompanied by fear. Especially thoughts of Mia. My feelings for her became entangled with it.

Having Mia had taught me that love is expansive, that its strength and magnificence come in unleashing it. Fear's potency is nuclear, it comes in harnessing it, in compression, density. It generated the heavy fuel I needed then. Because vigilance is a hungry animal.

There were two bright spots in the midst of this. I got accepted quickly into a local university and secured grants and scholarships to pay for it. And I found Elaine, a lawyer who was just the kind of woman Nick hated. And just the kind we needed—brilliant, principled, unyielding. Our very own gladiator.

Nick needn't have worried about the family name. Their reputation followed them thousands of miles away, right into the deposition of one of Nick's doctors. I noticed that the legal stenographer there seemed uncomfortable. She followed me to my car when it was done, making sure no one saw her.

"I can't believe this," she whispered. "This is the P. family from Philadelphia, isn't it?"

"Yes, how did you know?"

"I was good friends with his sister in high school when I had a boyfriend my parents hated, who, by the way, his sister slept with behind my back. Her mother called me one day to tell me that since I couldn't bring my boyfriend to my own house, he and I could go to their house and have sex anytime we wanted."

Something on my face made her pause, then say, "You did know the family was . . . you know, . . . kinda weird? You know, sexually?"

The reports from Moran's experts started rolling in. They'd spent months with Nick, with Mia, with me, and they all concluded to varying degrees that what Mia reported was true, and once she was sure Nick couldn't hurt her again, she reported plenty.

I found out what "plenty" was in a cold, dim court hallway. I opened the file Elaine had given me and read the things he'd done to hurt her, things I hadn't known, things she "patected" me from.

My heart twisted, my lungs felt as if they were being wrung. I sobbed going into Moran's chambers for the hearing. Which greatly annoyed him. Until he read the report himself, snapping from page to page. The recommendations in the report were no less painful. They recommended treatment and immediate supervised visitation; after treatment, well, Mom and Dad should make some rules, say, like no nudity between father and daughter.

"You mean he can still see Mia if he gets *therapy*? And you think this time around he's going to follow rules?" I asked outraged.

Dear naïve, stupid Claire. How unsophisticated. How primitive. Don't you think the experts know what they're talking about? Don't you know that a hundred years of psychology has allowed us to *evolve* in our understanding of human behavior and the laws that govern it, made us wise in these matters?

And our wisdom, our bottom line is this: we don't think molesting a child is a *choice*—we don't think he could *help* consciously calculating for months to hide what he was doing or stop himself from telling Mia not to tell on him. We think it is a *disease*.

Of course you do. To a hammer, everything is a nail. If the almighty psychologist can change a gay person's desires, as they thought they could then, why, of course they can make someone stop finding little kiddies irresistible, too.

"You mean you really think you can cure this 'disease'?"

Well, okay, maybe not *cure* it, maybe just *control* it. *Maybe*. So, we're also recommending therapy for your violated child so she can learn how to avoid future molestations. We recommend that she understand her *"private zones"* and what to do if she is touched inappropriately.

We'll give you the opportunity to do it again after treatment, Mr. P, but with a new vocabulary. After all, a man is entitled to his biological child, even one he betrayed and violated in the worst possible way.

What about what *Mia* wants, you ask? Why, Claire, she's hardly four years old, how can she *possibly* know what she wants? We'll tell her what she wants.

And as for Mom, well, she'd best learn to cooperate with you and to control her angry expressions.

This was how they protected our children in family court. It made me sick to my stomach. Who it protected was themselves; it was men scratching each other's backs. It still is. It's not so hard to figure out. Men become politicians and judges: politicians and judges make laws.

Elaine no doubt told me what I could expect, but it didn't stick. Even though we were in family court and jail was never a possibility, I was sure that once the judge got at The Truth, Mia would be safe for good. What a fantasy. Perhaps what she needed protection from were my own delusions.

The following week I ran into a very upset Carrie in the courthouse. She'd just learned that a respected judge was found fondling his granddaughter. She told me of another judge who watched a videotape of a visitation between a little girl and the father who molested her. When the father entered the room, the girl started screaming and tried to force herself under a low coffee table to hide. It was horrible to watch, she said.

"What did the judge do?" I asked, afraid Mia might face the same fate.

"He shook his head and said, 'We just have to find a way to get those two back together as a family.'"

To his great credit, Judge Moran did insist Nick complete a full course of MDSO therapy, as in Mentally Disordered Sex Offender, before any kind of contact with Mia, even supervised. Nick got the judge to change the wording to just Sex Offender therapy.

Mia never saw Nick again. But not because of anything the system did. Because he decided not to go to the therapy as ordered.

In between all the madness, Mia and I moved on campus and began what would be two of the happiest years of our lives. When I wasn't battling my ex, I loved my life. Mia attended the campus nursery school; I majored in art history and film studies.

A few months after starting school, Mia began to smile again. For a long time, she started every day by asking if she'd have to see "him" today. One day she was climbing a slide and said, "Are you really really really sure I won't have to see him today?" Really really really, little monkey. She reached the top of the slide, looked down, and smiled her gorgeous wide smile, and I thought my heart would burst.

The university became Mia's big playground. The generosity of everyone there was wonderful. Cafeteria workers fed Mia for free for two years, financial aid worked miracles. Mia made friends at school. She rode through our new world on the back of my bike in her shiny red helmet and decided her name was really Queenie Princess Arosia. For weeks, if I didn't call her that, she didn't answer.

If one part of me was discovering what was rotten in the world, the mother part of me felt like it was always spring and each new day was green with laughter. I had the joy of looking up from writing a formal analysis of Gericault's "Raft of the Medusa" to see Mia clonking about in my high heels and fur coat as she whispered to an imaginary person, "Does it get cold in your spaceship?" Here, she said kindly, taking off the fur, this should help, and my coat is off to Mars. I watched her from around a corner as she solemnly pledged allegiance to the refrigerator, with liberty and dust is for all.

I looked for the flag at her nursery school and, sure enough, it was beside the refrigerator. How vast and inscrutable the world must seem to a child, even their small corner of it. They need for it all to work, so they simply remake it as they go, as it suits them. Why wouldn't people pledge to honor the big white box where they keep the food?

They remake themselves as well. I overheard her talking to her stuffed animals, "her children" as she called them—"Amember when the mean daddy cut up all the walls? And I patected mudder from all those fings he frew? Well, you don't have to worry nooooo more, 'acause he can't come see us!"

I was astonished—where had she kept the memory of that night? I thought she'd forgotten it forever. She'd simply buried it twelve months deep. Until the moment she was able to recall a night of terror as a night of heroism. Till she could transform paralysis to courage. I felt as if I were witnessing the actual creation of a human trait—confidence. She was creating herself anew in a way that all the therapy in the world couldn't.

I didn't share any of the dark clouds with Mia, the fear or sorrow. She never saw that face, the alert, frightened one with eyes in the back of her head. She saw the singing face.

I had a clear and ringing voice and sang to her all day long. Singing expressed our joy in each other, it knitted up our frayed edges. At night, just the two of us in the dark, singing created sanctuary, my lullabies were as hymns. It was the closest I ever came to praying.

She still had nightmares of Nick, still acted out what happened. She'd say she wants to kill her dad without even looking up from her fingerpaints. We were sitting in a theater watching a Maya Deren film when I noticed Mia on her back with her dress pulled up, her legs in the air, and no underwear on. I pulled her quickly onto my lap, glancing around the dark for her panties. They were on the floor by the door, where we'd stood waiting in line.

She continued to see a wonderful psychologist named Ella, and her sexualized behavior faded slowly. She grew stronger and happier as I headed for graduation.

I'd formed a friendship with a gentlemanly professor who became a kind of father figure, at a time when fathers weren't high on my list. He was mortified that I had no intention of ever getting married again. But, Claire, he said, you can't possibly want to live alone. My marriage has been the best part of my life for forty years. You just need time, he assured me.

I met Paul at a downtown film gala. He was handsome, fair, and dark-haired, with huge dove-colored eyes that turned down at the corners. A talented designer without the artistic personality that usually goes with it, Paul was the kind of Southern gentleman that's practically extinct. He stood when a woman entered a room and still called his parents ma'am and sir. We dated for six months, until I was certain it was a lasting relationship, before I introduced him to Mia.

At their first meeting she was so possessive of me, she slid off my lap, whacked him in the face with a stuffed animal, and crawled back into my lap, scowling. Still, she agreed to let us take her to the zoo next time. She had a screaming tantrum the entire car ride there. Well, I thought, there goes Paul.

After we parked, she got out, sniffled herself quiet and put her little hand up for me to take. Then she put the other one up for Paul to take and we never looked back.

Paul's appearance in our lives meant that she got doted on by two. She was the center of our lives and she loved it, loved that she had a kind man who would protect us both from what she now called her "old dad." She had a new father. But she never called him Daddy, he would always be Paul or, after enough years passed, occasionally "Dad."

Sometimes it was his arms that held her and walked her back to sleep after nightmares of Nick pulling a long needle out of his jacket and sticking it into her while he laughed in his curly blond wig.

Paul taught her to paint, to pitch like a boy, to skateboard. To fly. Literally. She was so fine-boned and light that he would throw her up in the air high above his head and catch her as she sailed down, squealing with delight.

I took photos of Mia looking like she was falling from heaven. Photos of her making big muscles and ferocious faces, of her galloping, laughing, waving a sparkling magic wand. Of Mia the Powerful.

Mia ruled.

5.

Paul, Mia, and I moved to Los Angeles when she was five so I could pursue a career as a screenwriter. I worked regularly, and in genres women rarely wrote in then—action and futuristic thrillers. But my primary ambition was to be a great mom. I knew these were magic years and reveled in them. So did Mia. She thought it was Herself that magically controlled the TV. She turned it on and off and changed the channels because she had The Power. Mia would swing her arms around, zap the TV with a "Poof!" and it obeyed.

We thought she'd outgrow it, as children outgrow the tooth fairy. She didn't, and by age six, we were afraid she'd be humiliated at some friend's house. So the TV began to disobey her little by little. It was both heartbreaking and comical to see her keep swinging and poofing to no avail. I told her the TV grew up and had its own power now.

"Oh, no, it didn't, Mother, TVs don't grow up!"

There are so many ways we commit crimes against our children, even out of love. She didn't want to grow up and leave her magic behind. I didn't want her to, either.

She eventually realized she didn't have The Power, but she wasn't ready to give up magic yet. So, God got the job. But how could we be sure He was qualified?

I had no idea what to tell her. I'd never talked to her about God and she'd never seen me pray. *I'd* never seen me pray. My experience of the divine was entirely culinary. Potato pancakes at Hannukah, matzoh at Passover, starvation at Yom Kippur.

Absent any help from me, Mia decided to prove not just God's existence, but his usefulness. "If there is a God, why doesn't he do something already? I mean like *now*, not fifty years ago when he parted the Red Sea." She came up with a True Test, one that would vastly improve her life.

She had a terrible fear of toilets "overflooding and drownding" her. We always had to flush it after she was a safe distance from the bathroom.

"Mother, Paul," she announced grandly, "I'm going to the bathroom and I'm going to ask God not to overflood it and drownd me when I flush. Weeee'll see if there's really a God."

We waited in the hall while the exam was administered. She went. She flushed. We could just picture her waiting for the rising tide with her hands over her eyes. She finally emerged, beaming and proud.

It's not every child that's able to prove that there's a God. And she expected Him to be darned grateful she did.

It was in her play that I saw remnants of the abuse in her emotional life. A recurring theme in Mia's psyche was of evil lurking behind good. The clown of her nightmares always pulled off his blond wig to become Nick. When she played with her horses, the kind, strong stallion would suddenly become evil and try to devour the younger horses. The mother horse was always shuttling her foals from one "secret cave" to another to protect them.

I heard Mia muttering after midnight once and went in to find her combing her stuffed animals. An evil man made an oil slick on purpose, she whispered, and left them to die, so she was cleaning their fur to save them. Her horses and stuffies had as many calamities as they had tea parties.

Her nightmares had stayed behind in Chicago, but her memories apparently hadn't. Her second-grade teacher, Sara, a gentle, perceptive woman in her forties, called us in to show us Mia's weekly journal.

"Sometimes I feel bad when I think of certain events," Mia wrote, "such as when my old dad did bad things to me. But all I have to do is not think about it and then I feel better."

She assured us she'd keep Mia's journal confidential should she want to continue writing about "certain events." Sara and Mia forged a deep bond that soon included Paul and I. She had a calm, spiritual presence that was often an anchor for our family.

I asked Mia if she still remembered what Nick did to her. She looked at me as if I was daft.

"Of course, I do, Mama," she said. "I just don't remember which birthday it happened on." Then she wagged her finger at me and scolded, "You know, Mother, you shouldn'ta got married with that man."

How could I reply? Tell her that if I hadn't, she wouldn't be here? What a terrible truth for her to one day realize. The price she paid for her existence.

"He did *what?*" said Judge Moran, outraged.

I had flown back to Chicago to settle a child support dispute, and my lawyer told him that Nick had remarried and had more children. I had just found out myself and was half hoping the judge wouldn't, because I knew he'd have Child Protection investigate him again. Then, Nick would blame me and would want revenge.

Which is exactly what happened. For years, Nick hadn't paid for any psychological care related to the abuse, as he was court ordered to do, nor his share of doctor bills, but now, to get back at me, he wanted visitation rights.

My happy life collapsed and I didn't know how to shore it back up. He had the means to outspend me in court. Going to court in California was risky anyway. Fathers got visitation no matter what they did or what the child wanted. I could just see Mia screaming and trying to crawl under a coffee table in the name of family unity. I'd sooner disappear than leave her alone with him ever again. And I knew how.

I'd heard of an "Underground" that secreted away women and children when courts wouldn't protect them. The only other option I saw was doing what Dr. Elizabeth Morgan did in her well-publicized case. She had her parents spirit her child to New Zealand, and she went to jail for it.

I was prepared to do either if I had to. I felt so emotionally overwhelmed that I called a social service agency for counseling. A therapist named Fran called back and I poured out the whole saga in between sobs. As we were making an appointment, I asked her full name. Fran Blair, she said, then spelled it out for me: B-l-e-y-e-r. That's an unusual spelling, I said, are you related to a Peter Bleyer, from Philadelphia?

Why, yes, as a matter of fact, he's my husband, she said, why do you ask?

I'd come all the way across the country to escape from Nick and the *one* psychologist in the entire state of California I *happen* to call is the wife of a P family friend. Who had been at my wedding. I don't know who was shocked more, she or I.

Paul came home to find me staring at the phone, practically catatonic.

If I had any doubt Nick would learn where we lived, I didn't anymore. It took me exactly one day to find the Underground. I met a well-dressed young woman at a café and explained my situation. She listened quietly, then led me to her car without a word.

She drove to an apartment in a seedy part of town, locked the door behind us, and then told me this was the first stop in going underground. I looked around and thought, here I am again, at the nexus of Nick, desperation and dirty orange shag carpet. The worn sheets on the bed matched the one strung across the window. We stepped over toys and sat on the sagging plaid Herculon sofa to talk about the mechanics of "disappearing."

We could take nothing of our old life, not even a stuffed animal. There'd be new histories, new hair colors, a new profession. Every day would be a lie. Paul would be watched.

I wish I could tell you that you'll get used to it, she said, but you won't. And if you ever do, that's when you'll get caught, because you'll get careless, it'll be good-bye Mia, hello prison. Once she was eighteen, Mia could resurface, but I never could, I'd face charges. I would go to my grave looking over my shoulder. Underground was an apt name, I was feeling cadaverous already.

We would wait here until she got everything set up for us. There was a doorless closet against one wall full of Goodwill cast-offs. She pointed to them and said I could pick out new wardrobes for Mia and me once we got settled in.

I scanned for the least drecky choices. Triple-pleated, puce trousers; a flowered sweatshirt; and a slick, thin blue belt that looked like a Tupperware cake dish handle.

Or I could hold the pants up with that Navajo beaded belt and use the Tupperware belt to hang myself. God help me, it was vanity that made my decision.

Forget it, I told Paul, Mia will have to lie every day knowing that if she screws up, Mommy goes to jail. And it'll flat out kill me to become Jane Smith, tight-lipped blond bookkeeper for Frank's Fuel-n-Feed.

I found another lawyer in Chicago who established that nothing would happen without the Sex Offender therapy Moran ordered. Nick finally withdrew his motion.

But the damage to Mia was done. Because I made the single worst choice I'd ever made in raising her. From the start, I felt it was best to hide all this from her until I had no choice. My hope was that it wouldn't come to that. But, for some reason, a sister-in-law kept harping on me to tell Mia, saying, "You must always be honest with your kids." I was of the opinion that your kids didn't need to know some things. But I was so exhausted and fearful, and she so insistent, I gave in.

I took Mia outdoors, by her favorite fountain, and somehow managed to force the words from my mouth, "Your old dad wants to see you again." She grabbed me and started to cry. She shrunk into a ball in my lap and I knew immediately that I'd done something I'd regret for the rest of my life. It didn't matter that I told her that I was going to fight hard to stop him; her safe world was shattered. I was furious at my sister-in-law and myself. I could see in Mia's face that her little life was snapped in two. Her first Before and After.

Mia was never the same. Sometimes, she'd stare off into space and a fleeting melancholy would pass across her features. She began to pick at her fingernails and jiggle her knee, or she'd get these shudders up her spine, like someone cracked the whip from her tailbone to her neck. Her nightmares returned, either with Nick chasing her in that wig or snatching her off the playground or scaring her with snakes (Freud got that one right).

One night as we walked to her favorite restaurant for dinner, she galloped in front of an alley without looking, just as a car was pulling out. The car's brakes squealed and Mia froze inches from the bumper. It was the second time in a few days she'd done it. We scooped her up and scolded her about looking both ways. By the time we ordered dinner, she seemed fine. Then her mouth and shoulders suddenly sagged. I asked what was wrong.

"I just have this feeling that I don't like being a person," she said quietly.

I took her to see a child psychologist, Colleen, a very caring woman who spent over a year helping Mia through this time. Though Mia grew to feel safer, she remained a changed girl. She became a nervous child. There was a shadow across her heart.

She was afraid something would happen to me; her fear of being alone in bathrooms got worse. Until she was twelve, she wouldn't shower unless I was in the bathroom or Paul was outside in the hall. "A bad guy could come in, and I can't see through this shower door, you know!"

The fallout from Nick finally hit me as well. Not long after, I woke up crying every morning, with a sick, mushy feeling in my stomach that was inexplicable, followed by losing ten pounds in as many days. The CD from the film *The Piano* became the soundtrack to the depression movie I starred in, *Crying in Three Positions*. Standing, sitting, lying down, it was all I did. When Mia got home from school, I'd somehow pretend to be her smiling mother, make dinner, read stories, ask about school.

I learned why most people committed suicide. It's impossible to describe what it is to have your heart *literally* hurt so much that only the stopping of it will end the pain. Stopping it becomes the bright and shining light at the end of the tunnel. Just the thought of it, with its secret, thrilling promise of release, is enough to lift you up to where you can perform basic functions, like brushing your teeth or eating or drawing that pricey chef's knife across the jugular. Somewhere in the mountains where it wouldn't leave a mess for someone else to clean up.

I finally got on an antidepressant and in six months I no longer needed them, but I knew a hole had opened up in the terrain. And that if I wasn't careful, I could fall in.

It was little things, it always is. Things only a mother notices. A subtle withholding, waiting too long to wash her hair, a book choice, red cheeks.

When Mia was thirteen, I noticed her cheeks were often red. It was winter, it couldn't be the sun. My cheeks aren't red, she'd say. Paul agreed, as he nearly always did.

But they were. I had no idea where the thought came from, but out popped, "I think you're scalding your face." As soon as I said it, my brain agreed with my intuition.

Did I catch hell. What a mean thing to say, leave me alone, leave her alone, they said. I didn't say anything else about it, but I had sprouted a new antenna. One that would cause increasing discord in our home as it picked up the subtlest things in her behavior.

Her heroes had always been Jane Goodall and Audrey Hepburn. Suddenly, it was Sex Pistol Johnny Rotten. She read his autobiography several times. "For a school assignment," she said. She began to let her personal grooming slide. She'd stay in the bathroom forever, but whatever she was doing didn't involve soap and water.

It's odd, I told Paul, something's off. It's typical teen behavior, Paul said, leave her alone. No, it's not, I told him, teenage girls are fanatic about their appearance.

"You can't keep at her like this, Claire," he said irritably, "for heaven's sake, she's a great kid, she's not doing anything wrong."

It's true, she wasn't *doing* anything wrong, but something *was* wrong. I felt the same way I did when I met Nick's family, something was wrong with the picture. I couldn't see it but I could feel it.

Then, one day, out of the blue, Mia said to me, with cold curiosity, almost with contempt: "How could you have married *him*?"

I arranged for her to see Colleen again, to deal with whatever was coming up for her about Nick. Mia was old enough then that the sessions were confidential.

Mia asked to see the court papers; she wanted to read all the reports for herself. We decided she would read them in Colleen's office, where she could ask me questions and deal with the emotions that were sure to come up.

Mia seemed appropriately angry, curious, bothered. Some things she remembered well. Some she remembered remembering. All of it she remembered feeling. She remembered how the abuse made her feel most of all. I told her it was okay to be angry with me, it was normal. She was surprised—why would I be mad at you, Mommy?

In her mind, we escaped him together, we were the crusading duo triumphing over evil. My question challenged the bond that had defined us. I realized that she couldn't conceive of me as being fallible.

"What a pervert!" she said on the way home. "It's not fair that he's not in jail. I can't believe he could do something like that to a little kid and get to go on with his life."

"A little kid." Maybe talking about herself in third person made it easier. At bedtime, she thanked me for being her mother, for going through "all that," as if *I* had the biggest burden.

She never spoke of him again and it seemed the issue was behind her, though she did want to continue seeing Colleen. I thought they might deal with some of the things that continued to bother me about her behavior. The problem was, what had been bothering me still wasn't bothering anyone else. Which meant the problem became me.

She began hanging out with a new student, the one who was into witchcraft and push-up bras. For once, Paul and I weren't at odds about Mia.

"I've got a bad feeling about that girl," he said.

Mia became even more slack about her hygiene and grew more sluggish and quiet. Thus began a few months of a duet that went something like this:

"Colleen, she won't shower for days."

Claire, her hygiene is fine.

"Colleen, she's withdrawn, she's dropped all her old friends, and she's reading Johnny Rotten for the twentieth time—that's not normal."

Claire, you can't control everything she does. You must let her make some of her own choices.

"Colleen, she's lost so much weight her ribs stick out, and she's always tired. Are you sure she's not depressed or doing drugs or still having issues about her old dad?"

No, Claire, Mia is not depressed and her weight is fine. Mia's not doing drugs. And she never talks about her old dad.

The stress level at home had escalated, and Mia seemed increasingly determined to provoke me. As only a child can do, she had the dynamic between Paul and me down to a science.

Paul and I had let little things between us fester for a long time. He hated conflict so much that even a simple disagreement made him squirm. He liked staying under the radar at all costs. Which is what makes submarines so deadly. He punished with such graciousness and refined manners, it was almost possible to believe him when he'd say, who, me, passive aggressive?

There's little that's passive about me. I'm expressive, the barometer that gets blamed for the storms. Granted, I did cause some of the storms. I practically had my own weather system that summer. I felt like I was in the middle of a tornado, barely hanging on while my life blew out of control around me.

* * *

"Paul, she's been in that bathroom for an hour and I don't hear the shower running. I don't care what Colleen says about her privacy, I'm going in there."

Don't come in, she yelled when I knocked. My antenna shot up and I pushed on the door. Noo!! she yelled. Paul was hissing at me to leave her the hell alone. I pushed harder and found her standing there with her razor.

"Mia, what are you doing?" I asked, puzzled.

"What do you think I'm doing!"

"I have no idea," I said honestly.

She looked angry at my ignorance. Then she started crying and said, Mommy, I've been cutting myself. I put my arms around her and said, what, when you shave your legs, honey? We'll get you an electric shaver. She sunk down to the floor and I sank with her, bewildered.

No, Mommy, cutting as in self-mutilating.

Self-what??

Neither Paul nor I had ever heard of such a thing. She may as well have told us she grew a third arm. As if the looks on our faces weren't bad enough, I blurted, "But, it's so weird! Mia, why would you do such a thing?"

I wanted to understand the feelings that drove her to do it. But, all she heard was "you're weird," and it was downhill from there. Everyone started crying and she was so upset that I was upset, she ended up comforting me.

"Don't worry, Mommy, Colleen said it's not *that* unheard of."

"Colleen knew?" Paul and I blurted in unison.

We were appalled. I thought therapists of minors had to divulge something like that. Colleen later said that Mia wanted to deal with it on her own. And the implication was that I was largely the cause.

Really? I alone had the power to make my strong-willed daughter ladder her thighs with so many slits they looked like a giant grosgrain ribbon? To make her stop showering, become obsessed with Johnny Rotten, drop her best friends to hang out with the Wicca queen, and lose ten pounds in a month? Wow, all that power in one single mother? Why bother with therapy, all Mia needed was a surge protector.

Maybe all that power sizzled my synapses, but I'm wondering, doctor, there's no chance that this has anything to do with her being molested? I mean, maybe it's a stretch, but all this having happened after she asked for the reports of her abuse, there's no chance at all? Call me thick-headed, but I just have to ask.

No, Claire, this isn't about her old dad, Colleen told me. Again.

Some part of me must have had enough dismissal, or maybe it *was* all my fault; maybe I was simply tired of it all. Because I didn't do what I usually do, which is to get information, gather knowledge, so I can ana-lyze, judge, execute, fix. I just wanted Mia to stop doing it and she did. I knew because she showed me the countless red slashes across her upper thighs and stomach as they scabbed over and faded to pink. Rosy ribbons of proof that I wasn't in denial, that my family was healed, my child was whole.

Life returned to normal. Mia became her cheerful, funny self again. I was hired by a revered producer to adapt a book I loved. We were putting a bid on our first home and Mia was choosing the breed of dog she'd fi-nally be able to have. At midnight on January 30, I sang all the way home from my office, under a sky full of stars. I sang down the walkway to my back door.

I was singing when I noticed that her bedroom window was open.

parttwo

6.

"Test her for every possible drug you can test for."

I'm with the admitting clerk in the hospital's psych ward. A day after we found Mia in Venice, she's still stoned. I wish they could test for the gene for split personality. This déjà vu of my life with Nick is just the first of a series. The next two weeks will make me think I'm cursed.

I keep Mia locked in my vision while I admit her, in case there's an exit beyond my sightline. She sits listlessly on a gurney with her flushed face and matted hair.

I corner a doctor and tell him I want a full STD panel, too. Her journal made it clear that the wholesome ski trip to Mammoth with her classmates was anything but.

"I can't do HIV without her permission," says the pasty-faced doctor.

"*Her* permission? She's a minor."

Apparently in the sunny State of California I can't have my minor child's blood tested for AIDS, even if her life's at risk. I have no right to ask them to hold her against her will for more than three days, even if her life's at risk. And, I have no right to force her into rehab, even if her life's at risk. Only *she* can make those decisions.

"You're putting a fifteen-year-old on drugs in charge of her own welfare? If she had cancer and I didn't make her go for treatment, I'd get arrested for child endangerment—what's the difference?"

"There are good reasons for these laws," he says as he scribbles.

"Really? I'll tell you what, Doctor, if my daughter is the one making all the decisions, then why don't you send her your bill? Better yet, why don't you send it to the ACLfuckingU."

I rarely curse but right now I want to do it in three languages. I want his children to join cults, shoot heroin, end up in the gutter. I want him to suffer a Saturday night with a voodoo-eyed kid. I want to keep feeling this anger because it feels better than the sick-hearted pain.

A nurse takes Mia to get settled while someone gives us a tour of the ward, which is fifteen minutes of beigeness. We're given a stack of information and a cheery good-bye. We have almost no idea what her treatment will be and we don't get to talk to a doctor. Which means their primary source of information will be her. We're afraid she'll do what she did with us for the last year, and no doubt with Colleen, figure out what they want to hear and give it to them.

Mia refuses to come out to say good-bye to us. It is a knife.

What the hell is wrong with her? Everyone here's anorexic, except for an OCD who wipes himself bloody every time he takes a shit. All I did was run away, so why the FUCK am I here? God I hate her. Two days ago everything was perfect and now I'm locked up with Twiggy and the ass-wiper in what's gotta be the creepiest place on earth.

Paul and I navigate the sterile halls for our first visit with butterflies in our stomachs. I feel like I'm going to a maternity ward to see my new child, the one I didn't know I had. I see our faces reflected in the chicken-wired glass of the visiting room. We look like basset hounds.

Mia's physical presence had always been sharply defined, vivid with contrasts—light eyes, dark brows, light hair, olive skin; her live-wire limbs carved a big space in the world for herself. People always noticed Mia.

Now, when Mia slinks into the room and scrunches into a chair, a darkness emanates from inside her that's blurred and blackened her edges. My bold-contoured Matisse of a girl has become a smudged Mona Lisa, mysterious and unknowable. She doesn't even sound the same, it's as if she, like, dropped, like, fifty IQ points, like, overnight, dude.

We ply her: Are you sure you don't want to go back to Hopkins, sweetie? Do you want to try Beverly High? Do you this, do you that, can we this, can we that. We're begging is what we're doing. We'll do anything because we're scared. And she knows it. She's got the power of a teen with terrified parents.

She answers with snotty shrugs, sarcasm. Rain and Talia are already gracing some alley in Haight-Ashbury. Without her. And it's all our fault. We rained on her parade. Mainly me. I ruined everything, I spoiled her Big Plans.

"This place isn't going to change me. You're wasting your money," is what she leaves us with.

We walk back to the car in the rain. How appropriate the weather has been, the sky dumping buckets on us. It makes me feel even more pathetic. Paul starts to cry.

"I can't get the look in her eyes out of my mind," he says miserably, "when she was on the floor in the kitchen. There was a flicker of the real Mia in her eyes, just for a second. She looked so scared."

We stand there holding each other up amid the shoppers and the rain and the traffic, two sad parents huddled under an umbrella. We drive home and the whole city is full of Mia. That was where she played soccer for five years, this was where we walked her to school, here's her best friend's street. Even the car makes me ache. In LA, mothers and daughters spend half their life together in the car; we'd talk about sleepovers, which trail has the best wildflowers, what she wanted to be when she grew up.

Homeless drug addict wasn't on the list.

What a joke. They can't possibly think a psych ward is going to do anything besides waste enough money to feed a small country. Even if I needed "help"— which I don't—why would I talk to anyone here? All they do is nod and pretend to listen, while really trying to figure out if you're better labeled as having a mood disorder or acute paranoia. Which really just means you're bitchy and irritable or worry too much. Nothing that couldn't be solved with a joint and a shut the fuck up.

Helen, my social worker, now she's another animal altogether. She's not interested in labels or pills, she wants to reach out and touch someone! People like her all love being able to "reach a troubled youth," it makes them feel good or some shit, like their lives have meaning because they've figured you out. She'll be so easy to bullshit.

Mia's treatment consists primarily of sessions with a social worker, Helen. I guess the anorexics get the PhDs. I tell Helen I think this may be linked

to Mia's early molestation. In the two weeks she's there, they never address it at all. Because Mia says it has *nothing* to do with it, it's ancient
history, my mother's crazy. And Helen believes her.

Mia's back to no showering, she wants to drop out, do drugs, and live
among homeless gutterpunks but they think she's fine, she needs more independence, I'm too controlling, her school's too rigid. And the pièce de
résistance—we're supposed to agree with Mia's plan of action: if she goes
straight home she'll do drugs and run away, if she lives somewhere else
for a while, she won't. Helen is proud of Mia's "reasonable solution."

"That's not a solution, that's a threat! Can't you see Mia's manipulating you? Am I the only sane person in this room?"

I had no idea my life with Nick was training camp. Back down the
rabbit hole.

Helen looks at Mia sympathetically. "Mia feels you don't acknowledge
her feelings," she says in that gentle therapist tone that makes me want to
strangle her.

You nitwit! Mia's not running away because I don't acknowledge her
feelings. It's because I *do*. It's not about the drugs or her school or arguments with me at home. My daughter is running because she's in pain.
And I know why. She hates me for that.

*They don't get it, I'm NOT going back. She's psychotic, she always has to make
it about* him, *dredge up the past for no reason. She's the one that's driving me
nuts now, that reads my diaries, asks me if I'm in a cult, sticks me in this shit-
hole. She's the one who's always nagging, questioning, commenting. I'm weird,
I'm dirty, I'm lazy. It's like living under a giant microscope that sees any minor
flaw in cosmic proportions. I accidentally leave my shoe in the doorway and the
next thing I know I'm the spawn of Satan. Which maybe isn't too far off—that
would make her the Devil.*

I may have won a battle in capturing her, but she's got the will of Patton,
this girl. In our last session, Mia pulls out the big guns. She's also not
coming home because there is A Man in our building who was "bothering" her, you know, sexually threatening her. In unison, Paul and I go bug-
eyed and swivel our heads at her.

It is a comically strange moment, Paul and I looking from Mia to each other to Helen to Mia to each other. Paul and I know she's lying, the only man it could be is gay. Mia knows we know, and all three of us know that we can't say so or we look like horrible parents. I'll prove everything she's said about me, how I never believe her.

Paul starts to ask her about this Man but Helen cuts him off— Mia's not ready to talk about it, it's too upsetting, we must respect her privacy.

I needn't have worried about Mia's IQ. Her tactical brilliance is stunning.

Paul and I stagger out of there like it's Groundhog Day and we have to keep reliving one bad Mia day after another.

"Goddamn idiots," Paul says angrily. "She's too upset to even *talk* about what some 'man' in the building did, but they haven't called the police?"

"*Now*, you're saying this, in the parking lot? You couldn't have said it to Helen? God forbid you cast any doubt on what Mia's been saying about me. Now you know how I felt the last year when you all told me nothing was wrong with Mia!"

I fume the whole way home. I hate it now, walking past her bedroom window to the back door. I hate walking into my own home. It's the same place, the same high ceilings and crown moldings I've always loved, the same antiques and gleaming oak floors, but now it feels like it should have crime scene tape around it, the site of recent carnage.

I storm around the kitchen making dinner to let off steam. I finally slam the frying pan down on the stovetop.

"I'm not the reason she ran away and you know it!" I yell at Paul. "What none of you idiots get is that I'd be thrilled to death if it was all because of me! Because if I caused this, then I could do whatever it takes to uncause it!!"

Paul looks like a deer in headlights, staring at me with his big celery-colored eyes. I don't have a physical temper, I'm not pot slammer.

"Okay, Claire, you were right," he says softly, "but we can't go back, it's done. What can we do now? There's gotta be something we can do now to turn this around."

Yeah, right, and I know what it is, I just forgot to tell everyone. He's doing what he usually does—leave all the decisions with consequences to me.

Something suddenly occurs to me: Mia writes everything down. I march down the hall to her bedroom and flip on the light.

"The truth is somewhere in this room."

While the rain pounds outside, we scavenge for Mia's inner life. And little by little, the clues come out. Random slips of paper tucked in a science notebook, entries between math assignments. A tiny blue spiral jammed inside a binder pocket.

I pick up a diorama Mia made last semester, showing her outer and inner self. The outside is covered with trees, the ocean, her friends. Inside, she's made four quadrants, four selves. There's a jungle, tigers, her *National Geographic* self. There's a palette, guitar pick, horses. And there are two little houses, in a blackened corner painted with red slashes. One house has flowered curtains. This must be her happy house, I think, the good memories. I pick up the roof and inside are the words *lies, depression, pervert*.

The other house has a black roof with a red eye, carefully glued down. Outside are two men. One is a magazine photo of a man's face, with the horns of a devil pasted on. The other is a little ragdoll man. It reminds me of the anatomically correct dolls that haunted me for so long. There's a strand of yarn attached to him that disappears under the roof. Already, my heart is sinking.

I carefully tear off the roof and find the sad buried treasure. The yarn is attached to a girl doll inside the house. She's such a tiny thing, rammed in upside down, with her bare legs sticking straight up. I suddenly see Mia's four-year-old, skinny legs sticking up in the air. Curled around the girl doll is a poem she wrote, called "Him," on three little pages with Mia's writing:

> Why did he do it to me? Dreams now about the abuse, no blocking anymore, can't ever be happy, life sucks. I feel so depressed and angry. I hate myself.

I carry Mia's writings to the hospital as if I carried her very salvation in a nine-by-twelve brown envelope. I carry it like Helen's head on a platter. Hail, the conquering Mother, riding high astride the steed named I Told Them So.

I might as well have arrived in a tumbrel.

First charge: Invasion of Privacy. How dare you read your daughter's journals?

Second charge: Making Assumptions About That Which You Know Not Of. Those writings mean nothing, you aren't trained, you have no ability to judge.

Third, on asking again about the mysterious Man who's threatening her: You Have No Respect for Boundaries. Mia will speak when she's ready. Bad mother, baaad mother.

She'll talk when she's ready, she'll come home when she's ready, she'll stop doing drugs when she's ready. Meantime, Helen and her supervising psychologist have agreed with Mia that she should live with our friend, Sara, her old second-grade teacher, for a spell. We're not to ask Mia about drugs, forbid her to smoke, or bring up anything she doesn't want to talk about.

In fact, the most helpful position we can take now is "sitting back." Let her make her own choices, they say. I think a much more useful thing is to remind these two Einsteins what Mia's choices have been lately. This does not go over well. I finally just give up. My blood pressure's gone through the roof and I've ground the enamel off my molars but I smile and say Fine! Sure! Sara's might be just the thing! It'll give everyone a little break! It'll keep me from killing my own daughter is what it'll do.

"Ms. Fontaine, we laud you for being so open!" Laud, they actually use this word. Oh, it's paeans and laurels for me now. Then they thank me for "sending Mia a message of trust." What I've sent is a message of stupidity and weakness. I want to bang their heads against the beige wall. Better yet, I should bang my own, leave my blood as a warning to the next unsuspecting parent.

My memory is visual, my feelings are recorded in images. This exact moment, when being Mia's mommy ended, will be remembered as an iron gray sky, as Mia's averted eyes, as Paul's fingers gripped on the arms of a stainless steel chair.

This is what is recorded when the cord is cut and the blissful bubble that was always my life with Mia lifts up without me in it for the first time. And with it goes my anger. My fury melts and recasts itself into something that feels much worse. Resignation, defeat, *acknowledgment.* That we will never again be to each other what we were.

Thank God they're gone. I feel like shit. They look so miserable and confused. That's why I never wanted them to see this side of me, why I kept it hidden. And they wouldn't have if they hadn't tried to find me! That's why I get so mad, they fucked everything up and now I end up feeling guilty!

Two days ago I was so happy. Rain took us to the beach, across from the tide pools, to this huge drum circle. Joints and bottles were passed around and the beats being pumped out were so strong the sand seemed to shake. It was all so primal. It was a castaway circle filled with shouting Rastas, angry punks, hippie girls in flowing skirts twirling about like dancing fireflies. It was so alive.

It was awesome, one minute I didn't know a soul and the next I had a group of friends and a place to crash. That's what I love about the streets, how unpredictable it is, how chaotic and raw.

And now they want me to go back? Back to Hopkins' manicured world? Back to hiding under a straight-A face, to walking around smiling and hollow? I'd rather slice my hand open to remind myself I'm flesh and blood and not plastic.

I leave there feeling motherness drain out of me with each step. I'm skin in the shape of a woman but nothing inside feels solid, wet, living.

It materializes suddenly, as if I turned a corner and there it was in my path. Something I laughed off long ago, then let slither along in our shadow for a dozen years, just out of memory's reach, but licking at my heels. Now, here it lies, coiled and patient, waiting all this time for my certain arrival.

Ella's warning. Ten years ago, she had told me so. On a balcony outside her office in Chicago, just before we moved to L.A. Mia was galloping around the courtyard below us like a giddy pony, stopping to whinny and throw her head back. It was two years since she'd last seen Nick.

Ella told us Mia was doing well and didn't need therapy anymore.

However.

When Mia becomes an adolescent, she added, and becomes sexually aware, issues will come up for her about Nick and the abuse. She'll have problems. Have her see someone who deals with early incest trauma.

I only half listened to her. Adolescence? That's years away, she'll have had so much time to heal and be happy. Adolescence is a lifetime away!

I call the hospital in the morning and request a psychiatrist specializing in Mia's issues. The day of our appointment, Paul and I return to the ward with cautious hope. If, as Ella said, this behavior is so predictable, perhaps a treatment for it is, too, by someone with appropriate training.

The tall, blond doctor is waiting in the hall for us. I don't know what I must have been in a former life to have earned this karma—a warthog, Caligula—but she extends her hand with a kind smile and says,

"Hello, I'm Dr. P."

Oh. My. God. Paul and I stand there with our mouths hanging open. She stares at us, waiting. We can't even stammer a reply.

"Is something wrong?" she asks patiently.

"Yes!" I finally manage. "Are you related to Nick P from Philadelphia?"

Twelve years later and thousands of miles away, the *one* psychiatrist in the entire state of California that I *happen* to get is Nick's cousin.

History isn't repeating itself, it's stuttering.

"Him"

He enters my room and the eyes on my dolls shut, stuffed animals bear
  witness with glazed eyes
That can't shed tears.
With his every footstep I watch the footprint permanently imprinted
  in the tufts of my carpet.
He stains it gray.
Somewhere in the background, I hear running water and wish it
  would wash over me,
Like thousands of hands calming me, streaming over me with my
  mother's angelic smile.
But instead of her laughing, joyous face, I can see only his leering grin
  towering over me,
Like trying to coax a fox into a trap.

But, I have tricked him, my father,
And I leave, dissipate into the air.
He finally leaves after eternity has ended but I remain paralyzed on
    the floor.
My stuffed animals' eyes are frozen open in shock.

MIA, AGED 14

7.

"Mia is a very troubled girl."

Dr. Kravitz is one of the doctors in charge at the hospital. He saw us right away when he'd heard what happened. He's also seen Mia.

"Of course, this all stems from the sexual abuse. It's a very durable trauma, very significant in terms of Mia's self-perception, especially when it occurs at such a young age. The self-loathing and disgust she's expressed is typical. No matter what a parent does or doesn't do, by fifteen the problem manifests itself. Kids don't connect it, they don't see the effects played out in their behavior. Like the cutting, for example. She has no idea why she did it, only that it made her feel better."

Why would she? Trained professionals twice her age didn't.

"Cutting serves many functions," he continues. "It's the embodiment of distrust of the body. It relieves tension. It's a way of achieving mastery; it says I will control the harm inflicted on me. It had nothing to do with communication problems with you."

This should feel like a victory, but it doesn't.

"Coupled with her enmeshment with you," he says, "she got a double whammy."

"Her what?"

Okay, let's rewind, go back to the chapter in the *How to Mother an Abused Child* manual I never got to read when all this started. Here's the drill:

- Child is abused, perpetrator threatens to hurt mother. Child feels protective of mother.

- Struggle to escape perp reinforces feelings of mutual protection. It's Mom and I against the world.

- Something necessary at the time later creates "enmeshment." Child doesn't see her actions as separate from mother. Even during normal adolescent individuation. But—

- Normal individuation doesn't happen in abuse survivors. They don't feel normal, so they—

- Act out in unhealthy or self-destructive ways, which creates—

- Fear and pain for mother, which creates—

- Guilt for child who still feels responsible for mother's emotional health.

- Child seeks release from the guilt and from not feeling normal, which leads to—

- Escape to the world of other not normal people, where mother can't see her child self-destruct, which leads to—

"The bad news."

"That was the *good* news?" I ask.

"Understanding all of this isn't going to help, very little will," the doctor says. "She'll go back to the streets, the drugs. It's the only thing that offers her relief from her own misery, the only way she sees to protect you."

Mother horse can't save her pony anymore. She's charging off into the unending night that you buy in little plastic bags. She's leaving because she loves me too much to hurt me? Then, I wish she hated me, that she wanted to destroy me instead of herself. That she would do to me whatever it takes to scratch the itch of the sullied child.

Staying at Sara's lasts two weeks. When my sister Vivian asks if Mia wants to stay with her for a while, Mia jumps at the offer. Maybe it'll be a good thing, I think. Vivian lives in Larkin, Indiana, a tiny town in the countryside, certainly a more wholesome environment than LA. Mia will have her little cousin, the public school there will be less pressure than Hopkins. It'll also give Paul and I time to recover.

Mia's back in her bedroom tonight, but only to pack her things for Indiana. I don't recognize anything she's packing, she must have gotten these things in the last two weeks. Grungy druggie clothes, combat boots, shapeless knitted beanies. Different clothes for a different girl living a different life. One without me.

She doesn't seem to mind my presence, though I can tell she's glad we're not talking. But she's leaving tomorrow morning and I have a nauseating suspicion I won't speak to her again for a long time.

"Mia, I know you were unhappy inside for a long time, but right before you ran away, things seemed better, you seemed genuinely happy before you left."

She looks up from her packing. "I *was* really happy, Mom. I knew I was leaving."

It's funny. I used to be terrified of hurting my mom, it was my worst fear. Then it came true. That night she saw me cutting changed everything. It was one of those moments that define your life in a new way. Her look of pure horror and disgust, it was like she ripped me open and laid bare a gremlin. That was when I knew I had to go, that her house was too bright. I had already been hanging out and partying with street kids on the Promenade enough to know I made sense in their world, that I fit. Once I made the decision to go, I had found a thread to hang on to, to follow to salvation. Of course, I seemed happy, the last days of something are always the sweetest.

She goes back to packing, turning her face from me. My throat constricts. The stupid thing is, I get what she's saying, I know how she feels. It was how I felt when I thought about suicide, that promise of release. Only I was seeking escape *from* the darkness, I wanted the light at the end of the tunnel. She seeks escape in the opposite direction. Either way promises oblivion.

Our most intimate conversations have always been while I was sitting on her bed like I am now, usually at bedtime. I remember how terrified she always was of monsters in the dark, of bad guys under the bed or in the closet. I remember all the ways I tried to banish her fears—telling the monster he had the wrong address and sending him off with directions and a cookie, turning on the lights to show her the empty closet, magic wanding them poof! into dead mosquitoes, see there he is smushed on the screen. Nothing helped. One time she began to cry and told me not to bother, pointing to her head and saying sadly, "You can't make them go away, Mudder, because they're in my head."

Now, she'll do anything to get rid of the monsters in her head, even if it kills her. God knows it's killing me.

8.

I don't know what about animal dissection inspires this teacher but he's practically two-stepping his instructions across the room. I glance around to see if anyone else finds this weird, but no one's the least bit fazed. Of course not, Mia, you're in fucking farmland, they all probably killed a chicken this morning to bring for lunch.

I do a quick inventory of my new class. I brought neither bible nor shotgun, so between the religious and the rednecks, the snot-nosed nerd in the back is increasingly appealing. I'm beginning to wonder what I've gotten myself into. Then I notice the arm-crossed, slouching girl in the back. She smiles at me, runs a ring-filled hand through short and spiky bleached blonde hair. She's pretty, with heavy eyeliner, electric blue eyes.

When I pass her desk on the way out, she says hi.

"I'm Melanie. You're that new chick from LA, right?"

At least I haven't been mistaken for a local.

I've only been in Larkin about a month but I'm really happy, trailer parks, hunting, cornfields, and all. One kid here actually pulls up to school in a small tractor. A fucking tractor! Like I should talk. I show up in a yellow school bus.

Melanie and I hang out almost every day. I don't know where she gets her drugs but her supply seems never ending. After school, I walk the now-familiar path to Melanie's house and follow her singing to the bathroom, a cluttered crack of a room filled with hanging clothes and a sink dyed rainbow from years of spilled hair dye and makeup. Despite the dirt, I love the mess in her house, it feels homey, easy to squish into and disappear. Our house has hardwood floors, hard angles, and uncomfortable, yet attractive, furniture.

"Mel?"

Two surprised blue eyes peep out from the curtain. "Oh! Hi. Listen, Jeremy's folks are gone for the weekend, he's having a huge party. It'll be awesome. Tell your aunt you're staying at my house, my mom will cover."

One thing I'm still getting used to is that no one here has parents—even if they have them. Lying for my friends certainly wasn't part of my mother's parenting. When I was little and didn't get my way, I would fantasize that I had "real" parents somewhere that never said no. It suddenly feels like I've walked into the golden land of those imaginary parents.

I love it here. I finally feel free. I have some space from my mom, I have a cool group of friends. I have no history.

"I think she smokes pot with her new friends, but she does go to school," my sister says to me optimistically.

If the worst thing she does is smoke pot in the cornfields, it's an improvement. My, how my standards have changed. Hopkins is out the window, too, she'll never go back. We look at public schools all the way into the Valley. They all look the same, the same dingy halls, same tired teachers, the same gang-banger boys and slutty girls I sent her to a private school to shield her from.

Mia steadfastly refuses to come to the phone when we call. We haven't spoken to her once since she left. Six weeks later it still feels like a kick in the stomach.

"Are your teeth brushed?"

My little cousin Sophie nods her head vigorously.

"Okay, go pick out a bedtime story."

Sophie loves when I read to her because I always do the voices. Cockney street urchins, evil wizards, I can be just about anyone. Of course, being high helps. I've learned to lower my voice halfway through the book, so that she's asleep by the end of it.

"And the little princess lived happily ever after."

I fold the book and watch her sleep. She's so fragile but at the same time seems so much stronger than I am. I want to protect her, so bad things never happen to her, so she's always clean and glowing. I touch hair lightly, afraid to disturb her, to rub off.

The doorbell rings. I run down before it wakes up Sophie. Melanie's there with two guys I've never seen. She smiles and shakes a baggie of white powder in front of her face. She probably fucked them for it. A month ago I would have gotten mad at her for doing that, but I don't even care now. It keeps stuff coming my way.

"Oooh, Mia, you're gonna LOVE this shit!" she giggles furiously. "This heay's the pure, uncut co-cai-een-a."

An hour of partying later, I'm throwing up the "uncut cocaieena." My tongue's bloody from biting it while it was numb and the acid from the vomit stings. Shaking, I push through the medicine cabinet and find the Nyquil bottles so I can fall asleep. Thank God Sophie gets so many colds.

Melanie's free drug supply no longer baffles me. His name is Trevor Wilkinson. Most things don't live up to their reputation. The Wilkinsons leave theirs in the dust. Local legends, Trevor and his brother are both dropouts and are usually in trouble with the law. The most anyone's seen of them is a glimpse from their black Impala, a flash of face, a whiff of smoke, a blaring song.

Their house looks like a ghetto crackhouse airlifted and dropped in the middle of a cornfield. Blue paint is peeling and faded, a rusting pickup truck sits dying on the front lawn, and a mangled dog is chained to the front porch. It lunges for me when I walk by.

"Shut it, Samson," someone behind me growls.

I turn and there's a skinny, blond guy standing behind me. His hazel eyes look gentle despite the devil lock hanging between them and a badly scarred eyebrow. He looks twenty-six, twenty-seven.

"Who's she?" he asks, blatantly checking me up and down.

"Mia," I say. "You gonna keep staring or invite us in?"

"Feisty," he says, flashing a grin. "I like that. I'm Derek."

He reaches for the front door but it flies open on its own as a guy bursts through and hurls himself over the porch, retching.

We walk down a dingy hallway into a smoky room filled with people in various stages of oblivion. Condom wrappers litter the floor, along with empty plastic baggies, tin foil, and soda bottles.

Melanie struts in like Cleopatra, laughing as she pushes a potato-faced kid with a bull ring out of the way to clear a spot on the sofa. A small pile of heroin sits on the coffee table. Suddenly, Mel goes silent. I watch, intrigued by this new side of her, precise, focused, and serious.

Just as I lean in to do a line, the door slams open and a squatty woman with hair shooting out in all directions is silhouetted in the doorway.

"Hi honey, I'm Linda."

"Mia," I say, waiting for her to comment on the small mountain of dope.

"Nice meetin' you, sweetie." Her smile vanishes. "Derek, did you take my cigarettes?"

This place is nuts, awesome, but nuts. I lean back in and cut out two lines. The high hits me totally unexpectedly. It's not that instant rush you get from coke, it sort of melts over you slowly until it feels normal to be weightless and floating, like life has always been slow and beautiful. My body comes and goes, tingly and prickly one minute, normal the next. I sit zoned out like that for hours before I realize I have to puke.

Derek gives me a ride home, Melanie being "occupied" with Trevor. I pass Linda curled up on the sofa, dazed and drooling.

"Is she sick?" I whisper.

"No," Derek answers. "Not sick . . . just weak."

I spend time in Mia's room each day, exploring her old books and toys, her collection of handmade boxes, her photos. It soothes the ache in a part of me I wasn't aware of yet, the way your sternum or spleen doesn't exist until it hurts. I have a new organ now in the shape of my daughter's absence. I'm learning the anatomy of new life.

Late one Saturday night, I find a pretty wallet that she never used. Or so I thought. I notice a seam has been opened to make a secret place. I dig inside and find a folded white 3 × 5 card. I unfold it to see, written in blood traced with a fingertip: ROTTEN.

"Hey, Mia, I'm gonna mix you up something special, 'kay? It's better than straight H. Speedballs are seriously like communing with God."

"Sure," I mumble, half stoned, half drunk.

Derek comes over with a needle and a belt.

"Here, tighten this around your arm," he says. "Make sure it's really tight."

The needle comes toward me, slow and weaving, like the circles my mom used to make with a spoon when I was little to get me to eat. It finally makes contact with the vein and plunges in.

It's the most mindblowing pleasure, the rush of coke minus the agitation. And when the coke wears off it leaves just enough of an edge to enjoy the heroin, which is ten times more potent than snorting.

* * *

There's nothing like personal calamity to find out just how small your town is. Somehow, everyone knows what's happened to our family, friends, colleagues, school moms. I run into them everywhere, in library stacks, at the Writers Guild Theatre, at the Farmer's Market herb stand. I've become a human car wreck that people can't help rubbernecking.

They're all kind, concerned, but sometimes I need to not be who I am. I've ducked out a restaurant kitchen, slipped through an employee lounge, hidden behind display racks. I've escaped through the produce doors at Whole Foods twice.

I know they all care, many of them deeply, and I'm grateful. It's the pity in their eyes I can't stand. How careful they are. It's such a thin line between I'm sorry it's you and I'm glad it's not me.

We go to the Wilkinsons so often now it's become routine. Time's hard to distinguish there, nights blur with days, this week with last week with last month. It's like a continuum, you know whenever you go back you'll pick up right where you left off, snorting, smoking, shooting. It's its own world, that house.

Derek's become like a big brother. Sometimes he takes me on drives and shows me stuff, the best cliff jumping spots, places where deer gather, secret caves. We talk about things, his mom, my old dad. He lived on the streets for a year before coming back home. He's been on heroin for six, but he says he's trying to kick it. Kick it and leave this place for good.

I know what he means about this place now. Being young and doing this shit is one thing, but here half the parents do it, too. I know one guy whose forty-five-year-old aunt gives his friends head as long as they dope her up first.

"No," Derek says, ignoring the ten I tap against his shoulder.

"What the hell's your problem? You mix me speedballs all the time."

"I know, but shooting straight is different. You think I haven't noticed your legs?" he asks, sucking the liquid into a needle. I tug down my cutoffs. I'd forgotten about my scars.

"That don't matter, I already seen them," he mumbles, one end of a belt in his mouth. "You got enough to figure out without fucking yourself up even more. Don't wanna end up like me now, do ya?"

I'd normally continue to argue, but something in his tone silences me. He jerks his head sideways, pulling the belt tight while pumping his fist. Tapping his bulging blue vein, he shoots up. His blood replaces the junk in the needle and I watch the bright red mix with the fluid, like jellyfish tentacles. For some reason it reminds me of a womb, something about the blood curling up into the fluid and swaying gently. It seems warm and cozy and I want to be in there, just for a moment.

I start to say so but his eyes are already closed, his back slumped against the wall and he curls on his side. I push his devil lock to the side to see his profile. He looks young all of a sudden, small. I saw him curled up like this last week, only then it was because he was sick from withdrawal, his sheets covered in his own filth. He didn't even make it six days.

I've been in Indiana visiting Mia for three days and haven't looked into her eyes once. She won't look at me and barely speaks to me. I know nothing of her now, what she thinks, what she does, where she goes. My daughter's made me irrelevant. I need new skills. I need all-seeing eyes, I need the ears of a dog, I need clairvoyance, armor. I need many things to be Mia's mother now, love least of all. Now, love is a liability.

She doesn't know who I am, either, and I think it angers her. She doesn't recognize this woman who is scared, who doesn't know how to make her pain go away.

We share the same guest bed, and some nights she scoots over and puts her arm around me. The night before I leave, she says good night, Mom, I love you. I cry till long after she's asleep.

I gotta get the hell out of here. By the time Derek picks me up, it takes two fat lines before I even begin to calm down. I'd forgotten how bad it is between my mom and me now, either awkward silences or pointless lectures.

When we get there, I'm thankful for the chaos that is the Wilkinson house. For Samson's barking, for Linda's hollering, for everyone high as hell and getting drunk.

I go to the corner where Melanie's at and blow some coke while matching shots with Derek and Trevor. I lean back and the room splatters into pieces. Furniture and people's faces and bodies all swirl together to dance a dervish and I see my mom's face floating in the middle of it all, with her sad, defeated look. I hate that face, it's a lie. She was never like that until I ran away. She was never weak or helpless, she's usually a fucking banshee.

A familiar rage builds, my hands clench. I stumble to the bathroom and fumble around until I find a razor. It pours out of me in a torrent, every thought and feeling leaving a red gash on its way out. I cry red until I can breathe again.

"Whooohoooo!"

Melanie's on the bed in her underwear and a T-shirt, rocking her hips in tempo with the music. Five guys are crowded around the bed, shouting and whooping. Every couple seconds she stumbles, then giggles and keeps dancing. I want to leave but I shot some shit and am too fucked up to move.

Melanie's really into it now, whipping her hair around like a rock star and leaning over far enough for everyone to see down her shirt, sans bra.

"Hey, Mel!" Trevor yells, pumping his hips. "Show them what you show me!"

Melanie turns her back, then whips her shirt off, cascading giggles. How can she do that? I can't take off my shirt in front of one guy, much less five. She's running her hands over herself and shaking her hair and feeling so good and . . .

I come to and the room's empty and dark. I'm so thirsty. I go to sit up but I'm pushed back down. I can't . . . I can't breathe. Gasping, I try to sit up again, but something's pushing me down. There's a weight on me and this pushing, on top of me, inside of me. In a haze, I see Derek's face floating above my own, wincing. What . . . what's his face doing there?

Sun streaks through the curtains. I pull the blanket up over my head and curl up in a ball. Shit! I feel last night's activities coming up. I grab a bag from the floor and let it go. I'm sweaty and shaking, my teeth chatter.

"Mia?"

Melanie gets up and comes over to me, pulling my hair from my face and stroking it. Her hands are refreshing and cool.

"Come on, sweetie, let's go eat, you'll feel better."

Nodding, I pull the cover off to get up and immediately throw it back on. I'm naked from the waist down.

"Did I fall asleep like that?"

Melanie grabs my jeans off the sofa. "Damn, Mia! You don't remember anything, do you?"

Well, no shit. I pull on my jeans and suddenly Derek's wincing face flashes. I stiffen and push his face out of my head.

Fuck it Mia, what happened, happened. Just forget about it.

When Melanie calls next I make up some excuse for not wanting to go to the Wilkinsons. I'm afraid to be around Derek, of him pretending nothing happened. Of me going along with it.

"Brian Starcher told me about a party tonight, he'll pick us up at my house."

I've seen Brian at school. He roams the hallways in his wife beater, muscles bulging, chains and cigarette dangling beneath multicolored spikes.

We go to some guy's house and party until late. Brian and I drop acid under the stars and have one of those "deep" conversations. There's a fair tomorrow, he says. By the time the acid wears off, it is tomorrow.

"Mia's run again, Claire."

The phone call we've been dreading. Paul knows before I say anything, by the way I drop into a chair with the phone. He slams his fist on the cabinet.

The police find her later that day outside a raunchy bar in another town. The officer tells me she was with ex-cons. Parolees at a biker bar. It's Venice, country style. Vivian picks her up from the police station with her bags already packed. She can't put her on a plane fast enough.

If I thought she looked bad at Vivian's, she's even worse now. Her eyes are always pinkish, her nose runs, her cheeks and eye sockets are sunken. She barely weighs a hundred pounds.

She's coarse, rabbity, aggressive, secretive. Sometimes she cackles with hoarse laughter that's so unnerving, I'm almost afraid of her, of this Indiana Mia. She's picked up the accent and mannerisms of rural druggies so well, I think she needs an exorcism rather than therapy, which she refuses anyway. "No freakin' way, I don't need no therapist."

Sometimes she's so blue and quiet, it's painful to see, painful that she refuses to open up to me. Other times, she's beaming and fizzy, saying I'm so glad to be home! Of course, she's high when she's like this, so it poisons my joy. It's obvious she's completely addicted now. Her unspoken threat is that if we say anything about it, she'll run again.

She's become both stupid and cunning. What I've come to realize is that she doesn't need to be any smarter. Just as a scholar thrives on how much she knows, a druggie thrives on how little. Their knowledge and energy constrict around finding their next high, their brilliance is measured by it. If you only need to be smart about one thing, any junkie can be a genius.

It's frightening to have no parental authority, no power to help her. Still, we're thankful that she's not on the street. That she's not a crime scene photo on a Venice police officer's desk.

She agrees to finish tenth grade at an alternative school, "for fuck-ups," she says, not bothered by the label. The director, Maddy, likes Mia, she likes them all, they're creative, misunderstood, they march to a different drummer. They march to their dealers, I add. Then that's their path, Maddy says, you must trust that your child will find her way.

What if that way leads to permanent addiction, to jail, to the funeral parlor? Or just to the shabby half-life of those who never fully rose up from the level they sunk to in their drug days? Like the men with graying ponytails who hand you your groceries. Or the women with cigarette laughs, funky toenails, and sagas to tell.

"I'm taking a bus back to Indiana."

It's early Sunday morning, her duffel's already packed.

"I didn't want to sneak out again. I promise I'll call every few weeks to let you know I'm okay. But, if you guys or Aunt Vivian do anything to find me, you'll never hear from me again."

You said you'd finish school, I say weakly. Paul, the easy parent, the one who was always a sucker for his little girl, has had it.

"You don't have to worry, we're not going to look for you this time!" he yells at her. "You want to go live with scum, go! You want to throw away your future, fine, go, leave now!"

This has broken him. There is a flash of hurt on her face; it's the first emotion she's shown since she got home. Still, she walks to the door with her duffel.

"Mia, wait!" I rush after her. "The bus station's in a dangerous part of town! Your dad will take you. Paul, please!"

I can't believe it, I'm volunteering to take her to a bus station to run away. But she'll escape no matter what we do. At least she's offering to call. No one speaks on the ride downtown. The ticket line is full of migrant workers, drifters, a group of nuns. Mia stands outside my car door in the seedy parking lot, hoping I'll come out to say good-bye.

"Please, Mommy, it's not about you, it's not, I just have to do this, I have to be on my own. Please, hug me good-bye."

When she starts to walk away, I jump out and clutch her. We're both crying for this good-bye, the way we cried when she arrived in the world.

"Promise you won't look for me, I promise I'll call from the road every day so you know I'm okay," she says as she hugs me then pulls away.

"Please call us, Mia." She's already walking away from me. "Please call! I promise I won't look for you!"

I am lying.

9.

"I can't believe she hasn't called yet, she promised," I whisper to Paul in the middle of the second night. There's no need to preface it with, "Are you awake?"

"You actually believed her?" he says.

"She doesn't want to feel guilty. She thinks calling us lets her off the hook."

Till now, "waiting for the phone to ring in the night" was just a cliché. Now, we're torn between dying for it to ring and be Mia, and hoping it doesn't because it might be the police or the morgue.

I'm on a bus in the middle of nowhere, high off my ass. This tweaker saw me popping Coricidin the first day and we've been sitting in the back getting high ever since. There's shit else to do on a bus for three days.

There's a group of nuns singing praise to Jesus on my left, a cluster of screaming babies up front, and pacing the aisle is some sketchy guy muttering to himself in Spanish. Thank God I'm high because I couldn't handle all this straight.

My anger at Mia for doing this to herself has pulled me out of the fog of parental guilt. A depressed, drug-addled fifteen-year-old has manipulated and intimidated all of the adults around her into collaborating in her self-destruction.

I juggle writing and feigning good cheer for the producer with researching a way to help Mia nearly every hour of the day. I have the phone company put a trace on our line and alert Vivian that she's headed for Indiana. I call police officers, probation officers, and state social workers to find a rehab program for her. Until Mia breaks the law, they can't help.

Insurance will pay for a month of inpatient rehab, but it won't be much different than the psych ward. I try calling the local high school guidance counselor, who recommends we go for family therapy. Right.

Dr. Kravitz suggests a therapeutic boarding school in the mountains nearby. Five grand a month, a lot of traditional therapy, and she can't be forced to stay. Not good.

Someone suggests joining BILY, Because I Love You, a support group for parents of runaways and missing kids. Oh, no, Paul groans, I couldn't take it. I agree. Our misery doesn't want the company of theirs.

I've learned to say she has a drug addiction stemming from depression rather than sexual abuse. Drugs are cool and half of LA is on antidepressants. Fallout from incest? You can hear them squirm through the phone. How easy it would be if it were only drugs. Drugs you can withdraw from. How do you withdraw from memories—a lobotomy?

"Mia!"

I step off the bus in Indiana and there's Brian, smiling. I race over and I'm so happy to be off that bus I kiss him. He explains the living situation to me on the ride home. He's obviously tweaked, talking and driving like a maniac.

"See, I technically live with my cousin and his girlfriend, who fucking hates me. So most nights, I just sleep in my van. So, I was thinking we could just live in my van and then for showers and shit we'll wait until she leaves and sneak you in. In about a month I'm gonna rent a trailer."

"That's cool. Oh, shoot, hold up. I gotta call my mom."

"Yes, we'll take the charges! Where are you, are you okay?"

"I don't know, Kansas," Mia says. "I just want you to know I'm okay. I gotta go."

She's not in Kansas, the caller ID box says she's in an area near Larkin. I call the Larkin police. Vivian says to tell them she hung out with the Wilkinsons.

The police tell us they'll watch for her, then tell us two things: not to search on our own because we'd stick out too much and Larkin County has one of the worst heroin problems in the nation. So much for the wholesome countryside. There's the 4H and the other H.

I ask them what they'd do if it were their kid. The general consensus:

slap the living daylights out of them, lock 'em in the barn, home school them, and let 'em out at eighteen. At this point, it's the best suggestion we've heard.

The girlfriend's gone so I get my first shower since I left home a week ago. I've been coughing a lot lately and the steam feels good in my chest. When I get out, Brian's standing there staring.

"Hello," I say, surprised. I feel both pleased and squirmy. We've had sex once before but I was high and kept most of my clothes on. When he finally hands me the towel I take it and run upstairs to dry off and change.

We cut a few lines and head over to a party at his friend Warren's place. It's loud and rowdy, an older version of the Wilkinson house. Warren's fun and kind of fatherly, but with an edge. He's telling stories about his latest escapade, a fight he and some friends got into.

"I took a bat to this one jackass, damn near killed him. And then his friend came out to get his back and I turned around and knifed the fucker!"

His eyes gleam with pride. I'm glad when he stops talking and goes back to drinking and manning the grill. He brings me a burger.

"As long as you're here you're family. I know Brian since he was a little shrivel dick. Hey, and just 'cause this jackass lives in his vehicle, you're a lady and if you ever want a real bed you come on over here."

I smile and thank him, trying to reconcile the image of this hospitable guy with someone who amuses himself by splitting people's heads open with baseball bats.

I've been afraid to call Mia's friend, Melanie, in case she alerts her, but we have nothing else to go on. I make girl talk, earn her confidence. She says she hasn't seen Mia. I drop casually that coke now and then wasn't so bad, but Mia's looking awful now.

"She's probably speedballing more," she says, as if I know what it is. "That can make you look pretty bad."

She promises to call if she hears from Mia. I research speedballing. Injecting a mixture of cocaine and heroin is one of the most common causes of death by overdose. The heart loses rhythm and fails. River Phoenix and John Belushi died speedballing.

Paul and I have been on two phone lines and two computers looking for help. We've googled "teen," "juvenile," "drugs," "delinquent," but all we get are porno sites—naked teens behind bars, naked teens in bondage, naked teen drug orgies. We've tried "Rehab," "treatment," "family"— nothing, nothing, nothing. I'm ready to don overalls, hunt her down, and lock her in the first barn I can buy.

When the phone rings.

"She do what?!" our French friend Yvette cries out. "Sanks à God you call to me! I know a mozer wiz a girl who do bad tings, so she lock 'er up in some place zat fix 'er! She a big model now, zat girl! I going to call to 'er right now!"

I have a new alarm clock: the slamming of my head against the van floor when Brian races over the railroad tracks on the way to work. I tap on the glass for him to pull over so I can come up front. I lift up the hatch and hop down but my legs give way and little white dots appear everywhere. I sit on the ground, taking deep breaths. In a minute, color and sound drain back like a slow wave. Still shaky, I hold onto the car for support until I feel the front door handle.

"It's extreme and expensive. You can't just go visit either, she has to earn it," Yvette's friend tells me. "But it worked for us. We have a very close relationship now."

Her daughter was at a behavior modification school in Utah for a year, a state that allows you to force your child into treatment. We naïvely assumed the laws were the same everywhere.

We've never heard of this kind of school but they've been in the news, on *48 Hours*, *Dateline*, and we get copies of the shows. Their portrayal is hardly encouraging. They sound scary, like they brainwash the kids. Though if they were like Mia, maybe they needed their brains washed.

We get referral names from the schools and talk to many families from an array of them, most of whom are happy, with some minor criticisms. But we're troubled by the conflicting portrayals. Do we believe the parents, whom the schools themselves chose for referrals, or the news?

On the one hand, the media's supposed to report with no bias. On the other hand, Woody Allen marries his daughter and the press still adores him. And just as schools pick their referral parents, reporters pick the kids they talk to. Kids with good stories would hardly sell. And Yvette's friend was not referred by a school.

We try Maddy, from the alternative school. Yes, she says, I've had parents send students there as a last resort, and they do seem to change the kids, but I worry at what cost. She says they come back with this cultish vocabulary and they seem just a little too polite. "I hate to tame these kids, Claire." Though I'm sure it wasn't her intention, she's just given the schools a recommendation—*a little too polite*? And psychotherapy's got plenty of its own slang—projection, overdetermined, fixation.

We find schools in Utah, Montana, and Oregon, all far from civilization, with "trails to success" amid towering pines and cinnamon-hued boulders. We study brochures, scrutinize websites, and call parents till we're dizzy. Some schools sound too warm and fuzzy. I don't want the counselors to be her "friend," I want her to feel like she's hit a wall. And I want that wall as escape-proof and as far from anyone she knows as possible.

Once again, like Glinda in her shimmering bubble, Yvette appears at our door, in her impossibly high heels and red lipstick, carrying a bottle of wine and glasses.

"You don't believe eet, Claire, she come 'ere, ze model! She going to be shot in LA and she want talk to you! She be at my 'ouse tomorrow night, I going to make a nice dinner for you." She pours three glasses of wine. "Come, my darleeng, we going to 'ave a leelabeet wine, because you look terreeble. I tell you, you going to find Mia by zis weekend, I know eet! Salut!"

From her French leeps to God's ears.

The rain pummels down outside Warren's living room. His son Devon's playing his favorite video game, Street Fighter. As usual, he's dirty and full of scabs from fighting in school.

"You're lucky, when I was a kid, my mom didn't let me play video games," I say, coughing in between words. My chest is on fire.

"That sucks. Here, play with me!"

I grab a controller and try to dodge the kicks coming at my character, an Asian girl in lime green. When Devon finally kicks the shit out of me, he jumps up, yelling, "Haha, I killed that dirty gook!"

I can't believe the little snot just said that! I'm about to ask him where he heard that when Warren reaches over and roughs up his hair.

"Way to go, Dev, that's what you gotta do to gooks, and niggers, get rid of

'em. They're a total waste of space that steal our women and tax dollars. Remember those dudes Daddy beat a couple weeks ago after I picked you up from school? Those were fag bastards, which are just as bad as kikes, gooks, and niggers."

My mouth goes dry and my high vanishes instantly as I realize that my new friends are probably the skinheads Aunt Vivian used to talk about. My heart is pounding so hard, I'm scared he'll actually hear it.

The twisted and misshapen body of the neighbor Warren beat to a bloody pulp last weekend flashes to mind. It was surreal to watch, a kamikaze blur of arms and legs until the man spewed red like a fountain. And that was just for asking Warren to turn down his music.

I am so stupid, so blind. And so Jewish. For some reason, a memory from childhood comes up. Of standing at the kitchen counter picking out unwanted raisins from my cereal. To make sure I would have a completely raisin-free breakfast, I invented a game where the raisins were Nazis and the cereal flakes were Jews. I'd sift through my cereal and pluck out the Nazis, who shouted and protested that they were really Jews. But I was not fooled by their lies and would throw all the raisins in my clenched palm into the trash and slam the lid shut. I solved the raisin question!

But now the tables have turned and I wonder if the raisins know there's one little cereal flake hiding in their midst. And what they would do if they found out.

I can't get Warren's words out of my head. Fag bastards? I was practically raised by lesbians and "fag bastards." And my first kiss was with a "gook."

The rain hammering down on the van and my flood of thoughts is driving me crazy. I count out the last of my money, a whopping two dollars and sixty-seven cents.

I hop out and walk to town in the rain. By the time I get there, I'm soaked and muddy. I also can barely see. I feel so weak and light-headed, I sit down on the side of the road in the rain and put my head between my knees. A spiked ball has settled in the back of my throat. Please, God, please, don't let me faint out here like a dog in the dirt.

I need to get out of here but I have no money and nowhere to go. I'm scared. Of Brian, of Warren, of the fact that I keep fainting and on some days can barely breathe. I light a cigarette and try to come up with a plan, but I keep drawing blanks. The van seems impossibly far away now, so I call Brian's work and a half-hour later, he pulls up, grinning. He got a big bonus today and we waste no time getting started on an eight-ball of coke.

* * *

"Mia! Are you sick? You sound sick, honey." Paul rushes over to listen. He points to the caller ID box—she's in a different area code.

"I need money." Her voice is thin and scratchy.

"We're afraid you'll use cash for drugs. Aunt Vivian will bring you food, anything you need!"

"I want cash, you fucking bitch!" she suddenly screams shrilly.

It's like a gunshot—she's never, *never* cursed at me.

"If you won't send me any fucking cash," she yells, "then give me his number! I want my fucking old father's phone number, bitch!"

"I—I don't know it." I'm stunned. "You're going to ask him for money?"

"I want to tell him what an asshole he is for ruining our lives! I want him to die!" she shrieks and hangs up.

Paul takes the phone out of my hand and looks at me anxiously.

"We're losing her, Paul."

"It was the hardest thing I've ever done. I hated it there for a long time. You go through some serious emotional shit and the other girls won't let you fake your way through. You can't lie to a liar."

"Zat model" has met us at Yvette's for dinner. I recognize her from magazines. She's candid, poised, kind. She's spending the little time off she has on this shoot with two miserable parents she doesn't know.

She tells us the first three levels in the school are more internal, about getting you to recognize how you got there. Levels four, five, and six are more about how you interact with the world, with peers and family.

"You become a mentor to newer girls and there's a lot more contact with parents."

"What prompted you to start changing?"

"After a while, you see that the kids who've moved up to higher levels in the school really are happier. You just get sick of your own bullshit, you know? I still use a lot of what I learned, it really does change you for the better, long term. I do occasionally have a drink but I haven't used drugs since, which is saying a lot in my profession."

Of all the schools, the parents from her school or their sister facilities are the most ardent in their support of "the program," as they call it, which surprises me given it's the strictest of the lot and the one the media slams the most. One woman returns my call after midnight. I knew you'd be awake, she says, I've been there. She's right, I'm wide awake, studying a map of Larkin.

Parents are honest about what they don't like—the food's lousy, communication isn't always good, academics are mediocre. They're also blunt in saying that Paul and I will be doing some behavior modifying of our own; the program involves the entire family.

The last woman I talk to, Trish, feels most like me in terms of personality and philosophy. She's a banker who also teaches yoga, with a happy marriage and a daughter much like Mia at their newest facility.

"I think it's actually the extremity of the program and location that works. They have to be stripped of everything familiar and comfortable, so their only comfort becomes internal. I especially like that the program includes visualizations and affirmations along with the strict rules. The balance is quite remarkable; it changes the way they think. The director, Glenn, is amazing. The girls adore her."

"You're sending her where?!" everyone says.

Morava Academy. In Brno, Czech Republic, near the Slovak border. The other side of the world. Locked doors *and* windows. A tracking dog trained by the German military. Only twenty students, a student-to-staff ratio of 2:1. Peer group daily, personal growth seminars regularly. The teachers speak English, many have PhDs. Students earn the right to take trips to Prague, Vienna, and Budapest. My mother's from Hungary, she and I can visit together and show Mia her heritage.

It couldn't get any better. All we have to do is find her. She hasn't called in a week.

"For heaven's sake, tell the police and your sister to stop looking for her. If anyone notices, she'll take off. I'm a former police officer, I'll coordinate with them when I get there. Try to get me a name, that's best in rural areas."

Jack Tyson is an escort. I had no idea there was an entire profession devoted to finding and snatching seriously wayward teens. When he finds her, *if* he does, he'll take her to a holding facility in Utah where she'll get a medical and psychological evaluation before being escorted to the Czech Republic.

Melanie hasn't called but I try her again, telling her that Mia is sick and we want to send money and medicine. She says she's sorry but doesn't sound like it and doesn't offer more. I think her tone's changed because she hears the desperation in my voice. She knows my small talk is begging and she's enjoying it.

I hear her light a cigarette. I hear her inhale.

"Well, you know," she says languidly, "I do remember her saying something about camping with some guy."

I can picture her narrowing her eyes as she blows the smoke out in her own sweet time. Then she sighs the words out slowly, "I think . . . it was . . . Brian . . . Briiiian Starcher."

She always knew. And she never would have called to tell me. I had to go to her, do a dance, wheedle. There's a learning curve to this that could cost Mia her life.

I find the Starcher's number easily enough. Fortunately, Brian's brother is young, polite, and intimidated by me. Unfortunately, he doesn't know where he is. But he does know where he works. Jack's on a plane within hours.

"He filled the door, Claire, literally. He could kidnap a gorilla."

It's late at night and Jack's just left Vivian's. She gave him and his partner, Beth, names and locations, local hangouts. They'll start their search early tomorrow at the campground. It's the first night I feel any kind of hope.

I've been wanting to go camping ever since we got here. I love being out at night like this, out in the wild. I look up at the stars. They make me feel alive. It's a welcome change from that dead feeling that only drugs or raw physical sensation like cutting wakens. I feel connected. I don't know what to, but I feel less alone. I didn't grow up religious and I've always been somewhat envious of people who are. I felt dumb whenever I prayed, like I was talking to a wall. I could just picture God sitting up high looking at his answering machine and seeing six billion unheard messages and then deleting them all. But tonight's different. I don't feel alone, even if it is just the stars up there watching me.

* * *

I wake up today so weak I can barely move. Or breathe for that matter, my voice is almost totally gone and I'm wheezing like crazy. I have no appetite even though I haven't eaten in days. I literally don't even have the energy to pull myself up to the glass to signal to Brian as he starts the van. He's helping a friend move some stuff into his shop, a friend he says can give me a part-time job to pay for food and smokes. What he doesn't know is that it's also go-ing to buy me a ticket out of here. New York's not far and it's full of other street kids.

I lay my head down and pass out.

Jack and Beth cruise Larkin on the way to the campground. The van isn't there, but a girl remembers seeing it. They hit the gas stations, the bars and pool halls, the convenience stores, cheap diners. He checks the park-ing lot of Brian's job twice, but he must be off today.

The convenience store nearby is run by someone Jack feels he can trust. The man recognizes Mia, says she comes in for cigarettes. He promises not to alert her.

Jack returns to the campground but the van never shows up.

My coughing wakes me after it's dark. I pull myself up to the window. We're still at Brian's friend's; they're probably all inside the shop partying. I just want to sleep. I'll figure out what to do tomorrow.

Jack focuses his last day on Brian's job and places near it. He pulls into the lot of the plant, drives up and down the aisles, then stops.

The van sits parked in the hot June sun. He gets out one aisle over and walks toward the front of the van. Beth pulls up behind it, blocking the path out the back. Jack walks along the front bumper. The front seat is empty. He turns down the side. No curtains on the back window—good. Jack moves silently down the side of the van, stops at the window and looks in.

There's a dirty mattress and pillows. And no Mia. He looks around the lot, gets in his car, and tells Beth to drive to the convenience store. They'll come back to the lot and wait for Brian to leave and follow him.

They pull slowly out of the lot, passing a grassy area that slopes down to a river. And in that river, just below his sightline, a sick, emaciated girl is cooling off.

* * *

On my back, in my underclothes, the cool water feels like heaven. I was so hot I dragged myself to the river behind the plant. I had to stop to rest twice. Now, submerged in water, I look up at the wavering sky from underwater and for a blissful moment forget where I am.

An hour later, Jack returns to the plant lot and cruises up the aisle. The van is gone. Gone! Brian must have gotten off early. They search everywhere else she could be until late into the night, with no luck. He leaves early tomorrow.

My God, he was so close! I'm so upset I can't stop pacing. I have such a strong foreboding that she's about to run to somewhere else or overdose or she's sick.

I slap open the back door and stagger out into the night, barefoot and in pajamas, like a loosed asylum inmate with her robe flapping behind her. I burst into tears and stop in the street and beg—

"Dear God,

Please help me find Mia.

Sincerely,

Claire."

A letter? My first prayer in my adult life comes out like a letter? Like it was to Santa Claus?

God must have checked his mail. An hour later the phone rings. It's Mia. Can Aunt Vivian bring medicine and groceries? Yes yes yes! Antibiotics, antipsychotics, money, whatever you need, help is on the way, Mia, we love you please come home!

"Mother, I just want some money and antibiotics. Tell her to meet at the convenience store tomorrow at eleven. If she says one word to me, I'll take the stuff and I won't call you again."

I promise Mia she won't, trying to keep the happiness out of my voice. Jack generously agrees to stay an extra day to pick her up.

I think I've found a new pen pal. I send a Him thank you card immediately.

My mom finally did something right. My aunt's van is there, and there's a grocery bag sitting in front. I go to open the door and grab the bag, but it's locked.

Aunt Vivian gets out and walks around to where I'm standing. Shit, I didn't want to talk to her.

She unlocks the passenger door, reaches for the bag, hands it to me and hugs me, saying something about how much my family loves me. Just then I hear a door open behind me. I go to turn around but my arms are grabbed and I'm lifted in the air. My heart skyrockets out of my chest and I start looking around in every direction, panicking.

"Aunt Vivian, help me!"

She's saying something and looking at me sadly but isn't doing anything to stop this. What the FUCK is going on? Who is this guy? I vaguely hear him say, "It's okay, your mother sent us." Right! I'm sure those are the last words heard by every abducted girl from here to LA.

I'm pushed into a car, which speeds off immediately. My hands reach everywhere, the window, the handle, I'm trapped. They keep repeating that it's okay, I haven't been kidnapped, my mother sent them.

"Prove it, you fucking assholes!" I yell, on the verge of tears.

The guy turns around to me and says with a smile, "Twinkletoes."

I freeze. That was our secret family password when I was little.

Everything falls into place, the sad look on my aunt's face, my mom's willingness to send me money, the locked door. I feel like I've been hit by a truck. My own mother had me kidnapped.

10.

"Our 'A' student was drug addicted. . . . Renee graduated from the program having rediscovered self-esteem, respect, love for her family and her incredible talents."

". . . Jonathon is loving, patient, respectful, powerful, truly the magical child he was many years ago. This has been the greatest gift we've ever received."

I'm addicted to them, the testimonials. We're in a frenzy trying to find Mia's passport but every time I pass the dining room I have to stop and read some more, like a gerbil hitting the food lever. I can't get enough. My child will be saved, they say to me, they'll return her to me, to herself, to happiness!

Paul's been swamped with work, so our friend Karin has been staying a few days to help me through this. She's sunny and optimistic, a boon to our spirits. She's also extremely practical and organized, which is a huge help to a frazzled mother trying to get everything together to send her daughter halfway across the planet.

"I'm going where?"

The "escorts" dropped me off and now these people are telling me this isn't rehab and I'm going to the Czech Republic! They might as well have said I'm going on an expedition to Jupiter—do I prefer a blue or pink jumpsuit?

"But Jack said I'm being sent to rehab for two weeks," I repeat, praying they have me mixed up with some other kid.

"He lied because your mom said you might run."

That bitch!

"But what does the Czech Republic have to do with rehab?"

They explain it to me again. Behavior modification program. Typical stay is around one year. The rules will be explained when I get there. Held here until I have my passport. That last part is the only useful thing out of their mouths.

"How long does that take?"

What I'm really asking is how long I have to plan an escape. The answer: about five days.

If I wasn't so tired last night, I would have noticed this wasn't rehab. No "rehab" is a log cabin in the desert, with dead mounted animals on every surface. Monkeys, elk, a leopard, the entire front half of an impala. The table we play cards on is an elephant's ear perched on its own foot.

There are eight kids here, some going to Samoa or Jamaica. Three of us are going to the Czech Republic. Two once I get out of here.

The next couple of days go by really slow. I have so little energy I pretty much sleep through most of it. They gave me some medicine so at least my fever's gone. The worst part is I can't smoke. Not having any dope is bad enough but quitting smoking at the same time is a bitch. I'm not the only one. It's amazing no one's killed anyone else.

I've decided to wait until Sunday to run. I'm still weak, and I need more time to figure out the pattern of the place. I've been pocketing food, but all the windows I've checked are alarmed. Plus, my mom obviously said something to the staff, because they've been watching me like a hawk.

When I wake up this morning, it's still dark out. I got to the bathroom and bump into someone. It's the new girl, Hollie, the tiny, redhead that came in last night. She's at the window with her arms up. I quickly go in and shut the door.

"Hey," I whisper, "are you trying to run?"

She starts to deny it but I cut her off.

"It's cool, I am too. I have some food saved up but so far all the windows I've checked have alarms on them."

She looks at me a second and then opens up her palm. There's a battery in it.

They fax us Mia's psychological test results. On the Incomplete Sentence Blank section: My nerves—are fried, My mind—is fried, The future—seems bleak, People—piss me off. They report her attitude as demanding and contemptuous, with a general disdain for people. Gee, d'ya think?

They've started her on antibiotics and she was found to be clinically malnourished. She's jittery with withdrawal, but is cooperative, which makes me nervous.

"That's her MO," I warn Loren, the owner of the holding facility. "If she's behaving well, she's thinking of running."

They assure me she's being watched constantly, even at night. She's leaving in the morning. Thank God it's over. I sing to myself as I get ready for bed, my voice resonating with joy and relief. It's the first time I've sung since the night I sang her lullabies over the phone. The night before she vanished.

It's become my frame of reference, that night. It is my Before and After.

The night watch person just shined his light over the beds. When he leaves, I look over at Hollie and nod. We pull off our pajamas and stuff them under the blanket, along with some other clothes. He shines the light around so quickly that as long as it looks like a body, we're fine. But there's a motion sensor that's going to be tricky.

We pull socks over our flip-flops to make running easier and quieter. Then we slide off our beds and crawl on our bellies VERY slowly, to the bathroom.

The bathroom window opens soundlessly. Hollie goes up with a boost from me and I follow, hoisting myself up and over before jumping outside. We take off running as fast as we can in sock-covered flip-flops. Suddenly, Hollie stops short. There's an enormous, cactus-filled ditch. We climb down, plow through the brush, climb up the other side of the ditch, and see three more ravines just like this one. Shit! Just that one cost us an extra ten minutes! An hour later, we finally spot the road.

Out here, all roads lead to Hurricane, a town the size of a tumbleweed and equally exciting, I'm sure. By the time we reach town the sky's changed from black to gray. My socks look like Hellraiser—*thorns and bristles stick out from every angle and my legs are a bloody mess.*

While Hollie calls her boyfriend in Salt Lake from a pay phone, I notice a small house across the street with a For Rent sign. Enough slats are missing from the pulled blinds for me to guess that it's vacant. Two narrow rectangular windows by the ground around back will be easiest to break. I motion for Hollie to come over, pick up a rock, shatter the window, and crawl in.

By the time she climbs down, any fear about someone living here is gone. An inch of dust covers everything and cobwebs are everywhere. If I hadn't just walked five hours in thorn-covered flip-flops, I'd probably be weirded out. But right now, all I can focus on is a sofa at the end of the room. The last thing

I remember hearing is that her boyfriend is sending two of his friends to come get us.

"Ms. Fontaine, there's been a staff error."

It's the supervisor, Monty. He's spent extra time with Mia and called many times to reassure me.

"Staff error, what, on her application, do you need me to send something?" It doesn't occur to me that it's too early for anyone to be doing any paperwork there. Paul's sound asleep, so is Karin.

"No, Ms. Fontaine. Mia has fled the facility."

Karin will tell me later that I kept screaming. All I will remember of this moment is the color red. Karin will tell me later that she had been trying to grab hold of me and she had on red pajamas.

"How long has she been gone?" I yell into the phone.

"Seven hours, we didn't know they were gone till wake-up."

"Seven hours?! Who's they?!"

"She ran with another girl named Hollie who has a boyfriend in Salt Lake; we think they've contacted him. We have people checking it out. It's our fault, I can't apologize enough. It was a new employee on night duty. We're all out searching, people in town, the sheriff."

Karin grabs the phone. "The FBI's looking, too. I've told them the girls are underage and we're worried about prostitution. You'll be hearing from them."

She'd called the FBI, thinking it would put extra pressure on them. It did. Loren, the owner, calls back angry. Tough shit, Karin tells him, you should take better care of your charges. He argues with her, saying that *he's* annoyed with our daughter, what a bad girl. As if he's running a Girl Scout camp.

I put the Larkin police on alert. We contact all the trucking companies who travel Utah, who put out bulletins to all their drivers. We fax missing person flyers to the Salt Lake Greyhound station, then throw together a suitcase and head to the airport.

Before we leave the house, Jack Tyson calls. Turns out Hollie is Jack's niece; he'd just escorted her two days ago. It also turns out Karin wasn't far off about prostitution. Hollie is a crack addict whose pimp/boyfriend forces her to prostitute. Jack's found out that Hollie's boyfriend paid a couple of guys to get the two girls and sneak them over state lines into

Kentucky or Tennessee, where it's easier to prostitute them. He's already done time for transporting minor girls over state lines.

My God, what else? How much lower, how much worse, can she possibly end up? Turning redneck tricks in some shack at the end of a dirt road. Mia, what have you done to yourself now?

Sunrise wakes me up. I get up and look around while Hollie sleeps. We're in a basement with a kitchen. On a wild hope, I check the cabinets. There are some cans of beans and a box of cereal—cornflakes with a picture of a groovy black kid sporting a huge Afro. I look at the expiration date. 1979. I'm not that hungry.

The morning crawls by. We take out some knives from a drawer and make a game of throwing them at the big orange flowers on the wallpaper. Whoever hits the center first wins.

"When Aidan finds out where I've been he's gonna be so pissed," Hollie says, grinning. "He would have killed them. No joke. He's the most amazing person I've ever met."

Something about her smile, I don't think she's joking about the killing part. Whatever, it's just a ride out of here and then I can go my own way.

Every flight to Salt Lake is full. We blubber out our plight to a Southwest supervisor, whose eyes tear up. His fingers fly over the keyboard and he makes calls till he all but orders passengers to be bumped for us. We're over the Mojave in an hour.

Within another two hours we're speeding down I-15 south of Salt Lake City to meet Jack and his wife Rebecca. We're going to stake out the boyfriend's house and the apartment of the guys who have the girls. Paul will go undercover as a cowboy in the bus station at sunrise before the first bus leaves. This feels like a really bad cop drama, the episode where "angry parents take the law into their own hands."

The cell phone rings and my heart jumps—maybe they've found her!

"Bubbie?"

"Vivian told me what happened. Listen to me, Mia's got no money, no food, and right now no brains. She's either going to steal something or do something else stupid and she'll get caught. Girls that age think they're smart but they're not, they're full of shit. I had four of you, I know. So, don't worry, you'll find her because sooner or later she's going to get herself arrested. And I'm not your bubbie."

Oookay, I'm flying down a freeway in Utah listening to my mother reassure me and scold me at the same time with her Boris-and-Natasha accent. She's normally about as demonstrative as Clint Eastwood, so coming from her this is not only incredibly supportive, it's positively mushy and it does comfort me.

We're being pulled over for SPEEDING. I look over at the idiot driving.

"Hey man, I'm high!" he tries. Two friends of her boyfriend picked us up about an hour ago. It was probably dumb to get high but I was already getting the shakes and have been irritable enough to kill someone.

We smile real big at the cop, all four of us in this two-seater. It doesn't work. Besides going 100 mph, there are cigarettes on the dashboard. And in Mormonville, you have to be nineteen to buy smokes. The oldest of us is eighteen, which means the cop is now searching the car for other "contraband." I remember these guys saying they had to make a drop-off on the way and suddenly I get that you-know-you're-fucked-beyond-belief feeling.

I've never seen this many drugs in one sitting. They pull them out of the glove box, from under the seats, in the seats themselves. And the weed's in little plastic baggies. With names on them. And scales, he's pulling scales from under the backseat! Their license might as well say DEALERS in big red letters.

Somebody please tell me I'm not standing on the side of a freeway, handcuffed and leg-shackled, watching this fat fuck of a pig laugh as he adds scales to a stack of drugs the size of a small child.

It was odd enough finding myself happy that Mia was *only* smoking pot. Now, I'm turning cartwheels because she's been arrested.

Paul and I stagger into a Provo convenience store, pick out some frozen burritos, and stand in front of the microwave studying the buttons like two complete morons. We've never used one. I have just mobilized truckers, bus employees, and police in two states within a matter of hours. But, right now, that the only thing between me and a dead faint is a metal box with a few buttons is suddenly a catastrophe of such proportion that I burst into tears.

A group of teenagers immediately comes over to help. They are all so rosy-cheeked, sober, and friendly they seem like another species.

"Here, ma'am, I'll do it for you," says a boy Mia's age. They help us microwave, they help us get drinks, they point out the direction of a hotel, and two boys offer to drive us there and walk back.

I notice most of them have on bracelets or rings with CTR engraved on them. What's that stand for, I ask. Choose The Right, ma'am. Choose the right what, I ask.

"Always choose the right thing to do, take the higher ground."

I want one of *them* for a child!

An hour later, I'm sitting on the edge of the hotel bathtub, murmuring, "Please forgive me for saying that, God. I'm so mean and—"

Hey, wait a minute—I never *said* the words, I just *thought* them. So what, Claire, you think God doesn't know what people think? This is a Disturbing Realization.

My mind's a chaotic, overcrowded station with a thousand trains going every direction, some of them going very dark places, some on tracks bloody from running over people I don't like. All I need is the Almighty Omnipotent One setting up surveillance cameras. Isn't there some kind of off button, an ecumenical lead shield?

Aha, my 3 a.m. wide-awake brain says, that's it, that's why all this happened! Four decades of wicked thoughts. But, I know people who are a lot worse than me, I'm related to some of them, and they've never had this kind of trouble—why me?

Claire, Claire, comes a little voice, don't you see? Can't you stop your fizzy brain for one second and see? Mia is safe, she's been found. You've been blessed beyond imagining. Ingrate.

I get one phone call. A woman answers breathlessly, "Hello?"

A woman who is not my mom.

"Um, is Claire Fontaine there?"

"No, she's in Utah, can I ask who's—

"She's WHAT?"

"Mia?"

"Sara?"

"I can't believe you'd do this again, Mia! You should be glad your mom and Paul are already in Provo, you have no idea who you were with!"

What is she, ex-CIA? The woman is fucking everywhere! Melanie and

Brian were always paranoid about seeing cop cars. I was on the lookout for a
rental car with my mother in it!

We have to be at juvenile hall in an hour and Paul needs his morning caf-
feine fix. We walk into a café full of the happiest people we've ever seen.
There are children everywhere and all the parents are tall, young, and
beautiful, with pale, luminous complexions. I want to ask what their skin
care regimen is when I notice a CTR ring on our waitress.

Are you kids here all in some youth group, I ask her politely. Oh, no,
it's a Mormon thing. Paul and I have no idea what about being Mormon
makes everyone so happy but he wishes it came in a cup with cream and
sugar. Because there's no coffee here and his head's pounding.

"Juvie" is a big, modern building outside of town. Paul and I pass through
pat-down to see a red-eyed bitch in a brown jumpsuit that I wish like hell
wasn't my daughter. She's so foul that Paul finally yanks me out of the
chair and pulls me out the door.

"You're not going to talk to your mother that way, you little brat."

He's so disgusted and angry he leaves to find coffee somewhere.
Nevada's not far.

I meet with Mia's probation officer, a sympathetic middle-aged
woman who informs me that, "Scales mean intent to distribute in the
state of Utah, which is a felony."

For a second, I almost burst out laughing at the complete, total weirdness of Mia/Pimp/Prostitute/Handcuffs/Probation Officer/*Felony*. At the
tragic absurdity that's become my life.

Luckily, Mia has no prior record. The judge releases her to my custody
on the condition she go straight to Morava. But she has to graduate or I
can ask him to reinstitute charges and hold her till she's twenty-one.

I'm happy because I finally have some authority to help Mia but upset
because it took a judge in another state to give me any. Jack has shown up
to deal with Hollie. He tells me he had a feeling the judge would release
Mia to us. How did you know—oh, wait, you're Mormon, aren't you? I
bet that judge is Mormon, too, isn't he? Jack smiles, amused.

The whole state's jumping with Mormons anxious to help us and I ask
God to bless each and every one of them.

* * *

From the time we get back, I know running isn't an option. My mom and Monty are by my side every second. When I go to the bathroom, she's in the stall with me.

It's hard to keep from crying. They moved my bed out to the middle of the main room. My mother's made them handcuff one of my wrists to the bed frame and sleep in my bra and underwear. There are wooden beams across the ceiling and a leopard is perched on the beam directly above my bed. He's crouched, with his fangs bared, and you can tell from his look that he knows he's cornered. I know exactly how he feels.

I sit beside Mia to say good night. She's drained, sad. Maybe she's just as tired of it all as I am, maybe inside she really wants help but is embarrassed to say so. She asks softly, Mommy, what if I become the fastest bunny ever? It's a paraphrase from one of her favorite bedtime books, *The Runaway Bunny.* I smile back and paraphrase the Mother Bunny's response: Then I will become the biggest fucking brick wall you have ever seen, my little bunny. Have a carrot.

partthree

11.

Mia's draped across me asleep on the flight to Vienna. I study her face like a specimen, a mutated species of daughter. I would give anything for a glimpse of my beautiful girl behind this ruined mask of leathery skin and sunken eyes. I inhale, eager even for a smell that's familiar, but that's gone, too. A user smells like drugs; her pores exude a wet copper stink.

Who is the girl in my arms I'm so desperately afraid of losing? This Mia who's twitching from withdrawal while she sleeps could have grown up in the rural shacks with the rest of her Indiana pals, with their puke-stained, prison-visit, cow-tipping lives. I'm afraid Mia isn't buried, but gone altogether.

I feel gone altogether myself. I hardly remember myself before all this began. They say our children raise us and it's true; my circuitry's been entirely rewired. Now, for example, when I see criminals on the news, I don't think first of their poor victims, as I used to, I think of their mothers.

I also used to think that nothing, short of death, could be worse than my little girl molested, and that only angels worked miracles. Oh, what I have learned. Listen: a man takes a child in his hands and does things, rams their little life like a freight train. *He casts a spell*. But the devil's miracles are both wondrous and sly, because he lies low, he bides his time. Far in her future, this child will defy physics, will *herself* become freight train, conductor, tracks, and target. She will lay her head on the tracks, keep one foot on the pedal and head straight for herself, laughing, calling it *freedom*. No mother can break that spell. Nothing but to lay my head down beside her, to be there when the end comes as I was there in the beginning and for every little sufferance in between.

After a few hours, Mia wakes up, takes my makeup bag, and heads for the bathroom. She returns made up like a whore. I glance through the makeup bag to be sure she hasn't kept the tweezers.

"Afraid I kept the tweezers as a weapon?" she snorts, reading my mind. "I'm not stupid, I know they're gonna confiscate sharps."

"Sharps? Two days in the slammer and you've got the lingo down."

She chuckles, yawns, and conks out again. Fury-laughter-sleep, in less than thirty seconds. "Mood highly labile."

Still, one thing hasn't changed, and it's the only mercy granted me in this long night. She seeks me out in her sleep, finds her mommy's lap. I should sleep, too, but I have so little time left with her. I stay up to let my eyes trace along her slender fingers, the tip of her nose, let my hands circle her tiny, bird wrists, feel her still-childish puff-breaths.

I'm memorizing her before I leave her.

The first thing I see coming off the plane are five soldiers with the biggest guns I've ever seen. Either Vienna gives everyone this warm a welcome or she's hired them. She glances at me for a reaction, but I won't give her the satisfaction. The whole United States is available and she picks the Czech Re-fucking-public.

She keeps looking around like she's expecting the Messiah and holding my arm so tight I'm sure I'll have permanent nail imprints to remember her by. When I feel her muscles relax I look up to see a tiny grinning lady with a live Ken doll beside her, dumb smile included. I stifle a laugh. My mom sent me all the way here to be disciplined by them?

I don't know who I was expecting at the Vienna airport, but it wasn't Peter and Zuza. Maybe people more official looking, certainly older. Not attractive young blonds in summer togs with soft Czech accents. And they're the *heads* of the staff at Morava. If I was looking to avoid a typically therapeutic setting, so far so good.

Frankly, I don't care if she never sees a therapist again. I don't care if they use shamans and chants. I hope they bring in a Feng Shui master to rearrange her mental furniture, locate the seat of trauma, and reposition it to deflect the poison arrows Mia keeps aiming at herself.

What a group we must make, the two of them flanking the two of us, Mia looking like a scrawny, pubescent streetwalker, me gripping her hand as if she were a toddler. I feel bad for her, to have this humiliation added to the anger that simmers beneath her tough surface. But, beneath the anger, where she's pretending she can't feel it, is fear.

Mia has never liked feeling weak or afraid. Her profile now, the erect head, the forward chin, is the same one I saw when she was eight, on a visit to a friend's farm in North Carolina. She hoisted Mia onto an old horse to mosey around the corral, but before she could get the reins on, he bolted toward the woods an acre away.

We watched helplessly as Mia ducked down tight into the horse's mane as he disappeared into the trees. After several frantic minutes, a black speck appeared far down the opposite field. Mia, approaching at a gallop. The horse looked like he was going to trample us all, but Mia yanked up on his mane and stopped right in front of us. With her head erect and her chin stuck out, as if to say, "I meant to do that."

When I was kissing her good night, I asked if she was scared. She pulled me close and whispered, "Ooooh, yes, Mommy, I was! And I knew he would run right to the trees so he could knock me off with the branches! So, I just ducked!" She shivered with excitement at the memory of it.

If the drugs have done one thing most of all, they have made her forget what she knew as a child—to duck. To recognize danger and protect herself.

After Peter locks Mia and Zuza into the back of the van, he says to me, "Only driver has door that can be opened from inside. We know that she is a runner, and very smart."

Someone finally gets it. As he walks me to my rental car, Peter says, with genuine caring, that Mia will be happy and healthy again, that I will have my real daughter back.

It has been my fate to be comforted by young men in strange places this week.

The van doors shut with a thud that echoes in my bones. I feel clammy, nauseous. I try to memorize the names of towns we pass to orient myself for when I run, but the Czechs don't fucking believe in vowels. The view out the window gives me no landmarks to help, it's one vineyard or sunflower field after another.

The view begins to flicker and fade, I can't tell if I'm watching a dream of this world or the real thing. I know the name of that big thing in the field out there is a cow, but I have to keep staring at it to remind myself. Cow. Spots plus udders equals cow, Mia. Fuck, I need a fix.

I follow Peter's speeding van past Brno, a blur of Byzantine, Gothic, Renaissance, Baroque, and Nouveau architecture. As we pass through the suburbs into a rural outlying area dense with summer foliage, I begin to feel a strange exhilaration. I feel buoyed and jittery with purpose. I'm speeding closer and closer to Mia's salvation. A place that awaits us with a system! With levels, seminars, consequences! With groups with names like Purity, Innocence, Clarity! They'll isolate, modify, confront, reveal, redirect! They'll do whatever it was that I couldn't do to help her.

We finally reach a lake ringed by low mountains and snake up into hills carpeted with sixty-foot fir trees so dense you can hardly see into them, Hansel and Gretel woods. Woods a girl could disappear into and never be found without a tracking dog.

Buried in them is a Soviet-era hotel, a faux chalet that's now Morava Academy. The glass vestibule has two sets of bolted doors, a good sign. A man joins Peter before they open the van door. He's wearing running shoes. I love it already.

And then Mia steps down from the van, dwarfed by the men, the building, the sky, her life. I've just been kicked in the heart. She looks so small and, for an instant, scared. I'm seized with panic and regret. She'll be so far from anyone who loves her.

This is no relief, I don't want this salvation, I'm choking on it. I want to go back, far back, I want to breathe her back into me, into my body again, the only place she was ever truly safe. Every mother knows this feeling. From the moment we let them go, we know they're never safe again.

This place looks like a bad dream after seeing too many shagadelic seventies films. Orange-flecked sofas, corny-ass posters, a tripped-out carpet hung up as art, and a coffee table covered in wood-grain shelf paper. I hope she's beginning to realize how lame this whole idea is.

No such luck. Zuza takes me to a room.

"This is where you will be sleeping."

There's nothing but two beds, a long empty shelf above each one and someone's ratty teddy bear on one pillow. The walls are totally bare and hospital white, the only homey things are nylon lace curtains. Zuza starts going through my backpack.

"Hey! Leave my shit alone."

She looks at me calmly. "Attitude is not tolerated here. If you want to do well, you will change it quickly."

If I was doing what I wanted, I wouldn't be here in the first place, bitch. I hold my tongue; if I show I'm mad they'll start watching me more closely.

She tells me I have to be deloused and puts on rubber gloves before touching me, even with my clothes still on. I know it's procedure, but still my cheeks burn.

"I showered before I got on the plane, you know."

"This is to be on the safe side."

The safe side of what? Me?

Mia's led away from me quickly. The place is Spartan, Joan Crawford spotless, with handmade inspirational posters, very Phil McGraw, very Dale Carnegie. It is unnaturally quiet.

A man appears from a dim hallway. He's extremely tall, handsome, fair, about thirty. I know immediately that he's (a) American, (b) Mormon and (c) not the director, Glenn. Brendan is a codirector from another facility, in charge till Glenn returns from having back surgery.

"But, I need to talk to Glenn about Mia; there are some things she doesn't know."

"Mia's behavior will tell us exactly where she's at," he says, unconcerned.

Like that's supposed to be encouraging? I also wanted to meet the person I'm leaving my child with. I ask to see her husband, Steve, only to learn that he's in Germany for two weeks, in special training with the famous sniff dog, who finished top of his class.

"You mean, the dog's not here, either?" I blurt.

Who cares if it's valedictorian as long as it can sniff out one fearless, foolish, fragrant girl? The honeymoon is definitely over. His whole demeanor says he's used to scared, nervous parents, and he feels no need to explain or assure. This is either arrogance or confidence. He adds that Mia's first two weeks will mainly be getting settled in, learning rules, getting her equilibrium. Equilibrium? It's chaos Mia loves. I'm the one who needs equilibrium.

He must have figured as much because he gives me a security tour. All doors are locked and guarded 24/7 (I notice staff with walkie-talkies posted all over), meds and drugs are locked and guarded, windows open only about five inches (I check most of them). There's no interaction between boys and girls. The dog will have no contact with kids to keep their scent fresh. They think his name is Ify—they don't know that's just short for I'll Find You.

The Czech staff is young and university educated; many speak English. Like Zuza and Peter, they are soft-spoken, polite, more formal in manner than Americans their age. Fine with me. The less like American culture it is here, the better.

The bedrooms are like college dorms between semesters. The lack of décor is deliberate; they want the kids to miss home. Throughout the tour, I ask endless questions. How often is peer group, how long till she earns a visit, how long does it take to move up levels, what if she doesn't pass seminars, and on and on. Most of it answered by a version of "It's up to her."

"If everything's up to her, then she's never getting off Level 1," I say as I follow him back through the lobby into the cafeteria, a large, airy room with beautiful views and Mozart playing.

"Trust me, she'll get sick of Level 1 quickly. No shoes, no dessert, no privileges," Brendan says as I look out the window to a rec area just below.

A group of teen boys with crew cuts sits in a circle on a blacktop with a staff member. One starts crying and two others put their arms around him; others kneel in front of him and touch his knee, his hand. It's odd to see teenage boys acting like this.

A very tall chain-link fence holds back the lush, towering woods pressing in on them from all sides. The setting's both gorgeous and oppressive. There is no view to the outside world at all.

I turn back from the window. "Mia doesn't care about dessert or shoes. She ran ten miles through the desert in flip-flops. Her feet are still swollen."

"Does she know you have such great faith in her?" he says, not without sarcasm, looking directly at me.

They weren't kidding about confronting attitude. Okay, so I'm faithless and cynical by now, you would be too, buddy, I want to say.

"I'm sorry, I'm just worried. She can fake her way through anything."

I'm obviously still not getting something because he laughs.

"Sure, because she's had a lot of folks she could manipulate, like her parents and therapists. Who's she going to fool here? The other girls were as bad as your daughter or worse. Kids here can't hide out emotionally; they've got to take themselves on or they don't get voted up. You'll understand the process better when you've taken the seminars."

"The process," "voted up," "take themselves on." I see what Maddy meant about the vocabulary. He's called away and I'm left standing alone in the lobby, feeling useless and anxious, like I'm onstage awaiting my cue in the play called *The Bad Mother*.

On impulse, I walk to a door and peek in. It's a classroom full of girls working silently at their desks, fresh-faced, innocent looking. Oh, is Mia going to hate this place. One girl notices me, her eyes fly open and she gasps. The whole class notices me and they all start grinning and raising their hands excitedly. Uh-oh, I've done it now. The teacher introduces me, then says something I don't catch.

In a flash I'm buried in squealing teenage girls, all fighting for "a mother hug! Can I have a mother hug!" They take turns hugging the breath out of me: I got Level 3 today, ma'am! Oh, I miss my mom so much! You gotta do the seminars, they're awesome! You shoulda' seen me, Miss Fontaine, I was a gutterpunk! Oh, hug me again, Miss Fontaine! Don't cry, Miss Fontaine, she's gonna be fine! Please don't cry, Miss Fontaine, we'll take good care of her, I promise!"

I come back from a shower to find my clothes gone and a uniform on my bed. If there's a God, he hates me. Denim pants with an elastic waist and elastic cuffs, a red T-shirt I have to wear tucked in and Day-glo pink fuzzy slippers.

Zuza appears. "It's time to say good-bye to your mother."

"Just tell her I said bye and I hate her."

It doesn't work, she leads me back to the lobby. I see her waiting for me and already feel that cloud of expected intimacy. She knows there's nothing to say but talks anyway, some bullshit about thanking her in the end. She ought to be thanking me that I'm not strangling her on the spot. Her lips are moving, she's crying, but all I feel is a cold fascination at how little I feel for this woman I'm supposed to love. That and an anger I can hardly control.

* * *

I'm told I can't come back tomorrow, it will "set Mia back." I have to say good-bye now. I'm caught completely off guard, I thought I could visit the rest of the week.

Mia's brought into the lobby and stands there with wet hair, a scrubbed face, her eyes glassy with hate. I approach her awkwardly and put my arms around her. I try to hold her tightly, but her anger has condensed her into something hard and cold. She has disappeared into herself and left me this statue to hold.

"I'm doing this because I love you too much to lose you," I whisper to her. "You're angry now but I know in my heart that you'll thank us later."

Without moving a muscle, my stone-child whispers back to me, "No, I won't, because once I get out of here you will never see me again. Ever."

I shut the car door and sobs burst out of me that shake the whole car. I cry like I haven't cried since the Saturday night we found her. I thought the relief from knowing she was locked up safe would mitigate the pain, that it would finally yank out the spearpoint of fear that's been jabbing so relentlessly in my back for so long.

But finding and losing her all these months, the constant vigil and pursuit, has been like dancing on a fire pit. Bearable only as long as you keep it up. Relief in this situation merely means being able to finally collapse onto hot coals.

"This is Lupe. She will be your buddy and teach you what you need to know."

Buddy? They can't be serious, I haven't heard that word since kindergarten. When my "buddy," a stocky Latina with bright, black eyes, walks in, chest out, arms swinging, with two fat, brown braids like Princess Leia, I nearly laugh in her face. This girl's probably never even had a cigarette.

Lupe smiles and rattles off some rules in a thick New York accent.

"You can't speak at any time unless the staff says so. You gotta line up heel-to-toe and do a head count before leaving any room. You can't smoke or drink. Until you're on the upper levels, you'll never leave this building except for PE or fitness. Looking out the windows is considered run plans, so you can't look outside. I don't even remember what the moon looks like."

The rules all drone into one big "you can't, you must, you can't, you must." I

*could give a shit. So far, all the doors have been bolted and the fire exits are
guarded, so the windows are the best way to go.*

*As if reading my mind, Lupe says, "Don't bother, you're never left alone and
even so, they only open a few inches."*

As she points to the window, I notice a large gang tattoo on her upper arm.

The Santon Hotel is a squat, white splat on a verdant hill sloping into the
lake opposite Morava. Nirvana is playing in the lobby. American rock is
ubiquitous in this country. My room comes with a lake view and Aretha
Franklin. Playing from a radio inside the wall with the knobs sticking out
of two crudely made holes. Talk about theft prevention. It won't turn off
and my head is splitting from crying.

English and Czech share no common word roots, not Latin, Greek,
Romance, Germanic, nada. Yes = an, ice cream = *zmrzlina,* there you have
it. Which renders the phone useless. Back downstairs I go, where I'm reduced to making knob motions and humming "Love in a Pink Cadillac"
to the desk clerk, a stunning young woman who knows all about us, we
shell-shocked Morava parents. She nods sympathetically and comes with
me to do whatever it is one does to turn off a Czech wall.

Normally, I'd be amused by this, but I'm so cracked and fragile now it's
just aggravating, it feels like a punishment, a further indictment. My life
as a Santon Hotel room, nothing works. For some reason, I think of
Anne Lamott, the "cranky Christian" whose books have been pressed on
me by a friend who thinks her spiritual wisdom and humor will help. The
things she endured, the accoutrements of addiction—vomit, snot, fear,
poverty—would have made me a pagan, a witch, an atheist at least. I can
hear Annie now, exhorting me in her best church voice to do what she always does when troubled, "Pray, child!"

What, I have to tell Him? Like it isn't obvious even for the non-
omnipotent? Some deity.

Well, now I've done it, I've snapped at God.

"Dear God, forget I said that, but more important could you watch
over Mia, please knock some sense into her before she—"

Stop, this is stupid, disrespectful. I have no idea how to pray properly,
but I'm pretty sure it's not in the epistolary manner. Once again, Claire, and
this time at least bow your head and use proper language: Lord, cleanseth

my child of evil substances. Maketh her thoughts of me not vile, that she may gaze upon my countenance with gladness, for it is not right nor holy that a little lamb should desire to killeth the ewe that hath nursed her.

I hateth this. I sound like Latka's half-wit sister auditioning Shakespeare. Religion's supposed to be a comfort; instead, it's turning out to be a skilled profession for which I am singularly unqualified.

I feel so throbby and irritable, I leave to take a walk around the lake. Fifteen minutes later, I realize my mother was right. Czechs really don't smile much and they don't have a taboo against staring the way Americans do. My sisters and I always thought it was just her. Growing up, we'd be embarrassed when she'd stare at someone. "What do you people have against looking at someone?" she'd huff. "You people" being Americans, like her children, for example. She also smiles less than most. "You Americans are always smiling. Only a fool smiles all the time."

Well, I'm sure as hell not smiling today, and I don't dress like a typical American tourist, so why is everyone rudely staring at me? I stop by a woman my age to make restaurant gestures, but she quickly shakes her head and hurries away like I have the plague. This happens two more times. I've never experienced anything like it. Is misery like drugs, exuded from the pores? Do they think it's contagious?

Then it hits me that, yes, I have experienced this. Every time I've skirted a smelly homeless person and avoided their gaze. As if their misery were contagious. Surely, they felt my unease and rejection, just as surely as I now feel the Czech's. Do I have to get this lesson now, TODAY?

Another realization makes me feel even worse. The beggars I avoided could have been how Mia ended up had I not found her. How she still could end up being if she escapes or if this place doesn't help her. Hustling for drug money, sleeping in hovels, dying young or getting old before her time. It never entered my mind that all those desperate vagrants, the dead-eyed women with rotted feet and scorched, peeling faces, were once someone's laughing, bright-eyed children. Like my child.

The setting sun has made the lake glitter and I have such an urge to wade in, to feel the cold water on my legs and the warm sun on my face. To short-circuit my emotions with physical sensation.

I remember Mia's laughing third-grade face on a lake like this one, canoeing at Mammoth. She was paddling and flinging her oar from one side of the canoe to the other, giggling hysterically, soaking us both. My God, that girl loved to laugh.

Happy memories are almost worse. I feel like my screenplay's protagonist, who found herself in a strange, unwelcoming land, where nothing held promise or tenderness, where everything, even the land itself, sang to her of her lost child.

Dinner is a bowl of something so oily I can see my reflection in it, served with six long, thin rolls. If my mother saw this she would die—"You call this food? Where are the dark, leafy greens?"

This is the first time I get to see who I'm stuck in here with. A dozen pimple-faced, silent girls in the same ugly uniform. They're my age, a few Asians, no blacks, one Latina, Lupe, the rest Anglo. A lot of them are pretty, even with no makeup and awful haircuts. One girl catches my eye and smiles at me. I stare back—what the fuck is there to smile about?

Suddenly, a loud Southern drawl fills the room. "Well, hello there! I'm Zig Ziglar!" Where Zig is coming from, I don't know, but his booming voice informs us that we "have the seeds of greatness!" The girls just keep on eating in silence as if nothing happened—some of them actually start taking notes! Whatever wrong my mother thinks I've done her is nothing compared to this.

When no one's looking the girl next to me points to my untouched rolls and looks at me questioningly. I slip her all six. I have no appetite anyway.

The lakeside restaurant is a Heidi-like affair nestled in the trees. A chorus of birds chirps back up to Barry Manilow and everyone stares at me when I enter. Big surprise. "Excuse me," I say politely, for lack of a better greeting. A surprised waiter hurries over. "You are American! Hallo! I speak English, leetle." I will learn two things tonight. One, an American here is always a Morava parent; the exchange rate and a broken heart means a tip equal to a night's pay. They'll trip over me the rest of the week. Two, when they say English a leetle, it is, in reality, far leetler.

Carp is a national dish, so I draw a fish. "Kapr, yes, good very!" He assures me no fried! Fresh yes total *never fried*! He bows and vanishes. He returns quickly with my fish, beaming. It's been fussed over, beautifully garnished. And very deeply fried.

After so long without food, the smell of the grease makes me queasy. I ask for a bag to take it back to my room.

A handsome young man at the next table who's been observing me leans over. He looks at me like I'm the Antichrist and sneers at me, actually curls his lip at me. At this point, I'm not offended, I'm actually interested, in an anthropological kind of way.

"American culture is *sheet*." As in "shit." He leans back, crossing his arms, quite satisfied with himself, rolling his eyes as Madonna's "Vogue" plays. He's wearing torn Levis, Nike knock-offs, and a black Metallica T-shirt.

You picked the wrong night, kid.

"Well, that's true," I say, politely, "my country does make a lot of shit. You seem to like eating it."

I leave a great, big American tip and feed my fresh yes kapr to the stray dog in the parking lot of the Santon Hotel.

"It's your complexion."

"My what?"

"They probably think you're a Gypsy," my mother tells me in her I-told-you-so voice, except she never told me. "They think all Gypsies steal."

"What, so they think I'm going to pick their pocket?"

"Well," replies my mother the communist, "Czechs avoid giving them jobs or apartments, what do they expect, serves them right. They couldn't get away with that when the Russians were there."

"They couldn't do a lot of things when the Russians were here, Ma. Like leave."

"Don't start with me. It's after midnight there. Go to sleep. Wear a hat. And don't smile so much, they'll think you're an idiot."

I haven't been in bed this early since I was ten. My leg is shaking and even though I'm shivering, the sheets are soaking with my sweat. I feel like a colony of ants is crawling around under my skin. I have to get OUT OF HERE!

Oh, for fuck's sake, Mia, calm down. There's always someone who can get stuff and you'll find them tomorrow. Just stay calm like you did at that hellhole in Utah until the right moment. I start taking deep breaths, like my mom told me to do before tests.

Mom. I see her as clearly as if she were in front of me. How she looked when

she said good-bye, my iron-willed goddess of a mother, bent over, shaky and small.
I want to console this woman, so unlike the mother I've always known, tell her to
give up. I want to tell her to move on with her own life and maybe I'll eventually
come back. She looked so pitiful today, so desperately hopeful. I feel a pang when I
picture those big sad eyes swimming in the hollows I've carved. I did this to her.

But fuck her for doing this to me.

It's after midnight, but I'm too antsy to sleep and I've already called Morava
twice to make sure she hasn't escaped. Around 2 a.m., my brain launches
into its new favorite game—obsessing over the moment our fates changed.
Finding the exact second in time, the One Thing. Do I think that finding
the tip of our history's funnel will narrow the focus of my guilt?

An event of such magnitude should be obvious, but it's tricky, the
choices are many. Such things are always and only visible in hindsight.
Which means that all of our choices are carried out ignorant of their true
significance, their final, lasting impact.

The exact second in time my hindsight focuses on tonight is this—
that my child is imprisoned here because I stood in a doorway thirteen
years ago and didn't understand the questions of a sad, puzzled monster
who wanted some explanation, some reason why decent people found sex
with children a problem. Because I didn't see his transformation any more
than I saw hers, till too late.

We carve our destinies blindfolded, with sharp knives.

I wake up and see the ugly brown carpet and Lupe sleeping across from me.
Shit. I'm still here. Then I hear Mariah Carey being sung in the hall.

"Dream lover come rescue me . . ."

"Sunny, SHUT UP," a sleepy voice yells.

A Czech voice calls out, "Who is talking, no talking, you have Cat 2.
Self-correct?"

Damn, they're serious about this silence thing.

"Good morning, girls!" Great, it's that bitch, "Miss" Zuza. "Everybody up!"

At this, Lupe leaps out of bed. I turn to go back to sleep but she rolls me back
over and tells me that we have thirty minutes to shower, dress, and clean the
rooms and bathrooms, spotless, daily.

"I'll do the bathroom, you clean the carpet. We only get the vacuum on Sun-
days, so you have to use your hands."

Twenty minutes later, I'm dressed and on my hands and knees picking up lint. In the Czech Republic.

"Line up!"

I step out of the room to line up but Lupe yanks me back.

"We have to ask permission to cross."

What? If they're the ones telling us to line up, why the hell do we have to ask to do it? I've never heard of anything so ridiculous. Except for not being able to talk, walk, eat, sleep, or pee without permission. Except for this whole fucking place.

I get in line in front of Lupe. I feel her chest brush up against my back.

"Get off me!"

Zuza explains that your toes must touch the person's heels in front of you. Okay, right, play along some more. We count off and walk to the lobby. Zuza peeks inside a door as if checking for enemy gunfire. Sure enough, danger lurks within.

"Girls! Face the wall, the boys are crossing out!"

I saw them do this yesterday but I didn't know it was because the opposite sex was about to pass!

"Mia, your nose must touch the wall so I know you're not peeking."

I roll my eyes and do it. My nose bumps the wall and I feel a chalky substance rub off onto it. I touch it and realize it's paint. Paint soft enough to scratch off. Snortably soft.

Just before I head out for breakfast, Paul calls to tell me my American Express card number was stolen at the airport in Atlanta, I can't use it. I call Morava to make sure she's still there and then head for downtown Brno to find an ATM. Wearing a hat.

Brno hasn't been spiffed up the way Prague has, but it's charming nonetheless, with old fountains and outdoor cafés. All of which play American *sheet*. There's even live *sheet*. On a platform in the main plaza, a band in cowboy gear plays Willie Nelson's "You Were Always on My Mind." In Czech, with a twang.

My ATM card won't work anywhere and no one in the banks I've tried speaks English. I can't find anyone that does. So far, the best thing about this place is that there are churches on every street I can duck into when I start to cry about leaving Mia or get too light-headed from hunger.

Growing up, I'd been to church with my paternal aunts far more than temple. Latin mass was enthralling and fantastic to a girl who lived in books—the ritual and incense, the graceful, cryptic gestures of priests in sparkling robes. I never tired of watching the sad, drooping Jesus on the cross, amazed and impressed that someone in such bad shape could have such a big following. I wanted to hold his hand, be a comfort.

All I want to do in these churches now is drink from the holy water basin when no one's looking. I can't believe this is happening to me. It's the twentieth century and I'm about to plotz in the gutter from thirst and starvation like some medieval peasant. I don't even have Czech coins to call Morava and beg for a spare potato to be left at the end of the driveway, where Mia can't see me and be set back.

Group therapy is the first time we can legally speak. A Czech lady named Tyna joins the circle.

"Hi, girls. Who wants to talk today?"

Unfuckingbelievable! Something here is voluntary. Four hands go up and she chooses a tense, pug-nosed girl. Even though she raised her hand to talk, she's silent.

"Last time in group you did the same thing, it's very nonworking," Tyna says. Non-what?

The girl sighs. "I've had stuff come up about my rape this week."

Christ, I don't want to hear this, I just found out this girl's name a day ago. I go over to Zuza and ask if I can go to the bathroom.

"We just came from there. There's another bathroom break in an hour."

Bitch. I distract myself by checking out the rest of the girls. It's hard to know who might have stuff because we're not allowed to talk and I can't tell by looks because they all look like matching nerds. They act like it, too, that's the scary thing. Because, either these girls weren't that bad to begin with, or they were and this brainwashing crap works. The girl finally stops talking.

"Feedback?" Tyna asks the group.

"I experience you as playing the victim, which still just gives your power away to him."

"My experience of you is that you use your rape to stay stuck, so you don't have to take on anything that scares you or is challenging."

This is so messed up. She opens up and her friends shove everything she said down her throat! Of course she's a victim, dumbasses, she got raped. One thing's for sure, I won't have any trouble maintaining the silence rule here.

When I stagger back to the Santon, I find that Paul's arranged for me to get some cash and I have my first meal in almost two days. I call Morava, and Zuza reports that Mia is quiet and cooperative, which makes me regret eating dinner because my stomach pitches. Fortunately, before I can say anything, Zuza continues, half amused.

"But I see her studying the windows and doors. I saw her studying the signs on the way here, too. Girls who are runners all do the same thing."

Brendan was right, they've seen it all. But, I still want that genius of a tracking dog there, ASAP.

I decide to spend my remaining few days sightseeing the area. As I dress in the morning, I find myself chatting with God about Mia, about my day, nonchalantly, without thinking. And it feels good.

I have no idea if it is theologically correct, but God's just going to have to settle for me chattering at Him like we've met for coffee in Starbucks.

Yesterday's grief and tears seem to have settled into a kind of numb peace, an acceptance perhaps. I know that somewhere I'm sad, still stricken I think, but in yesterday's body, the one that cried. Today, my body feels hushed and tender.

As I walk along the ancient ramparts of a ruined castle overlooking the city, my body feels memories as well. It remembers you now, Mia, as a vague ache across my arms, my chest and throat. The places you pressed against as I held you. Something done so often leaves a trace, an imprint that remains forever. Your cells rubbed off into mine and throb now like a phantom limb pain.

My prayer tonight, my last night near my daughter, is that Glenn will find the precious Mia that lies curled inside the dark cocoon she's spun around herself. That she will carve away from this stony Mia all that is not really her, the way Michelangelo released David from the marble by taking away all that was not David.

I still think that she is mine to fix, to save, by sheer force of will or by proxy. I still can't see that it isn't possible, that our paths have already been separated forever.

12.

"I honestly don't know how you could send your own fucking kid here . . . Dude! All they feed us is bread because it's cheap. I could kill somebody for a piece of lettuce . . . Get me out, I'm dying! If I'm not out before next summer, I'll burn the place down, NO JOKE! . . . If I come back and my books or other things of mine have been thrown out, I'll fucking kill you both . . ."

"I'm sure the food was much better in the back of that van!" Paul hoots as he reads her first letter. "And I guess she's just going to have to 'fucking kill both of us' when she sees her bedroom."

Yesterday, we threw out nearly everything in her room. The disgusting clothes, her Johnny Rotten books, bottles of Death Cola.

I check the parent manual, which gives examples of kids' typical letters as they go through the Denial phase, the Guilt Trip phase, the Anger phase. Mia managed to hit all three in one letter. She's so hateful and resolute I wouldn't be surprised if she just waited out her time till she's eighteen. Which would make this a pretty expensive babysitting service.

Mothering is a physical act, a dance of a thousand gestures performed and perfected over years. Hugging, hair brushing, oatmeal stirring, back-scratching, bed jumping, good-night snuggling, clock watching, carpooling. On autopilot, I keep starting to do things that are as outdated now as carding wool. My arms and hands are like dodo wings, vestigial appendages.

Even my voice has decided it's useless without Mia, because I can't sing anymore. Nothing comes out but hoarse, off-key noise. It's a minor loss given all that's happened, but it was a bond between us, another now broken, and it saddens me terribly.

My existence was structured around Mia. Her needs beat the rhythm of my days. There are only two real necessities in my life now. One is writing, which I do until dinnertime or I fall asleep having forgotten to eat.

The second is calling about Mr. Sniffy, das wunderdog.

I hate to keep calling day staff, who never seem to take calls anyway, so I call the night staff every afternoon. None of them speak even leetle of English. The first few days, I twist my tongue around *"německý ovčácký pes šňupat je tam ano?"* After polite chuckles and what can only have been, "Hey, Ivan, listen to this lunatic asking about shepherd of smell there dog is yes," I've simplified things. I say, "Madame Fontaine," bark a couple of times, make loud sniffing sounds, then say, *"Ano?"* (Yes?)

Each student has a case manager, who is the liaison between you and the school. Ours is Tyna, and each month we're to have one scheduled call with her and get three emails from her. Kids can write home as often as they like; parents can both write and email as often as they want. Paul sends emails, but half of them don't go through.

The few short emails I've sent have bounced back, and I haven't written more. What's there to say that hasn't already fallen on deaf ears? Besides, if I'm honest, I need a break from the Sturm und Drang. If I'm really, really honest, I suspect my short, and now nonexistent, emails are a way of punishing her.

The school recommends faxing Mia's letters to us back to Morava. It keeps staff and parents on the same page, making it harder for kids to manipulate. A few months ago, I would have had issues with doing this. Not anymore. Let her throw a tantrum.

Apparently, she has. Tyna has emailed us that Mia's just lost all her points. She does well, gains points, then screws up and loses them. The manual tells parents not to focus on points and levels, they're not always an indication of growth, but I ride her's like a roller coaster.

After a couple of weeks, I finally get Glenn on the phone. The first thing I ask isn't about Mia, it's about the dog. She says he was there for a few days but left again.

"What, is he going for a PhD?" I say, exasperated.

"No, the UN borrowed him to help find survivors in the Kenya embassy bombing. He saved eighteen people," she says proudly.

"Oh," I say, feeling stupid.

"Claire, relax. Your daughter is fine, she's learning every day. Now that I'm back, I'll spend some one on one time with her. You know, it's a big turning point for these kids to realize the world doesn't revolve around them. When was the last time you and your husband did anything fun? You need to get a life."

The realization that I can't run from here has officially tipped the life scale from pretty fucking awful to sheer hell. We do a head count every time we change rooms, so slipping away unnoticed is impossible. Plus, this place rewards people for ratting, so it's not just the staff I'd have to watch for. Which means I have a pen, paper, and thirty minutes during letter-writing time to convince my parents to take me home.

Dinner is Stephen Covey, fries, and something square that's been fried beyond recognition. I get up to get a glass of water.

"Mia!" Zuza barks. "What are you doing?"

Shit, I forgot.

"I was just getting more water."

"You cannot get up without permission, this you know by now. Self-correct?"

This is such bullshit. Consequences are divided into five categories, Cat 1–Cat 5; the higher the category, the more points you lose, some can drop you entire levels. Anytime you're consequented, you have the choice to self-correct, which basically means putting your tail between your legs in the name of saving points by filling out a form saying what you did wrong and what you'll do in the future to correct the situation. If you refuse, the consequence becomes staff corrected and you lose extra points. I could give a shit, I already lost all my points this morning.

"There's nothing to correct! I'm thirsty and I was getting more water."

"Fine, staff corrected."

I swallow a few choice words, sit down, and start scheming. Making my mom feel guilty or sorry for me won't work, she's too mad, and she's been here so she knows they don't torture us. Logic's the way to go, get her to see that this place is inappropriate and ineffective, a waste of retirement funds. I'll stress the poor education, lack of nutritional food, and absence of a real shrink. But I have to do it nicely, that's the hard part.

Tyna reports by email:

Mia lost her points last week so she start this week with 0 points on Level 1, but she promise me that she will be on Level 2 by 2 weeks. We will see. She was upset because she didn't receive any letters, yesterday she got email (from Paul) and she was very happy first but today she tell me that it wasn't so nice email . . . Her message for me to give you—'I need special face soap, bras and sandals. Thank you. Write me more!!!!' I am sorry about my bad English. I just hope you will underestand. Thank you. Best regards. Tyna

Mia's also written asking us to send her Harley T-shirt "to sleep in. They allow that, I asked!" She's assuming we're as dumb as we used to be. If she escapes, a Harley shirt won't stand out on the streets. We buy her the ugliest, most old-fashioned flowered nightgown we can find. Even if they left a door wide open, her pride wouldn't let her run in it.

By now, the other girls have noticed I have a package and come crowding around me. We're all part of a "family," who have named themselves the Band-Aids. As they explained in unison, the purpose of the Band-Aid family is "a group of sisters banding together to aid in creating present and future greatness." This place reaches new peaks of gayness daily.

We're on silence but from their big grins and wide eyes you can tell they're dying to know what I got. Teenage girls grinning like idiots over a heinous nightgown is frightening. They all blend together into one smiling blob. No one's distinct, it's like one corny personality with fourteen faces, like any individuality they might have had vanished with their voice.

It could be the silence, not being able to speak most of the time does things to you. It's driving me nuts. I think about everything from how much it sucks here to what Ruza the cook does in her time off, to what Melanie's doing right now, to if pygmies in jungles are happier than people in big cities. People say quiet is peaceful. They're wrong. It's the loudest place on earth.

Grief is a noisy thing. It is loud and stupid in hospital hallways and funeral parlors, in pajamas barefoot in the street. It repels others, helpless against your helplessness, your embarrassing lack of control. Grief is a refusal.

Sorrow, however, sorrow minds its manners. Sorrow has weight, grace. It confers a certain dignity; it implies wisdom. Sorrow is an acceptance. One our friends are no doubt relieved we've come to, and not just because Mia's safe. We cannot have been easy companions this last six months.

It's summer and they flood us with invitations, to parties and dinners, to picnics in the mountains, to the Hollywood Bowl. We've suddenly acquired a dark glamour. Inevitably, at one point someone says, oh, you're the couple! *That* couple, the Hopkins girl living in a van? . . . shooting up? . . . ran away *four times, kidnapped?* . . . *that* school? What an unbelievable story, how did you manage, and oh, how they admire us. Our strength, our courage! I'm given qualities I don't have and feel stripped of those I do. No one ever does the usual commiseration thing, the I-know-what-you're-going-through thing, my kid this or my kid that. Nobody's kid holds a candle to Mia.

We cross into the dining room and Ruza beams at us from behind her counter. A pretty Gypsy with long black hair that occasionally wanders into someone's meal, she's my favorite of the two cooks. The other, Jenka, a middle-aged woman with dirty blond hair, is as somber as Ruza is cheerful and boisterous.

I grab the bowl slid out to me and stare at the watery gray-brown liquid. Behind me I hear Sunny's now familiar whisper of "Kakao, Kakao, tac, tac." "Tak" is a word you learn very quickly if you ever plan on filling up—more. I could cry hearing Ruza tap out extra cocoa powder into Sunny's oatmeal. When everyone has been served and stands silently behind their chairs, Zuza gives a hand signal and we take our seats and begin eating.

From breakfast on, the day crawls by. It's the same schedule day in and day out. Wake-up; shower; cleaning; class; fitness; breakfast; class; PE; class; lunch; class; group; class; spelling or music, depending on the day; dinner; class; letter-writing; shutdown. When time's no longer your own, you think about it in new ways. Here, everything revolves around food and mail. 2 p.m. isn't 2 p.m., it's two hours until mail time and three hours until dinner.

Like clockwork, Tyna walks with a large stack of faxes and envelopes. Immediately, the mood changes as girls wait anxiously for their name to be called.

Mail is like a sentencing here, dividing the room into haves and have-nots. With no communication from the outside world, no magazines, newspapers, TV, or radio, mail is the only proof we have that we're not floating in some third dimension while back on earth Madonna's become president. It's also our only form of communication with our parents, whom most of the kids really miss.

As usual, my name's not called. I've only gotten three emails since I've been here, short, angry ones from Paul, making sure I know I'm here until I graduate.

* * *

PE here is a total joke. The girls vote between games like Mother May I and Red Light Green Light, then giggle like a bunch of third graders while spinning around to see if anyone frozen moved out of turn.

Today, a miracle happens and a girl named Roxanne suggests soccer. With long, thick, poker-straight golden hair, a sparkling smile, and a peppy attitude, she could have stepped out of a Pantene commercial. She's one of the more vocal girls—by vocal I mean she's constantly making facial expressions and hand gestures behind staff's back. You sort of have to change your definitions of things here.

Katrina dribbles the ball my way. For someone who's barely post-anorexic, she's fast. She has dark hair, deep olive skin, and a cute crooked smile; her thinness makes her big eyes even bigger.

I pass the ball to Sunny, who makes it about a foot before Roxanne charges and she runs away squealing. If anyone else did that I'd think they were a complete idiot, but Sunny cracks me up.

Her personality seems to have formed to fit her face. Round with high cheekbones, she has such smiling half-moons for eyes it's hard to believe she's Irish and not Asian. Sunny's obsessed with nature and anything female and has her head permanently stuck in a yellow submarine where everything is fluffy and fabulous. She used to be a really big cutter and even when she shared about that in group yesterday, she was laughing.

"I'd just make a little slash here and another there. Oh, how silly! And with a Lady Bic, too, isn't that just faaabulous!"

She got the feedback that she was smiling things off, but I liked that she saw the irony in self-mutilating with a pink razor with butterflies on it. At least she keeps it light. After Lupe, we needed it! She was crying so hard it took her five minutes just to stop shaking and form sentences. She was in a gang back home and had a boyfriend who used to beat the living shit out of her and force her to have sex with his friends. She was gang-raped and, still, she stayed. She acts so tough it's hard to imagine her letting someone do that to her.

I didn't even notice I was doing it. I was finishing a homework assignment in class when suddenly there's a bushel of armpit hair in my face and my paper is taken away. All because I was doodling.

"But I'm doing my homework, this whole page is done."

"You were not focusing on your work if you were drawing all over the page," the teacher, Miss Suska, says. "Begin again and you have Cat 1 correction for being off task. Self-correct?"

"Fuck you, you hairy bitch! How is recopying a perfectly good page of work learning anything? If you had even half a brain, you wouldn't ask me to waste my time doing mindless shit!"

Miss Suska is frail and proper, and she's trying hard to keep her composure.

"Okay, staff corrected," she squeaks.

"And would you also like to self-correct your Cat 2 major disrespect?" Sasha pipes up from across the room.

Sasha is a Level 4, aka junior staff, and, as such, she's expected to consequent us lower-level peons. She has her own room, can wear makeup and jewelry, and can roam around by herself. I never thought I'd be envious of someone's ability to go to the bathroom on their own, but that was before I had two minutes to go in a room where every drip and drop echoes for a line of girls to hear.

"Do you ever mind your own business, Sasha?"

"Okay, staff corrected. Come on, I'll take you up to worksheets."

I've been here about a month and at least two-thirds of it has been spent in worksheets. When you get a Cat 2 or above, you go to a room the size of a matchbox and listen to "educational tapes." Right, as if listening to shit I read two years ago is educational.

When I get up there, another repeat offender named Lara is listening to Robinson Crusoe. Last time we were in here we scraped some paint off the walls and snorted it when staff went to change the tape. I got a very minor buzz, but at least it was something. Some days I miss dope so much I don't even want to get up.

From the girls' faces you'd think every Sunday was Christmas. Why, I have no idea. After we shower, we spend FOUR hours cleaning the facility top to bottom. And by clean they mean immaculate, a single dust fleck or stray hair means redoing the whole area. Scrubbing for hours is awful enough, but being on silence on top of it's overkill so I start making melodies with the scrub brush. Sunny hears me, starts giggling and, thank you very much Zuza, we both get breaking silence, my fifth one of the weekend.

The whole silence thing is unnatural—even an involuntary laugh or burp is considered breaking it. The only times we don't need permission to speak are during group, cleaning and PE, but it has to be "on task" or they slap you with a fat Cat 2, bye-bye 50 points you just worked four days to earn. I've given up on ever reaching Level 2.

After cleaning we watch a movie, an activity that proves the dangers of taking away all media; girls are excited by The Sound of Music *and* Mary Poppins. *Then we get two hours of free speech. After a week of silence, it's like the Tower of Babel erupts out of fourteen conversation-starved girls. It's weird not to see cliques in a big group of girls. Instead, they group together over various activities—cards, watercolors, games.*

One girl, Samantha, usually sits alone in the corner, working intensely on some drawing. She's a petite, nervous girl with black hair that always hangs over her brown eyes. The girls playing cards wave me over.

"And is our lovely Morava Academy everything you'd hoped for?" Roxanne asks, batting her eyelashes and donning an English accent.

I roll my eyes in response.

"Yeah, it sucks," Roxanne says, "but once you accept that you aren't leaving anytime soon, it actually does get better. Except for the pants."

Lupe gives me an exasperated look and explains, "Her first two weeks here, all we hear outta this one's mouth is the pants! oh, the pants!"

"I will NEVER get used to these pants."

After Abercrombie and Bebe, no wonder. I thought she was going to be a real bitch, but she's not only down to earth, she's hilarious. Now that I know her I can totally picture her toking up to Sublime, blowing hits in her dog's face.

Sunny giggles. "Maybe not the pants but you sure as hell got used to the dinner rolls!"

We all crack up—yesterday morning Roxanne gave an elaborate blowjob to the long, skinny rolls they serve at every meal when staff turned their backs.

The door opens and in struts Sasha, perfectly made up and not a hair out of place. She walks up and taps Lupe on the shoulder.

"Want to talk now?"

"Cool, thanks. Here, Mia, take my hand, and don't fuckin' lose on me now!"

"Lupe!" Sasha raises her eyebrows.

"Dag! Yeah, sorry, self-correct, I won't swear in the future."

They walk off to a corner and we resume our conversation. When I look over a minute later, I don't believe it. The Lupe that was sprawled out across the table laughing and joking around now has her knees tucked up to her chest as she rocks gently and tears roll down her face. I can't hear what's being said but Sasha's gesturing and looking at her with a mixture of concern and frustration. I shake my head.

"I've never seen people talk about shit as much as you guys."

"Oh, you'll get used to it," Sunny says.

"Are you just in here for cutting yourself?" I ask.

"I actually put myself in here."

"You what?" She seemed normal.

"Yeah, Genius here even saved up to buy the plane ticket over!" Roxanne adds.

"I thought I found this cool boarding school in Europe. I could do some back-packing, stock up on Belgian chocolate . . . Wrong! By the time I realized what sort of place it was, my mom was all gung-ho on the idea, so here I am."

"Damn, that sucks. Why'd she think you needed to stay?"

Sunny giggles. "Oh, you know moms! Some pot—"

"LOTS of pot. And hippie drugs," Roxanne adds.

"Wasn't doing well in school, self-mutilation," Sunny adds. "I was sort of anorexic—"

"She weighed a hundred pounds!"

"And I sort of hated myself!" She finishes with a grin.

"What's her deal?" I ask, looking toward Sasha.

"Oh, Sasha's a doll. Not sure why she's in a program, but when they opened Morava last March, they brought her here so there'd be at least one upper level. She makes an excellent shrink."

Like they need one. It's weird and annoying how people talk about their "issues" 24/7. It's like they forgot there are subjects other than themselves. Even during free time, they talk about shit they shared in group a day before. Just getting through a day here is emotionally draining, and it's not even my shit I'm getting drained over!

Karin comes to stay with us while her boat, which she lives on, is under repair. She knows the effect Mia's letters have on us. She opens Mia's letters before we do and takes out the sting.

". . . Thanks for emailing me, Paul," she reads, affecting teenage snottiness. "It's good to hear from home, though three times in two months isn't the best track record. It really makes me feel great when all the other girls get long, nice letters from their parents—both of them. I thought you sent me here to work on our relationship . . ."

"Your 'relationship'? What relationship would that be, Mia?" Karin interrupts her reading, then continues, "Items number five and eight on her list of ten things you MUST send . . ." She bursts out laughing. "Dermalogica face gel and Victoria's Secret Pear body soap! Hah-hah!" she roars. "She wants to live on the streets with scumbuckets, fuck you Mom and Dad, I hate you! But please send me a bottle of thirty-five-dollar face gel!"

She's practically rolling on the floor. "Dermalogica, yeah, right!" She's right, it *is* ludicrous. It's also pathetic. That Mia can be so smart yet so clueless. She's been so cruel that sometimes it's hard to remember that she's reacting to a cruelty done to her.

Still, it is pretty funny. For the first time in what seems like eternity, I start giggling, then laughing. Pretty soon, I'm laughing so hard no sound's coming out and I can't sit up. I even join Paul and Karin in a toast an hour later at a sushi bar.

I can hear my mother already: mayonnaise on your bread, now you're drinking—you're starting to act like a shiksa, and what's to toast, look at your life.

I'm actually looking forward to group today, it means a break from pre-calc. Katrina starts with how hard it is to eat knowing she can't throw it back up. I feel like I'm back at the psych ward, minus the ass-wiper. Tyna turns to me.

"It's two weeks you are here now, Mia. Do you want to share with group?"

"No."

She keeps prying. "Maybe why you are here, how you feel about it?"

"I'm here because my mom's a paranoid bitch who's incapable of minding her own business and I hate it here."

"What makes you say your mom's paranoid?" Sasha interrupts.

"Because I don't need to be here, I was doing fine."

"Were you using drugs?" Sasha asks.

"Yeah."

"Like . . ."

"Coke mostly, weed, obviously, nothing serious."

Tyna interrupts Sasha's inquisition. "Your mother writes to me that you take heroin. This isn't serious?"

Bitch!

"I never shot heroin straight, it was always mixed," I say, borrowing Derek's line. "Not that it's any of your business. Or hers. I wasn't asking for

help. I don't give a fuck if I shoot dope three times a day and eat shrooms for breakfast, it's my life."

The girl that shared about her rape my first day raises her hand. Here we go.

"Look, I felt the same way when I first came in. That what I did was my business and I could control my life. But the bottom line is when you're doing those kinds of drugs as often as you were, you're not in control, the drugs are."

Then Lupe's hand goes up. What is this shit? I was playing cards with this chick two days ago.

"My experience of you is that you take your mom for granted. You're lucky you have a parent that loves you that much. Back home, I really took my parents for granted, too, but now that they're gone, I wish I had been a better daughter."

A better daughter? What the fuck is this, Lifetime TV?

Sasha's been quiet during the rest of the attacks but now she walks over. She kneels in front of me and quietly says, "My experience of you is that you underestimate the effect you have on other people because you don't know your own worth."

13.

"So, Mia, what is it about giving strange guys blowjobs that you like more than, say . . . helping your mom with the dishes?"

And so I meet the infamous Glenn. The way the other girls spoke of her, I was expecting someone softer, more motherly. Certainly not a spiky brunette with huge blue eyes and a tongue like a viper.

"I didn't give strange guys blowjobs."

"Really? You've never given head before?"

"Yeah, but it's not like I slept with them or anything."

"No, I heard you save that honor for strangers in the snow."

My face reddens. She's talking about the night I lost my virginity. She's obviously done her homework on me. Thanks, Mom, for telling my life story to a complete stranger.

"Mia, I'm a blunt woman and I expect the same honesty from you. Now, without having met you, I know two things. One, your mother loves you more than life, and two, you're one miserable kid."

I look up, startled. She sure cut to the chase.

"I know my mom loves me. That was never the problem."

"Or maybe it was," Glenn says softly, moving closer. "Maybe you wanted her to love you less. It would certainly make it easier to do the things you were doing, make you feel less guilty."

Is this woman psychic?

"It's very noble, using your suffering to shield your mom," she continues, "but the guilt game stops right here, right now. You can't use it as an excuse for your behavior anymore, that because you feel guilty, it's okay to do it anyway. It's fake redemption. The bottom line is you're selfish. I understand you have your own dragons to slay, but you don't do it at the expense of your relationship with your mom. Or yourself. I mean, can you honestly say you were happy?"

"I was before I came here."

"Well, that's interesting, because I'd be wretched if I was an addict living in some skinhead's van."

"What the hell's everyone's problem?" I can feel my voice escalating. "I like drugs, as a matter of fact, I love them and I was fine being on my own, so people should mind their own fucking business."

"That's the problem, Mia, I believe you. I believe you like drugs, that's why I said you're miserable. No happy person medicates themselves daily with lethal substances—don't use your BS I-never-shot-heroin-line with me, speedballs are just as bad, if not worse. No happy person needs to numb herself to life."

I keep thinking about my talk with Glenn. I can see why the girls like her, she doesn't bullshit like most adults. Her opening comment caught me so off guard, I think I was so open the rest of our talk because I was still in shock. I look over at Lupe, who is reading a book of inspirational sayings.

"Lupe, have you ever talked to Glenn before, one on one?"

She puts down her book and laughs.

"Your talk went well, I take it. I know, she's very blunt, sometimes to where it seems mean, but Glenn's seriously one of the coolest people you'll ever meet. Most people don't give a shit about you enough to be that honest. My old friends didn't and I'm guessing neither did yours."

"Maybe not, but anyway, Glenn said something about the night I lost my virginity and I've been thinking about it all day. I always thought of that night as fun, but hearing her talk about it really pissed me off."

I relay the conversation to Lupe, and briefly recount the night. A friend and I being picked up on the way to a ski lodge, getting high, drunken rides on four wheelers in the snow, and the grand finale, bouncing up and down on a giant red inner-tube.

"You had just met them?"

"Yeah, it wasn't the brightest idea, but we just wanted to party and they looked fun. You know, it's funny, when they picked us up I just had this feeling that this would be the night I'd lose my virginity. People make such a big deal out of it, I just wanted to get the damn thing over with. But hearing her say it like that made me feel stupid or dirty. I don't know . . . I think sometimes I regret it."

Lupe looks at me sympathetically.

"Hey, we've all done stupid shit. I was the opposite, I wanted to save myself for someone special. So I gave it up to Ricky and he was all romantic, I

love you, I love you, blah, blah, bullshit. Yeah, he loved me right into hospital visits and gang-rapes. Don't feel bad about how you lost it, that's done, you can't change it. But if you're acknowledging that the way you lost it made you feel bad, that's good because then you can choose different men and situations in the future.

"Listen, I know a lot of the things we say sound corny. But I'm telling you, some of the shit you learn actually makes sense. You'll see. Anyway, we have to go to bed now, but you should talk about this in group sometime. A lot of girls have fucked-up stories about their first time; hearing it might make you feel better."

I have to admit, hearing her talk about it actually did.

As soon as we're seated in group, Samantha raises her hand. There's a surprise. She won't socialize with anyone, yet constantly bitches about how much people hate her.

"I'm just not the sort of person people like." She stops to gnaw her fingernails and comb her hair in front of her eyes. "I just want to die. I tried it twice back home but someone always caught me."

I roll my eyes, half-wishing they hadn't. Tyna sees me. Great, worksheets here I come.

"Mia, what did you just do?"

"I rolled my eyes. Yes, fine, self-correct, in the future I will suppress all facial expressions."

Tyna laughs. "You're not in trouble, Mia, I call on you to show something. Why did you roll your eyes?"

"Because she sounds ridiculous and I've heard it a thousand times."

"Tell her, not me," Tyna coaches. "My experience of you is . . ."

I look over at Samantha. Christ.

"My experience of you is annoying because if you really wanted to die, you could have, I think you just liked the attention. And people wouldn't hate you so much if you talked about something besides how weird you think you are and how much life sucks."

The group all laughs and Tyna smiles. I'm lost, did I say something wrong?

"Samantha, Mia has been here one month. She just give you same feedback you hear since your first day. You don't trick people, they see you. From now on, you are to be silent in group unless you want share something real, no more drama for attention."

I'm sort of starting to see the point of feedback. It's not always an attack, sometimes it could actually help the person if they'd listen to it. Like Samantha. I look over at her, still chewing her fingers. She's not that bad, she just needs to lay off her bullshit and quit feeling sorry for herself. Still, I'd never share in group, so I have to give her credit for even doing that.

Nothing beats starting out your day by watching flab jiggle to "Jailhouse Rock." It's raining outside, so instead of regular fitness, we're watching Richard Simmons's "Sweatin' to the Oldies," on the covered patio. For once, I'm glad when Sasha calls my name out for laundry. I detest dancing.

When we rejoin the family, they're in group and Sunny's sharing about a letter she sent to her mom about cutting herself.

"Oh, yeah, that's gonna go over well. Hi, Mom, forget everything you've taught me about nonviolence and love, I slash myself to shreds with a razor! I tried to explain it but it doesn't even make sense to me. I don't know why I did it, I just felt better afterward."

I used to think I was the weirdest person in the world for cutting. I had no idea other people did it until Colleen told me. I've never actually heard someone else talk about it before and it's kind of reassuring. I want to tell Sunny this but I'm not sure how. I raise my hand and immediately regret it when fourteen heads turn my direction. It occurs to me I've never voluntarily spoken in group before.

"Mia," Tyna calls.

"Um, I used to cut myself, too. I guess I just wanted to thank you for sharing because I've never heard anyone else admit to doing it before. I know what you mean, about not knowing why or being able to explain it to others, but just knowing you'll feel better after. I would just get overwhelmed sometimes and cutting made sense of my emotions, it made the outside match the inside. It's like, if I can literally see my pain, I'm not so crazy for feeling it."

Everyone stares at me like I just told them I'm really a vampire.

"Wow," Sunny gushes. "I never thought about it that way, but it makes so much sense. It totally does that!"

"You oughtta talk more often, Mia," Katrina adds. "You're really insightful."

I suppress a smile, this actually feels kinda good. And then something occurs to me. If I start acting insightful and impress the staff, my mom might think this place is actually working and take me home.

* * *

Mia's right on schedule with the manual's next phase, Manipulation—

> Dear Mom and Dad—
>   I honestly don't think this is the best suited program for me. I want to
> know about something that's maybe shorter term, a situation where I
> could get more one-on-one therapy, I feel more comfortable . . . I don't
> know why you don't believe me when I say I'm not gonna run away . . .

We're not sure which feels worse, her honest, nasty letters, or these recent weasely missives.

Though we haven't doubted the choice to send her there, it's still dis-
comforting to have your kid so far away in a school that's, let's face it,
rather mysterious. The way it's organized, how progress is measured, all
the categories of offenses I've never heard of. I take a few letters to our
first parent support meeting to compare notes.

We're a varied lot: engineers, teachers, lawyers, doctors, a mechanic
who's mortgaged his house to pay for the school. Christians, Jews, a
Hindu couple, probably a few Mormons. We're all carefully made up and
impeccably dressed. As if to say, we couldn't control our own children, but
we're a good family, really, we are.

One couple sits apart with stiff faces that telegraph their shame. The
rest of us are excited and grateful to be with others in the same boat. We
eagerly exchange war stories, tales of woe that assure us our kid's not such
a freak—and for once, we aren't either. Boys who came after parents with
golf clubs and knives, daughters rescued from prostitution, ex-spouses
doing drugs with their kids, suicide attempts, devil worship.

After we're seated, a tall, attractive woman named Jan introduces herself to us and asks us what the purpose of our family is. Blank stares.
Most businesses have a mission statement, she says, we have a purpose for
nearly everything we do. How many of you ever took the time to do that
for your family? More blank stares.

This woman fairly radiates loving energy, but in two minutes she's
made a group of already fragile people feel even worse than they already
did. She whips out a fat marker and I suspect we're about to learn what
those two easels behind her are for.

She lists her family's Ten C's for a loving, joyful, supportive family—

the kind we don't have. Clarity, cooperation, choice, caring, change, ___ mony, comedy, communication, commitment, conflict resolution. I glance at Paul and wonder if his list starts with chaos, catastrophe, or crisis.

Jan makes two big circles on the other easel, labels one BELIEFS, then asks, "What are your beliefs about what makes a good parent?"

Well, Miss Ten C's, obviously none of us are qualified to answer. It's like pulling teeth but we help her fill the circle. "Good mothers are loving." "Good fathers are successful." "Good parents have kids that don't do drugs."

She goes to the other circle, writes "REALITY," faces us, and says, "The reality is that you've got a kid in the program. And here's what bridges the gap between the two."

She makes a little bridge between them, labeling it G-u-i-l-t.

Now, she's talking. Guilt we get.

"Now, your reality is obviously out of alignment with your beliefs about being a good parent. Reality isn't going to change; it is what it is, folks. What needs to change are your *beliefs*. Because I see a roomful of great parents. Who *also* happen to have kids in the program."

She looks at us sympathetically. "Look, I've sat where you're at. I had great plans for my daughter—she was going to be a doctor! What she became was a druggie with a heroin addict boyfriend. She was sleeping in a cave on the beach, eating from restaurant Dumpsters. She spent nearly a year and a half in the program and has been home over a year. She's stayed sober, has a job, lives on her own, and truly enjoys life. And while she worked her program in the school, I worked mine, at home. It may not seem like it now, but if you're open to it, your lives will change so much for the better that you'll one day thank your child for this."

We're all too surprised that an otherwise rational woman would say such a thing to even respond. There is *nothing* to be thankful about, except that our child is still, mercifully, alive.

The man who created the seminars that the schools use, David Gilcrease, introduces himself. He's about six and a half feet tall, in his mid-fifties.

"You've all found the program because you recognize that whatever you were doing wasn't working; something needed to change. And change is a complex dynamic; it requires education, challenge, and support. While the teens have various mechanisms within their program to support change, the parent program is wholly the seminars. It's critical as parents that we examine our roles in the breakdown of the family system. The seminars are structured to provide a safe environment for this self-examination."

He has us get into small groups on the floor for a "game," which we do with great relief. We feel like shamed children badly in need of recess.

"Unless you're willing to take an honest look at what's not working in your *own* lives, you're going to have a fixed kid coming home to the same family system they left, which is usually a recipe for disaster."

He walks around giving each group some puzzle pieces to put together. I raise my hand with questions about the rules. He answers, then says, "It's been a really long time since you trusted or validated yourself, hasn't it?"

"Is this a trick question?" I ask nervously.

He laughs and says no, just his experience of me. I don't know how he "experienced" this out of a few questions about a game, but I'm not about to ask.

As we struggle unsuccessfully to fit the pieces together, he asks us to notice our reactions, our inner conversation—frustration, failure, driven, smug, stupid, blame, perfection. My inner conversation is that I'm dying to snatch the pieces from our designated piece fitter, who is fitting much too slowly.

We, the unfixed, are sent home with a handout. "Ten Ways to Sink Your Child's Program—or—Ten Ways to Ensure a Repeat Performance." To name a few:

1. Talk about time with your child. Promise them they'll be home by a certain date. This way they won't be burdened with the need to make long-term changes. They can focus on just putting in their time.

2. Create your own special program. This lets your child know they are "special" and above any rules and standards.

6. Whenever your child has a problem or consequence, rush in and save the day. This will ensure your child knows your love and support is greater than their need for accountability.

7. Refuse to let go—try to control and protect your child's experience and progress. This has always worked so well in the past.

At least they've got a sense of humor, and they may have something there with that last one. On the drive home, I think about what David said. I'm decisive, assertive, hardly the qualities of someone who doesn't trust herself. It does give one pause, however, to be in the "Reality, you've got a kid in a program" circle. I've got that restless, snippy feeling I get when criticism hits home and I hate the person delivering it.

Normally, my thoughts would immediately switch tracks to the whizzing street scenery—why isn't there an Urth Coffee in Santa Monica, hey, Gap mannequins have nipples now, the sky's so pretty, let's go to the beach. Today, however, my mind's busy choo-choo stays right in the station listening to the following announcement: I have a long history of not trusting myself, with disastrous consequences.

Thank you very much, Mr. Gilcrease, the vocabulary word for the week will now be *self-recrimination*. Till now, Mia's bratty letters have allowed me to feel an infinitely more preferable sense of self-righteousness.

14.

Parents at the meeting encouraged us to join the Link, a bulletin board parents created to share information and support. It will become a lifeline in the coming year. A lot of the Link deals with our own personal growth, a lot of it is hysterical, a lot of it is, well, a lot, period. With several hundred parents on it, there are about thirty posts a day. I learn to cull the good ones quickly—there's a core of about twenty people worth reading, whether or not it's relevant to where Mia's at now.

They've just posted their most recent compilation of their popular "One Liners," excerpts from kids' first letters home. They're more than comic relief, they also serve to remind new parents not to take the first letters too seriously.

They fall into predictable categories. There's the pitiful:

If you let me go home, I will be Miss Good Student, I will be Miss Housework, Miss Helpful . . .
How could you do this to your only child, your pride and joy, the fruit of your loom. . . .
Even though you did this, I still love you internally . . .
There are certain animals that die without their moms and I've come to realize that I am one of those animals . . .

There's the creative:

I am in a group with mostly gays and murderers . . .
There are cannibals working here, one ate his father . . .
They feed us so little, I'm forced to eat grass and toothpaste . . .
One girl thinks she's really a reincarnated chimpanzee . . .

The place is full of crankheads and coke fiends, people with *actual* addictions, not like me . . .

Like Mia, they're all obsessed with their "stuff":

If I come home and one thing in my room is gone, there goes our relationship . . .

They beg, threaten, and manipulate in such predictable ways it makes you feel sorry for them. Until you remember what life was like when they were home.

My reflection in a pool of water catches me off guard. With no mirrors, the most you ever see of yourself is a passing glance in a window or glass door.

My skin's gotten terrible and my hair's complete frizz. I let Lara pluck my eyebrows yesterday with a rubber band we cut in half. Now, I look permanently surprised, thanks to two skinny commas above my eyes. Fuck it, whose gonna care here?

I think back to my first day here, how all the girls seemed so strange and dull, how they all looked like matching nerds, and want to laugh. Looking at myself now in these awful clothes, 10 pounds heavier, a hairy upper lip and broomstick hair, I feel fully assimilated into the Morava machine.

Tyna reports by email:

I spoke with Mia on Monday "one on one" and today she opened up little bit in group. I am happy it is her good start. She is sick of her lies. She wants to change and she is going to write you about it soon I hope she will do it.

Have a nice day Sincerely—Tyna

Mia's letter came a week later, and she did come clean, though she confined it to pharmaceuticals.

. . . I have only done pot, LSD, PCP, hash, coke, over-the-counter drugs (Coricidin and No-Doz), huffing inhalants, and drinking. Speed and shrooms, too, sorry. I guess barbituates, too.

Only? We're amazed she has enough brain cells left to remember her home address to send the letter to. And she didn't even mention the heroin.

"At least she's admitted lying in the first place, that's a first."

"Don't get too excited," Paul says as he puts his feet up and picks up his glass of wine. "She probably has no problem confessing to all these drugs because she still thinks it's okay to do them." Her letters and his nightly glass of wine have become inseparable. He says one makes the other one easier to swallow.

"I disagree. She has too much pride. I really think she's beginning to change a little. She writes two or three letters a week—there's even a second one in this envelope. And she's gone a few weeks now without going back to Level 1. I think it was a good thing she didn't get the emails I sent. Maybe not hearing from me has gotten her to take her actions more seriously. See, Paul, she misses home, listen—

I read from Mia's letter,

Just please write me. If you choose not to, tell me that. Just be honest. I know I've done a lot and will understand it if you guys don't want to start over with me. I love you both more than anything and I want to start a good relationship with you, I want you both to write to me. But, I'll be okay if you don't want to. *I really love you guys.* Mia.

"Poor thing's all over the place," Paul says sympathetically.
I pull out the second letter, written days after this one, reading,

Please, I'm seriously begging you to write me a letter with issues. *Please*, I want to start a good relationship with you guys and so far Paul's the only one who emailed me. Please just write me Mom, please. I want a two-way communication thing to start. I love you both. Love, Mia.

I know my child. This is not manipulation. This is a glimpse of my Mia, and she's afraid she's lost her mother. After dinner, I buy some mango-colored stationery, one of her favorite colors. I want a "two-way communication thing" to start, too.

* * *

"Trojan, T-R-O-J-A-N, a native or inhabitant of Troy."

Roxanne passes Katrina the dictionary.

"Lifestyle, L-I-F-E-S-T-Y-L-E, the habits, tastes, economic level, etc., that constitute the mode of living of an individual or group."

Clearly, the Czech Republic uses different brands of condoms, and the joke goes right over the head of our new staffer, Miss Olga. She has a sweet face and she's painfully shy, though she knows enough to know we shouldn't be laughing.

She walks over, smiling in confusion.

"Girls, I think there is no talking, yes?"

Suddenly, Tyna walks in.

"Girls, I have just come from speaking with Glenn. There is to be major change. From now on, you must talk in German only, no more English."

Are they serious? We take German classes here, but so far I can only say my name and count to ten.

Life in German means head counts have gone from ten seconds to ten minutes. Now, we all rush to line up because numbers under ten are easier to remember and pronounce. Asking for simple things sends girls roaring into laughter—cleanser: das Reinigungschmittel, *vacuum:* das Staubsauger. *The long rolls we get at every meal have become "das penis brot."*

Thankfully, Miss Zuza's got a sense of humor about it. Miss Olga, however, has become a drill sergeant. She must have gotten chewed out for being too lenient with us. We watched Sunny's favorite educational video today—David Attenborough on the sex life of a rare jungle flower—and Miss Olga gave her a breaking silence for squealing, "Aren't vaginas just fabulous!" Then, when Sunny kept smiling, she consequented her again. For smiling!

When the shift changes, we all complain to Miss Zuza about Miss Olga.

"What do you think made her change, girls?" Miss Zuza asks. "How many of you would be lying if you told me you didn't try to manipulate her?"

No one responds.

"You girls don't think about other peoples' feelings. Being manipulated is, what's the word, degrading. If you had not taken advantage of her, she wouldn't have wanted to overcompensate. And you might consider apologizing. It's not always easy working with you girls!"

I guess she has a point. Miss Zuza is strict but she has our respect. Once you stop trying to manipulate her, she's actually pretty cool.

A package arrives from Utah with a diary Mia left behind there. I've taken it to Kinko's to make a copy to send to Glenn along with the first letter I've written to Mia since she left for Morava.

As I flip the diary open to lay on the copy machine, my eyes fall on something obviously written while she was in Indiana.

The people she was hanging out with there were skinheads.

I look up from her small, cramped writing and stare outside at the world. Heat waves rise off the roof of a black Mercedes with a Nevada license plate. Skinhead. A woman in a taupe chemise hurries across Wilshire Boulevard. Neo-Nazi. A slender Persian businessman grinds a cigarette out under a brown pigskin loafer. Holocaust. A single yellow leaf falls. My mother.

The contents of Kinko's Dumpster have just increased by one sealed and addressed mango-hued letter.

15.

You'd think the president was coming to visit. The silence seems louder than normal as girls go about their morning chores anxiously, mysterious strangers scurry up and down the halls, and staff takes a sterner tone with us than normal.

Today is some seminar called Discovery, and a guy called David is running it. Just hearing his name terrifies those who went through Discovery with him before and "chose out," which basically means they got booted. Seminars are strictly confidential, so we know absolutely nothing about them, but when we line up outside the dining room, I have the distinct feeling what awaits us inside isn't Deepak Chopra and borscht. Suddenly, in one grand, sweeping motion, Miss Zuza and Sasha swing open the doors and usher us in to twinkling music.

The dining room has been transformed. Blackout material hangs over the curtains and two large easels stand in front of about thirty folding chairs. I get my first look at boys in months because seated on one side are about fifteen of them with shaved heads. They wear the same uniforms we do, which is unfortunate because blue jean sweatpants look ten times funnier on guys. Glenn, Steve, Sasha, Miss Zuza, and Mr. Peter sit at a table in back, hands folded, faces solemn.

Out of nowhere a voice booms, "Welcome to Discovery!" An enormous man with dark hair and pale skin walks up the aisle toward the front of the room. He introduces himself and goes over the ground rules.

"If you feel you cannot agree to any of these, please stand."

I scan the list. Maintain confidentiality, be seated by the time the music ends, wear your name tag in a visible location, no side talking, sit next to someone new after each break, follow the facilitator's instructions. They're straightforward enough, I stay seated and look around. No one stands.

"Well, that's settled, let's get down to work."

He starts going over shit that sounds like what we hear on the tapes. I'm half bored and half relieved. You get 100 points, enough for Level 2, if you graduate, so I pay just enough attention to look interested.

He tells us that we all started out as magical children, unfettered, confident, clean. Then certain events happen that inhibit us and from these events we form self-limiting beliefs, things we choose to believe about ourselves that limit our actions. How profound, I can feel myself changing already.

We turn to a page in our packet with two columns, one that says "I am" and the other that says "I am not." A list of adjectives is under each one. I scroll down the list, mentally circling a mess, dirty, and lazy under the "I am" column, and thin enough, good looking, and lovable under "I am not." I feel like that some of the time, but I hate how this place tries to get you to say you hate yourself. Whatever, if they want me to say I'm the scum of the earth, I will, just so I can tak, tak kakao *and salt.*

After a lunch break, we walk back in to the slow intro of the song "Also Sprach Zarathustra" from the movie 2001: A Space Odyssey. *Remembering we have to be seated by the end of the song, we all scramble to find a seat.*

"First things first, is there anyone with a broken agreement?" David asks.

When no one stands, he shouts, "I said, does anyone have a broken agreement?"

Lara stands. "I forgot my name tag. If I give myself a consequence, can I stay?"

David looks at her. "If I give myself a consequence, can I stay?" he repeats slowly. "Is that what you tried to do at home? Make a deal? I'll stay grounded one extra day if I can just go to this one party tonight. Please, Mom, please?"

Lara laughs sheepishly.

"IT'S NOT FUNNY, YOUNG LADY."

She looks up at him, shocked.

"I didn't think it'd be that big of a deal."

"Young lady, my experience of you is that you'll go to any length to get your way. You wanted to make a deal and move on, problem solved. WRONG! Making a deal doesn't allow you to look at the real problem—why you broke your word in the first place. This will be a more valuable lesson to you than anything I can offer you in this training. Lara, I'm inviting you back to the next Discovery. For your assignment I want one page, front and back, on why I broke my word and what I can do in the future to prevent myself from going unconscious."

On her way out, Lara's eye catches mine. There's no enjoyment in the connection; if anything, she seems almost ashamed. Mr. Peter removes her chair from the group. Jesus, this guy's a total asshole. I hate how they overanalyze everything here. Next thing you know, forgetting your notebook is actually projecting your subconscious fear of abandonment.

David turns to us, "Who else is just in here to slide by?!" he thunders, pacing back and forth and staring at us.

"Because I do NOT tolerate mediocrity. How you perform in here is a mirror of how you perform IN LIFE. You think it's just three days, some extra points? How many of you still think everything was just fine back home? I can do drugs, quit school, I've got it all under control. Well, how many of you know people that have overdosed, been murdered, how many of you were raped or beaten? Still think it's a joke? How many of you might be dead if you weren't in this room right now?"

I flinch when he says raped, but still think he's being dramatic. He turns to write something on the easel and we all exchange glances. Roxanne puts her finger in her mouth like a gun and Sunny looks too scared to even smile. David turns around, lowers his voice, and addresses us.

"You guys have more hurt than you know how to deal with. I'm here to help you uncover some of that and move on. But you have to be real, you have to be open and committed to becoming your best self. So now, who wants to play a game?"

No one raises their hand. He laughs. "See, even big, mean men like me like to play games."

He has us play one of those mind fuck games, the kind where the answer seems tricky but it's actually very simple. A boy named Robbie launches into a complicated answer and halfway through, everyone's lost. A cute blond kid named Jared patiently tries to explain Robbie's convoluted theory and keep order. I think he's their highest-level kid, though obviously not a Level 4 or he'd be back there with Sasha.

I laugh to myself, they're doing exactly what one of my teachers said cocky people do, go for the hardest answer possible to look smart. I stand up and suggest we think of it more literally, that the answer's probably simple. They ignore my advice. Halfway through the exercise I figure it out and write it down. Fuck 'em, if they didn't even want to listen to my advice, they probably won't believe the answer either.

After another twenty minutes of arguing, David calls time. He calls the *staff team to the front. This can't be good. They start giving us feedback about how quick we were to turn on each other, to act selfish and pushy. Sunny has acceptance issues, Roxanne's a control freak and perfectionist, Jared has approval needs. They nail Katrina for flirting with the boys. I did notice that when the boys came over she practically gave herself whiplash trying to flip her hair back. Then Sasha asks me to stand up. Wunderbar.*

"Mia, you gave great advice but when they didn't listen, you gave up immediately and sat back the rest of the game. In my experience, this is typical, leaving if things don't go your way. Look at how many times you ran away from home."

Glenn stands. "Mia, I saw you write down the answer. By not sharing it, your group lost. All because you wanted to get back at them for not listening to you. Sound anything like what happened between you and Mom? Knowing things that others don't makes you feel in control, powerful. You always have to be the one holding all the cards, laughing while others try to guess what's in your hand."

I want to say that's ridiculous, but I'd be lying. Growing up with a mother who exercised her intellect for a living, I accepted the oncoming verbal onslaught before arguments even began. Leading a double life not only allowed me to do what I wanted without hurting my mother, it was also an opportunity to level the playing field—for once, I knew something she didn't, something she couldn't argue away from me. I learned to view withholding knowledge as power.

"You think making yourself unapproachable protects you," Glenn continues. "But it just pushes people away."

I feel my face flush, being exposed in front of everyone is humiliating. I feel like a fool, and a bitch. I'm sure my team hates me now. And my mom, well, she's a whole other story.

"She didn't know who they were, Claire." Paul's been trying to calm me down since I got home from Kinko's and threw Mia's diary in her room. I'm filled with fury, disgust, shame most of all. My daughter, a Jew.

"I don't care! I hate her! You take care of her from now on."

"Claire, you've got to forgive her. She's your daughter. You know you don't hate her."

"Oh, yes, I do! I'm done forgiving her, this isn't forgivable! I hope she runs and never comes back!"

She's your child, she's on drugs, she's so unhappy. He begs on her behalf because we can't both be in the same place at the same time, it's always been that way. If I'm mad, he's gentle with her. If he gets angry, I plead her case. If one of us cries, the other's strong. But nothing will balance this, nothing he says, nothing anyone says.

I don't want my own daughter.

When Sunny's singing wakes me up, I feel hungover. I was up till one doing homework, journaling about how I ended up here and what my actions cost me.

We line up and when we hear 2001 start to play we perk up, rush to put on our name tags and find a seat, making mad-dash scrambles to switch seats if we sit next to someone we've sat next to before .

The group is considerably smaller and I wonder how many of us will make it through today. David begins predictably, with broken agreements. No one stands and, amazingly, Sasha doesn't have anyone to rat out.

"Samantha!"

We all jump—what the hell did she do? She stands, slumping over twice as much as usual. David walks over to her—and then smiles.

"Samantha, I'd like you to wear a headband the rest of this training to keep your hair out of your eyes. You up to that?"

Samantha looks at him for a second and then a miracle happens. She smiles and shakes her head yes. We give her the same feedback and she chews half her finger off. Go figure.

"Great," he says to her. He's actually starting to sound like a normal person. Until he explains the next process—we have to go up to every single person in the room and hear feedback about ourselves, namely what behaviors they notice in us that hold us back. Four miserable hours later, he calls stop and walks up front.

"You've all heard some pretty powerful feedback in the last twenty-four hours. There's a lot that's not working for you kids. How long has it been like this? Can you remember the last time you felt really happy? Truly carefree? You kids are in so much pain it immobilizes you, it's so obvious, yet you try so hard to stuff it down, drug it away. When's the last time you hugged your dad? Or yelled at him, pushed him away?"

As he speaks, the lights dim and a song begins to play. He asks us to sit on the floor, apart from each other. Staff scurries around us in the dark, dropping something beside us.

"Bring to mind a picture of your dad. Picture how he must have looked when he first saw you in the hospital, how it looked during a favorite memory of yours . . . Now bring to mind a picture of his face in a particularly painful memory. Maybe he looks hurt because he caught you drinking or in a lie, maybe

he looks mad because he's drunk, maybe he's about to hit you. Whatever that painful memory is, bring it up."

I think of the night Paul pinned me to the kitchen floor when I had the screwdriver, that combination of confusion, fury, and pain.

Then I think about my old dad. He's a blank, a mannequin head with no features. All I can picture is the nightmares, the clown wig, the needles poking. This makes me madder than anything. Mad in a way that I want to cry. Almost. I can always almost cry.

David's voice is escalating now. "Picture his face during those painful moments, picture how he looked, what he said . . . Now reach down. There's a rolled up towel next to you. Sitting cross-legged or on your knees, grab that towel and hit the floor with it, hit it as hard as you feel like hitting it. It's time to let go of all that pain and anger."

Some kids have started crying, and before he's even finished speaking, thuds can be heard across the room. In no time, it grows to loud, thundering thwacks accompanied by yells and cries. He's talking over them, urging them to let go of it all, of all the anger, all the pain.

I don't feel the urge to do anything, cry, scream, hit. Numbness has become so familiar that any sort of feeling seems like a virus my body immediately rejects. Back home I did anything to make myself feel alive—fight, use, cut. Nothing ever worked for more than a few hours.

As David keeps coaching, sounds start echoing that don't even sound human. It reminds me of watching Derek go through withdrawal. I haven't thought about Derek in so long. I guess when it comes down to it, all men just want sex. Shit, my own father did.

I pick up the towel next to me, kneading it between my palms. What gets me the most about my old dad, even more than the molestation itself, is that he didn't go to therapy, that he just gave me up. But only a sick fuck would do that, so what does that make me for wishing he had stayed in my life?

After awhile, the energy in the room dies down; everyone's exhausted themselves. Sensing the change of mood, David softens his voice and a song comes on. People collapse on the floor, some stay on their knees, heads bent over their knees. Looking at them makes me feel sad. That they can feel that intensely and I can't. That they have a father to cry over and I don't.

He goes through the exercise again, this time with our mothers. When he asks us to bring to mind a particularly painful moment, I don't even have to think about it. Her face after seeing me in the bathroom with the razor. I've never felt like such a freak in my whole life. Everything I had worried about was confirmed. I was a monster.

I pick up the towel again. The first couple whacks are weak, soft flicks of my wrist that hardly make a sound. I try it again, harder. It makes a satisfying thud that echoes up through my wrist and into my arm. I do it again, harder, and then harder still. Before I know it, a long-sedated voice comes out of me that makes me hit and hit and scream and hit. All the times she looked at me with disgust, all those times she would explode when she was having a bad day, it all tumbles out of me.

But then I start thinking of the life we had before I started distancing myself, before my model horses started collecting dust and my mom became too intrusive a presence. And I miss them, really miss them. I miss how close we used to be.

And then, in spite of promising not to, I cry. I cry for all the times I couldn't or wouldn't, for all the times I cried without sound. I cry for what my dad did to me and for what I did to myself. I cry for waking up naked and confused on the Wilkinson sofa. I cry for myself and I cry for my mom, for all the pain he caused her, and then everything I put her through. I want to cry away all the fights, all the drugs. I'm sorry Mommy, I'm sorry, I love you, I'm sorry.

I want to feel her brushing my hair, hugging me tight. I want my mommy. It's amazing, I'm fifteen and I'm sitting in a room full of kids all crying for their parents, the ones we had before we became cool.

At some point the rage and sadness drains out of me and I collapse and curl up in a ball. A pair of arms encircles me and I open my eyes and look up into Sasha's. I lean against her and we just rock and rock and rock.

David tells us softly to close our eyes and picture ourselves as children. A photograph comes to mind of me at age four, smiling in my pink dress that Bubbie made, with food all over my face and my eyes squinted up with laughter. Even in the photo you can almost hear the childish giggles. My little self jumps down from the chair and I take her hand and walk her to a forest, the kind I pictured when I still believed in unicorns.

I see myself galloping in Agnews meadow, at my first day at Hopkins when I was still excited about this new private school, swimming in the ocean waves, rubbing my pierced finger against my cousin Rosie's to become blood sisters, building forts and picking blackberries. Suddenly, I become conscious of light, joyous music playing.

As it gets louder, the lights brighten and I notice for the first time everyone *around me, blinking hard as they uncurl from the fetal position like newborns. We all stare at each other as though for the first time and smile. Not polite, cool smiles but big baby ones. We start laughing and hugging and dancing around the room. Jared and I hold hands and spin until we're dizzy. I roll into Sunny and we giggle and then giggle at our giggling.*

David gently tells us to crawl to our small groups. Every time I look over at Samantha we both start laughing again. I can't remember the last time I felt this happy. I stand up and start sharing with my group before David even gives us any instruction.

"I had no idea I had that much pent up inside of me! No wonder I felt dead all the time, I was only allowing a tiny, dark fraction of myself room to breathe."

I listen to the room become a chorus of "I didn't know I could feel this good," and it occurs to me how little we truly know people, even those we live with. We go through the motions during the day and return each night to our own private hell.

When I crawl into bed tonight, I think about how last night I was the same person in this same bed but in twenty-four hours something's changed. I think of us all romping around and try to imagine that happening in the real world. It's sad but I can't.

And that worries me. That what's created here can never fully translate into the real world. I push those thoughts out, I can worry about all that later. For now, I just want to fall asleep while I can still hear the laughter and giggles of twenty toddlers trapped in teenagers' bodies.

"Claire, it's not working," my producer says with both regret and frustration.

He's back from Europe, and we're sitting in his dining room.

"You know I love your work, but you keep getting behind, this thing with your daughter."

He's right. First Mia's diary, now my job. Losing this project isn't just a blow emotionally, but financially. I'll lose the remaining sixty thousand dollars of my contract. And I'm in no shape to look for another job at this point.

I hit Sunset and follow its green curves to the ocean. As populated as LA is, large stretches of beach are always empty. A perfect place to feel completely unmoored.

I've managed to cover half of George Polti's "Thirty-Six Dramatic

Situations" all in one lifetime: Erroneous Judgment, an Enemy Loved, Falling Prey to Cruelty or Misfortune, Self-sacrifice for a Kindred, Disaster, Pursuit, Recovery of a Lost One, Deliverance, Discovery of the Dishonor of a Loved One, and, finally, Conflict with a God . . .

What exactly do you have to say for yourself now, God?

I'm a writer to the bone. I make sense of the world narratively. There is always an overarching design, with recurring motifs, underlying motivations, opposing forces, fallen heroes, and fitting ends. A dramatic structure. Mine has unfolded thus:

Our cheeky heroine meets the unexpected, she suffers trials and tribulations, she wrestles the beast and rescues her only child! A period of calm ensues before calamity strikes again, but she's up to it! She pulls her from disaster's door, not a moment too soon! Happiness is on the horizon once again, but wait, wait! There's a major reversal, A Twist, oh, you clever scenarist! Just as the limo pulls up to paradise, the child, the one our heroine risked all for, the child *herself* becomes the beast! A changeling who vanquishes our gal with two swift blows! Oh, what a world what a world, all was for naught, the forces of evil have triumphed!

PAN across an expanse of beach as the sun disappears. To the lone figure seated at the water's edge. MOVING IN we see it's a WOMAN, with her head on her knees.

16.

Dear Mia,

    This is very hard for me to write and will no doubt be hard for you to read. That's tough luck for both of us . . . You have done what your old dad never managed to do—you have gutted my heart entirely. And if this makes you feel guilty, well, it should . . . Claire

My seminar high just ended. The sense of shame and stupidity I feel reading this is so overwhelming that I put it down several times. I'm such a shit. I want to cry but even that seems selfish.

I always assumed my connection with my mom was permanent. She was my mother, mine. It never occurred to me that mothering is voluntary. When I was little, even up to the time I first ran away, any sort of argument with her really upset me. We had a special closeness, and the thought of that changing or being lost terrified me. Then in the past year I shut her out and shredded the cord. But, I just wanted her to back off, not stop caring altogether.

She'll never forgive me, she shouldn't, what sort of masochist would want me for a daughter? The worst part, though, is where she wrote that until I take accountability for my actions, "I'm just a dirty kike, not your mother." This crushes me. I had no idea what Brian and his friends were until it was too late.

Her letter seems to have set the tone for the next two weeks. Coming out of Discovery I was on fire. I felt like Wonder Woman, I was never going to break a single rule, I'd graduate and live happily ever after—a great fantasy for the two days it lasted.

All the seminar did was open Pandora's box. I had so much shit come to the surface, Sasha and I made a list of my issues, so I could deal with them one at a time and not get overwhelmed. Group has become like a Jeopardy game for me, I'll take incest for 400, Alex, no, make that self-mutilation for 1,000.

The whole dynamic in the family's changed, too. We've all pretty much real-ized we're full of it and it's not only uncomfortable to be in our own skin, but embarrassing to be around everyone else who saw you pre-Discovery in all your shit and glory.

It's been almost a month now and she hasn't written a word since that awful letter. I must have apologized and begged for a response in a dozen letters by now, but still nothing. We have ten minutes before shutdown. I pull it out and read it again.

I hope that somewhere still inside of you is Mia—it is to that indescrib-ably wonderful person that I send all of my love. I can't wait to see her again.

Even after being so badly hurt, she ended the letter by saying she loves me. She should have signed it fuck you. That, I could understand.

Growing up, one of my favorite films was The Adventures of Natty Gan, *about a girl who travels across country by herself with her wolf dog. I used to stay up in bed at night pretending to be her. I was Natty racing to hop a train, I was Natty looking around to make sure that soup can was safe to steal, I was Natty grabbed from behind when out of nowhere my wolf dog flies at my attacker. I was captivated by her freedom and independence, by the adventure.*

I didn't think about the fact that she was traveling in search of her father. I guess we always want what we don't have. She traveled cross-country solo to find a parent, I did the same thing to leave one.

A friend of mine, a beautiful Polish producer, has arranged a meeting with director Tony Kaye. Lena's been trying for a while to set up a script I'd written, and he likes it.

I don't particularly care to go, I don't particularly care to do much of anything now, especially writing, which is too internal an endeavor. I'm finding apathy oddly relaxing. On the way to the studio, she fills me in on the film he's cutting:

American History X.

Of all the directors I take a meeting with, it has to be the guy who's just directed Hollywood's first major film about Neo-Nazis, about a skinhead?

Her tiny Mercedes suddenly feels suffocating; my armpits have started itching. She's going on about what an important film it is, how gorgeous the footage is. Yes, I mumble, pretending to stare out my window while I work on getting my features back in order.

We meet Kaye at a lunch table outside a cutting room on the studio lot. I feel floaty and dull-witted as the sun beats on my face and the top of his shaved head. He's quick-witted and gracious. Unfortunately, he also wants to talk about the controversy surrounding his film. The few English words I remember from Latin mass, Lord Deliver Me, are practically spelling themselves out across his bald pate.

"Claire, darling, you weren't yourself," Lena says on the way home. "You're always so high energy and creative in meetings. Is it Mia?"

Yes, probably, I say absently, apologizing.

"It must be hard to have her so far away. You must be dying to see her."

It's not far enough, and the only thing I'm dying to do is crawl in a hole.

Tonight, I dream of Mia. She's sitting in the pink velvet chair I had when she was little. She's shrunken and the whites of her eyes are solid red, like old depictions of the devil. I'm talking to her and she's high and belligerent; she mocks me. This makes me so mad, I lean down and grab her arms. I squeeze them so hard my fingers start to hurt and I know I'm hurting her. She tries to get away but I squeeze those little arms until I hear her bones cracking in my hands.

The sound of her bones breaking is so horrible it wakes me up with my hands clenched so tight that when I go to the kitchen I see nail marks in my palms. This feeling of her bones crunching haunts me for days. My own child's bones.

I'm ashamed of this anger. She's written me a dozen letters begging me to forgive her, but I can't; my heart feels as rigid and cold as steel, and as unforgiving.

Please, please, God, soften my heart. Who else will be her mother?

Hollywood is divided into two kinds of people: those who practice yoga and those who practice Zanax. I hate taking drugs, and yoga's right up there with chanting and feathered Dreamcatchers. But, after two weeks of incapacitating panic attacks, I'm learning to chattarunga with the best of them. Monday/Wednesday/Fridays, I inhale a column of red energy up from mother earth's core. Tuesday/Thursdays I suck calming blue breaths into my cranial cavity and down my spine. In between, I surround myself with purifying white light.

And I am still seized with a racing heart and pinched lungs. I recall an article about something called neurofeedback for anxiety and track down the information.

Two days later, I'm in a darkened room with three electrodes attached to my head, staring at a slowly turning star on a video screen. Every time my brain does the good thing, whatever that is, the star glows and I'm rewarded with a little beep! After so many beeps, a burst of twinkly sparks shoots out and showers the spinning star with happiness. A harplike interlude accompanies the twinkles.

Maybe I've become the cheapest date in town, but I begin to await those twinkles and sparks like a junkie. I practically start sucking my thumb the minute they hook me up and give me a lap blanket. Each half-hour of brain training is like a month in the country. I walk out of there feeling like Buddha.

It's almost enough to make me forget the rest of my life.

"Side—put your booty back—side—front!"

Five girls' backsides come swinging around toward me. We have a new exercise video, MTV's The Grind, *and we're loving it. Sunny looks like somebody oiled her hips.*

"Mädchen! Die Post ist hier!" Tyna comes in with a stack of mail. We stop dancing and wait for our name to be called. Except Sunny, who's oblivious, swinging her arms and shaking her hips, shouting in German and English.

"Jah, booty back, auf und ab, turn it around, yeow!"

"Sunny!" Tyna yells.

She stops, surprised to see Tyna holding out a letter with an exasperated look.

Sunny starts reading it immediately and shouts without permission, "Mein God! Meine mutter hat Discovery ge-passed!"

Fan-fucking-tastic, her mom just went through seminar and mine won't even write. I hate mail time. I've given up on them ever writing and am beginning not to care.

As we line up for class, I notice Sunny break into a smile, then quickly cover it with her hand. Sunny got permission earlier to borrow a tampon from

Lara and she's staring at it like it's a magic wand. I sneak a glance over her shoulder and notice the tiny writing: "A little something from me to go inside of you."

Normally, I'd laugh, we joke around like that all the time, but this is different. Sunny's really blushing. And then it hits me. Sunny's gay!

Everyone stands quietly behind their chairs in the cafeteria. Miss Zuza nods and we take a seat. Lupe raises her hand, "Darf ich musik putten on, Frau Zuza?"

"Jah, Lupe."

Lupe shuffles out of the dining room and returns smiling demurely. We begin eating in silence, save the clinks and tinks of eighteen girls' cutlery. A classical song begins to play, a sweet melody I recognize but can't name. Just as I begin to drift along to the song, a man's vibrato voice starts crooning, "Is this the real life? Is this just fantasy," and I suppress a laugh. Soon the whole table recognizes "Bohemian Rhapsody" and is waiting for Miss Zuza to as well.

By "doesn't really matter to me—to meee . . . ," we're all at the edge of our seats.

And then the rock part breaks out and we all bang our heads up and down in unison. Ruza, the cook, starts conducting with her wooden spoon and even little Jenka plays air guitar with a big spatula. Miss Zuza starts laughing when the door swings open and a worried-looking Peter rushes in. He stares for a second at the dancing cooks and headbanging girls and, seeing Miss Zuza unconcerned, shakes his head and retreats back to the boys. I guess his intrusion was enough for Miss Zuza, because she waves her arm, yelling, "Das reicht, Mädchen, das reicht (that's enough)!" But she's still smiling.

It's moments like this that make it bearable here.

I haven't gone on the Link in a while, but I do tonight and find a post from Sasha's mother.

> We both have had periods of great difficulty in coming to terms with the anger and pain that continues to creep in when we think of how she treated us . . . This evening I pulled out a book of my favorite poetry . . . sticking out between two of the pages was a photograph of our then-six-month-old Sasha in our arms, a look of radiant happiness on all three of our faces . . .

I commit this day to relinquish my anger . . . to forgive my daughter . . . When she looks into my eyes I want her to see nothing but love, support, and pride . . . which is precisely what she deserves.

It's the first cool night in a while and before taking a walk, I dig out the big, black writing sweater my mother knit for me. It's oversize with a big shawl collar, burnished leather buttons, and deep pockets. I haven't worn it since last winter.

When I look down to button it, I see it—a long, wavy strand of Mia's hair, a part of her still golden, unblackened. The part of her I stopped seeing. My little monkey.

17.

The seminar room's easy to find. Waiting outside the doors are about forty of the most haggard, wary, nervous middle-aged people ever to grace a hotel hallway. There are several parents like myself as well, who are upbeat, excited to be sharing in our child's treatment, however distant.

I'm more than upbeat; I'm still basking in the serenity of having forgiven Mia. I feel cleansed and tranquil. In fact, I feel positively seraphic.

The easels should have been the first clue.

Posters on the wall with slogans like "Nothing Can Change When You Are Comfortable" should have been the second.

Duane Smotherman is a handsome, six-foot-seven African American in his late forties. He struts, gesticulates, and captivates; he booms, whispers, and gets in our faces. He's here to teach us about our beliefs, behaviors, attitudes, and assumptions, ladies and gentlemen. About accountability and possibility, about *con*sciousness.

"It's no accident you are here, this did not happen over*night*. Your children are not dis*eased*, your children's behavior is merely a *symp*tom of a much deeper issue," he says as he strolls down the side of the room. "They are reacting to a fundamental *disconnect* in the family system. So, they looked for connection in drugs, sex, gangs, alcohol."

We've been asked to remain in open body position—legs uncrossed, palms on our thighs facing up. The room is fast dividing into wide-eyed guilt with upturned palms and testy muttering with legs and arms tightly crossed.

"They looked everywhere," he stops in front of a muttering couple, "but to *you*, true? Do you get it?"

They do, though they're not happy about it. He looks at the rest of us to make sure we're getting it, too.

"Make no mistake about it," he declares, "we're not here this weekend to fix your children. We're here to *reveal, feel, deal, heal,* and be *real*. To learn about *the shadow you cast*. To get *con*scious about what you brought to the family dynamic that landed you in these seats. The question is," he pauses, "do you have the *guts* to do what you are asking your kids to do?"

Like anyone's going to say "No, I'm gutless" when they can just slink off unnoticed at lunchtime. Our heads rotate to follow him as he walks back toward the front.

"This weekend you are going to walk through a hall of mirrors . . . Where everywhere you look . . . ," he stops abruptly. He knows how to hit the beats like a trained Shakespearean actor. He turns to face us. "All you see . . . is *you*." He pauses, smiles.

"Ladies and gentlemen, welcome to Discovery."

I've never read or work-shopped anything remotely transformational. To keep us present and in the moment, we're not permitted to take notes. Which puts me squarely outside the Comfort Zone thing Duane's scribbling about at the easel. As he writes a long list of "where we grown-ups like to hang out," I cringe and mentally tick off Control, Perfection, Being Right, and Analysis/Paralysis, i.e., "Being stuck in your head."

"This is where your kids hide out," he says, pointing to his head, "oh, yes, they *love* living up here in the penthouse suite. Your kids are *all* about outguessing, control, manipulation, about *working their parents*. About staying up here in their brains, where they don't have to feel. Now, none of you wouldn't know anything about that," he looks in my direction, nodding, "would you?"

Was he looking at me? Could you repeat the question? Because I'm still trying to wrap my brain around the last lesson, the self-limiting belief thing, where I'm supposed to figure out how I got programmed.

"Your SLBs," he said as he abbreviated them, "*run* you, ladies and gentlemen. And our self-limiting beliefs are far more powerful than our self-enhancing beliefs. Because we're un*con*scious of them. Most of us have no i-*dea* (a stomp here) what drives our behavior. We have no i-*dea* (another stomp) why something keeps showing up in our life. Oh, it may look like it "just happened," but there are *no accidents*. Human beings are *"addicted"* to being right. And the thing they like to be right about most are their beliefs, do you *get* it?"

Not without taking notes, I don't. All of this is too much to get in one sitting, anyway. My eyes drift over to a poster that says "What You Fear You Create." It reminds me of a quote by fifteenth-century French philosopher, Montaigne, "He who fears he will suffer, already suffers what he fears." Duane's lesson clicks into comprehension: Mia's beliefs about herself had to be two extremes, I am loved and protected, and I am powerless, damaged, unsafe with men. Look which beliefs ruled her. Look who she attracted into her life. How much more powerless and degraded could she be than to be a Jew who found herself with skinheads, even if unconsciously?

My attention wanders back to Duane, now sermonizing about Accountability, labeling a line graph I can't make any sense of.

"Accountability is not about blame, it's not about being wrong, it is about owning the choices you've made, or are making, that create the results you have in your life. And you do create *everything* in your life."

Well, hang on there, Mr. Corporate Honcho up front says, waving and standing.

"You mean to tell me, if I'm in a plane crash, I created that, too?"

"Do planes crash?" Duane asks.

"Yeah," the guy answers.

"So, you made a conscious choice to travel in a conveyance that has been known to crash, sink, get blown up, or otherwise create the unfortunate result of your not making it home, did you not? Are you *responsible*? Of course not, you didn't *cause* it. But you *are* accountable for making a choice that helped set up that outcome. You could have chosen another means of transportation. You always have a choice."

The guy sits down with an expression that says Duane is full of crap. Half the room agrees. The other half looks like a light went on. I'm somewhere in the twilight.

"Folks, the deal with accountability is this—you either see yourself as accountable, that is, as *making* things happen or you see things as a victim, that things are happening *to* you. As long as you see your life as the result of someone *else's* choices, then you see yourself as having no control over your life, because you have no control over anyone else's behavior. You're no doubt painfully aware that you can't even control the human beings you brought into this world. The only person you will ever have control over is *you*. Once you're willing to look at the role *you* played in what didn't work, you put yourself in the driver's seat of your destiny, because you can make a different choice to create a different outcome. You will be at *cause* in your life, not effect. In terms of your kids, if you don't get conscious about the role you played in landing yourself in this room, you're going to keep creating the same results."

He turns to the easel again, flipping to a fresh page.

"So, when you look around at what's showing up in your life, your results, you either have your *stories*," he says loudly, writing "Stories" with one hand and waving the other at us dismissively to project his real meaning, i.e. you either have your bullshit,

"or your *rea*sons," he writes and waves his hand again, meaning more bullshit,

"or your ex-*cuses*," a wave and a stomp, meaning your biggest bullshit of all,

"or you have your RESULTS. And let me tell you something else, ladies and gentlemen."

He spins and leans toward us with his index finger held up. We lean forward, rapt, as if the meaning of life is about to be revealed. Or at least the reason for our child's demise.

"Results . . . never . . . lie."

He waves that raised finger at us. "Your results will always tell you what your real intentions are, or were, consciously or not. *Results never lie*."

He finally lets us out for lunch. He's been scribbling and flipping, he's had all of us doing "processes" and half of us crying. I feel blindsided and the first day's barely half over.

We stagger out of there feeling sucker-punched. But intrigued in a macabre way. Few things are more interesting to people than themselves.

After the break, he introduces the service team, or staff, several happy men and women at the back table who've been scurrying about handling lights, music, doors. Unlike us, they're allowed to take notes, which they've been doing from the start as they watch us.

With one exception, they have kids either in the program or who have graduated it. The exception is a woman named Wendy G. She's got an intense gaze and a dazzling smile, which she's graced us with only once so far.

Duane divides us into two groups for a "game." It's a brainteaser-type process. Sam's group stays in the room; I go with my group to another room, where we figure it out in an atmosphere of excitement.

When we bounce back into the other group's room it's like a slap in the face. They're yelling, fighting, and harrumphing as they struggle to figure it out, making nasty remarks about the service team—"They want to see us lose!" Or about Duane—"He's tricking us!" Or about the game—"Hey, let's cheat, it's just a game!"

Paul stands and quietly gives what he thinks is the answer and he's shouted down by half the group. He mumbles, "Fuck this shit" and sits down for the remaining time, and I have my first lightbulb moment—this is *exactly* what Paul always does when he meets resistance. He makes the other (usually me) an asshole in his mind and withdraws. Duane was right—how you show up in here *is* a mirror of your life. The woman feeling "tricked" probably never trusts anyone and Mr. Hey Let's Cheat probably isn't Mr. Integrity whenever push comes to shove. They're not even aware of it. I love this stuff!

Why wouldn't I? So far, I haven't looked in the mirror myself.

During dinner, Paul actually agrees with my observations about him.

"It's amazing the way they design these processes to expose your issues," Paul marvels. "You can't deny what you just did in a roomful of people. I wouldn't have listened if somebody had simply told me."

"Yes, you would have. You'd have nodded politely and pretended to agree, because it would have gotten them off your back. I *so* get what Duane said about silence being the biggest power play there is."

"I'll try to be aware of it in the future." He shakes his head. "You love to win, don't you? You always have to be right."

"I never thought about it, but I guess I do."

"You guess? You can't even stand to lose at Monopoly! To your own child!"

This seminar's either going to make us like each other a lot more or a lot less. I have a feeling it's going to make me like *me* a lot more or a lot less.

* * *

At the end of the first night, Duane has us get into "feedback arcs," nine little horseshoes around the center of the room. From above, we must look like the June Taylor Dancers in daisy formation.

"Feedback is one of the most powerful tools we have to assist us in becoming self-aware. It's not about judgment, opinion, or making someone wrong. It is simply information, your honest experience of someone— 'Sally, my experience of you is . . .' or 'Sallie, my experience of *myself around you* is . . .' Sally says nothing more than, 'Thank you for caring enough about me to be honest.'"

If it's so benign, I want to know why they just dimmed the lights. And why the service team has suddenly spread like seeds to the four winds to impregnate our groups. They who have been taking notes about us for eleven hours. All grist, grist.

I notice Paul in the next arc with a look of genuine terror on his face. We have to care and share until all forty-five of us know what we really think of each other. I'm glad it's Wendy who joins our group; she's been the most perceptive in her comments.

Thus begins two of the strangest hours I've ever experienced. The darkened room resounds with the din of the good, the bad, and the ugly, punctuated by sobs.

Our sharing of the first person, Patricia T, a serious, heavyset woman, consists of neutral observations. Wendy goes last. She fixes her big, dark eyes on Patricia T and with a loving gaze says:

"Patricia, my experience of you is that you fear rejection so much that you create it by using your weight to push people away. My experience of *myself* around you is that I want to back away from your bitterness."

I can't believe she said that! The poor woman ducks her head, nodding in agreement as she begins to cry, wringing her hands together nervously. Even if it's true, and I think it is, I wouldn't have been rude enough to say it! But, by the time *I* go around, everyone will be. I'm going to get reamed! Especially with Duane circulating, yelling over us, "How much longer are you going to lie to yourself or to others?"

Wendy experiences the next guy as "using sarcasm to make people wrong." Another staffer leans in to experience a woman as using her beauty to manipulate and control others. The man beside me experiences everyone as "nice." Boy, is he going to get it—"approval suck" is the term they've been using.

"How far did your kids have to go before you stopped worrying about their approval?" Duane booms over the racket. "How did it serve you to sugarcoat the truth? Ladies and gentlemen, it's time *to get real*, this is your *life*!"

I've always thought people found me good-natured, genuine, so I'm floored to keep hearing that I'm snobby, smiling but not real, too intellectual (can you be?). Wendy stares into my eyes and tells me, "Claire, you have so much anger, it feels dark and heavy to be around you. You use words to distance yourself, and you use them as weapons. You use them to be everywhere but here and now. I experience myself as almost invisible around you, because all I feel I'm getting is your mouth and your brain, not your heart."

I'm so uncomfortable, I wish my mouth and brain could make *me* invisible.

Wendy's relentless. She follows me to another group to add, "You think your brain keeps you safe." Right now, earplugs would. Still, I'm unnerved by how consistent the feedback is. As my mother would say, "*Ob drei menschen sugen als die bist shicker, geh schlufen* (if three people tell you you're drunk, you better go to sleep)."

The din fades as the last of us finishes but the lights stay low because Duane's not finished. With *me*. The room's silent except for his voice hitting me like bullets.

"Claire, you experience everything in your *life* in your brain, thinking you can control it all. You've been disconnected from your heart for so long, *you are dead inside*! You haven't felt joy in so many years, you can't even remember what it feels like."

My hands fly to my face. He's circling me like a vulture.

"You been burying your heart beneath your intellect, beneath your stories and drama for years! When did you first decide it was okay to kill yourself, Claire?" he says in my face. "Your heart is dying and the pain is exhausting you, *exhausting* you! I can see it in your face! You know it, don't you?"

I'm crying into my hands and can barely stand. I don't want to hear this. He's right, I *don't* know what joy feels like, I'm always waiting for a shoe to drop. Even when Mia was tiny, my joy was surrounded by the shit that was my marriage. I had a few great years with her and Paul, before Nick threatened visitation.

A few years in a lifetime! My heart has existed to feel pain and fear for Mia for so long, I don't know what else my heart is for, and he's shoving my face in it. I hate Duane for this. I'm sobbing so hard, I double over and he leans down and whispers in my ear:

"And you're scared to death that you're never going to come alive."

I move out of the room feeling transparent. I'm vaguely aware of stares of pity or mortification, of someone squeezing my arm gently.

"Claire, are you okay, honey?" Paul whispers. I nod and move off. I'm not ready to be with anyone. I find a solitary chaise by the pool and pull out the dinner I packed, two hard-boiled eggs, olives, walnuts, V8. What was I thinking? All I want is candy. I want three electrodes and a spinning star.

I feel like I've been roto-rootered, only the crap came out the other end of the system. This is too much consciousness-getting at once. I feel like I've swallowed ten self-help books in one sitting and someone needs to burp me. Since I'm not about to raise my hand and get reamed in there again, I'll just ream myself right here, poolside beneath the rising moon.

Why do I have to be napalmed before I'm aware of how I'm really feeling about most things? Why do I have to think about how I feel? Which is a perverse statement—how can you "think" about how you "feel"? Isn't that like eating an apple to know what the color blue sounds like?

I think about the first significant decision of my adult life, my first marriage. I thought then that maturity meant using your head to guide you, not your heart. But, how much safer I'd have been had I'd listened to my heart about Nick, *not* my bookbrain construct of what I *thought* would be a perfect mate.

My brain has been my sword and shield against pain, and where else is pain felt but in the heart? To slay one is to slay them both. Why did I stop trusting my own heart? When did I disconnect?

I remember getting hurt again and again growing up because we moved so often for my father's work. I'd no sooner make new friends than they'd be gone. I'd grow to love my teachers, only to have to say good-bye to them. But this feels too easy, it sounds like first-date personal history chatter.

A memory leaps up in front of me, an image: the back of my mother's apron. I am running behind my mother. I can't be more than three or four. I'm trying to grab the hem of her blue-flowered apron and I'm cry-ing, "Do you still love me, Mommy, don't you love me anymore?"

"No, I don't love you when you do something like that!"

I don't remember what "that" was, but it could have been anything, putting a Chiquita banana sticker on a new dining room chair, moving something on her dresser from *exactly* where she put it. I felt such utter fear of her not loving me, I feel a crushing sensation in my chest even now just thinking of it.

Why wouldn't I feel wrong-bad-stupid, not lovable? Why wouldn't it drive me now to have to be always right-good-smart, so I'm loved and ac-cepted? Deep down, I never feel that I belong or am enough just the way I am. I always feel I have to work at it, to dazzle as much as I can with brains, talent, humor, if all else fails, with gourmet cooking.

But, when you act like that, it shows. You're trying too hard. One thing nearly everyone has radar for is a fake—and nobody likes a fake. So, I *have* created exactly what I feared. I've been proving myself right about being unlovable my whole life.

Bing! Ms. Fontaine, you've hit pay dirt, won the SLB Jackpot! Pulled back the red curtain and exposed the Wizardess at the control panel, feverishly manning the levers.

You grab the hem of her robe and whip her around and oh, she's just a little thing, our Claire, and oh, no, look, she's started to cry. All the levers have stopped and she feels so sad. Her devastated little heart.

I was always afraid my mother didn't love me. Because she never told me she did. Not as a child and only once as an adult, after I told her I loved her, on a phone call a few years ago. Like a dating couple where one of you waits for the other to say it first. She waited forty years.

When I get back to the room at the end of the night, I don't feel like talking. Which means the room is practically silent. I look at Paul's homework before we go to bed and see that the feedback he got most was that he's detached, withdrawn, avoids risk. How transparent we are in spite of ourselves.

After lunch on the second day, a father who looks like the Marlboro man says he's upset at how little guilt his son feels about what he's done. We all nod in agreement.

"What *he's* done, huh?" Duane comments lightly.

"Yeah. If he doesn't feel guilty about what he's done to the family, what's to stop him from coming home and doing the same stuff?"

Duane glances up, ruminating on this. He draws a breath to speak, stops himself, puts his hands in his pockets and looks down, nodding his head. The room's getting nervous because we have no idea what to expect.

Duane starts out pleasantly. "You know, when I do this seminar with your kids, we're not in a nice, air-conditioned room like this. We're in a room that gets hot very quickly, and you know how teenage boys sweat," he chuckles. "That room gets hot and it starts to smell." His voice starts rising. "It stinks from sweat because your kids are working so hard. Because they're dealing with all the pain and the guilt and the shame they feel for hurting you!"

He starts pacing across the front row, booming and jabbing the air. "I get punched, I get kicked, they spit on me. Your kids are carrying around so much guilt, it would make you *sick* to see it, *sick*! They've been numbing it with drugs, with sex, with alcohol, with violence. They cry out in agony, they *cry out*!" he bellows. "And you know who they cry out for? They cry out for YOU, every one of them! They cry out for Mommy and Daddy! They cry so hard, they vomit. I watch your children *vomit*!"

Chins duck and little cries burst out from mothers and fathers whose arms want to hold their sons and daughters, their babies.

"And you know what they're biggest fear is?" he's yelling now. "That you won't forgive them! All your children want is YOU, do you get it? Not your anger and blame, not your judgment or your self-*right*eousness. They don't want perfection, either, they want you, the *real you*!"

A wave of shame leaves us rattled and silent. He stands for a moment before saying quietly, "Now are you ready to get to work? To dig deep and see what you were unconscious of prior to this event in your family? To ask what you were in denial of? To ask yourself, 'Where did I go blind?'"

He looks into one face after another. Yesterday, people recoiled. Not today. Not those who stayed.

"You know, one of the questions I like to ask is this: 'What are you pretending not to know?' He pauses, then repeats, "What are you pretending not to know? Because, you see, ladies and gentlemen, you *always* know. When someone says to me 'I don't know,' I say: Unless, of course," he leans down to the woman in front of me, "you *do* know."

This woman's been smug since she got here, but I can see a film of sweat break out between her shoulder blades. He's had her number from day one.

Before we leave for break, I ask Wendy for a few moments. She stands close and looks directly into my eyes. I half regret this already.

"I didn't expect so much . . . stuff . . . to come up, I'm not sure how to take it back to real life. It's overwhelming."

"'Overwhelmed' is a choice, Claire. How would it look if you chose excitement instead, like you found yourself at a banquet of new possibilities, new ways of being?"

"Are you this, uh, blunt, outside the seminars? Don't people start avoiding you?"

"I always ask first if someone's open to feedback. If they're upset by what they hear, they're punishing me for being honest. It rarely happens, though, because they know it's coming from a place of love."

"What, you love everyone in the seminar?" I blurt.

"I couldn't do this if I didn't," she says simply.

This just blows me away. Because I believe her. Only love could make someone fearless enough to say the things she did. Our children are probably the only people we are that honest with. The worse their behavior, the more brutally honest. What she and Duane are doing is no different. Except that we've been carrying around our garbage thirty years longer than our kids have. No wonder they need pickaxes.

The last night of the Duanathon begins like a 1970s episode of Mr. Rogers. He starts with a lecture about our "Magical Child," the amazing boy or girl we used to be. Before we buried it behind layers of Fixed Beliefs that led to layers of Fixed Emotions that led to layers of Fixed Behaviors and voilà! that's how you cooked yourself up into the great big onion you are now.

If they're trying to avoid the word "inner" child because it sounds too therapeutic, sounding like you came out of a box of Lucky Charms isn't an improvement. But if last night taught me anything, it's that Duane Smotherman knows something about being human that I don't.

The lights dim and we're asked to get comfortable on the floor. I have to leave my glasses on the back table during this process so they don't get whacked off my face by the flailing arm of someone who doesn't regress quite all the way to the magical part of their childhood. I'm legally blind without corrective lenses, which will regress me to a preverbal state without any help from Duane.

I lay back and close my eyes as Duane talks us softly through a visualization. A half-hour later I'm in the most glorious forest imaginable, feeling like happy juice has been injected straight into a vein. My brain has stopped fizzing for the very first time in, I don't know, my life maybe.

I feel more clear, aware, and open than I ever have. No, this isn't feeling *or* thinking. It's simply *being*. I feel whole, as if my heart, mind, and soul have found their way back to each other.

I'm walking down a path toward a shimmering golden light. And there she is, walking out of the light toward me. A little froggy-eyed girl with big hair, in her favorite yellow dress. And she's not wrong and she's not bad. She's lovable beyond imagining. She's beautiful. She looks up at me and holds her arms up. I pick her up and she looks into my eyes and asks, "Where have you been all this time?"

We walk hand in hand out of the forest into Agnews meadow, a storybook meadow near Yosemite. There's another little girl there calling to us and waving as she gallops toward us.

It's little stick-legged, wide-eyed, laughing Mia. She takes my hand, only my hand is suddenly very small. I realize I'm not looking down at my little self, I *am* that little girl and I'm holding Mia's hand.

We lift our arms and fly away, together.

18.

Dear Mia,

    Please know that yes, I forgive you. Yes, we support you. Yes, we have faith in you. Full trust will take a little longer, obviously, but it sounds like you understand this.

She finally forgave me. And in such a wonderful letter. I finally turned into one of those girls whose face lights up when Tyna walks in with mail, one of the haves. Tears come when I read and I don't bother wiping them away. Sunny, who sits to my right, reaches over and rubs my back silently. I'm thankful for the silence now. I just want to sit with this feeling. I need this to stay with me, as a reminder why I can't ever go back down the road I was on.

Since Discovery, I feel bright and airy, as if I had been spring cleaned. Life at home with Paul is lighter as well. We're feedbacking right and left, it's irresistible, it's our new toy. And there's a playfulness to it. I'm experiencing some hostility here, Claire, is this a pattern in your life? Paul, why are you choosing silence, I'm experiencing you as making me wrong.

    Karin's experiencing us both as scary and insufferable. "I think you've both been friggin' brainwashed. Gimme a beer—or is that not allowed now?"

    "Of course it is, dear. Here's a Corona." I hand her a beer and smile at her like a Moonie. "Lime wedge?"

    She snatches the beer, giving me a look. "Don't even think of starting in on me."

    "Karin, I'm experiencing you as threatened," Paul jokes.

    "Your marriage is what's threatened! I'd kill my spouse if he said half the shit you guys are saying to each other."

"Not if it was something you really needed to hear," I reply.

"Some things are best left unheard," she says.

"Have you noticed either of us getting upset by it?" I ask her.

"That's the scary part. Paul tells you you're controlling, read 'bitch,' you tell him he's being a wuss, in so many words, and you two are laughing and hugging like you just got married. It's like they sucked any self-respect you had right out of you. Mia's gonna get home and want to run away all over again."

"Karin, it's not criticism, it's about helping someone get out of their own way. I wish I'd have been more conscious of some of my behaviors a long time ago. I'd have made some very different choices."

That's probably the most important lesson I took home. I always blamed someone or something else because I didn't want to blame myself; I thought "blame" made me a bad person. In shifting from "blame" to neutrally looking at the choices that I made, asking, *how did I set this up,* I feel a sense of power in my own life that has till now eluded me.

As the weeks pass and the "seminar high," as they call it, wears off somewhat, what lingers is a profound shift in the way Paul and I experience each other and life in general. And Karin has not only stopped joking about it, she's decided to take the seminar herself.

Because I have so much time on my hands now, I've signed up for a pitching workshop with a local writing guru. As he's describing the protagonist's mythic journey, he draws a bull's-eye just like the one Duane did. And then he puts a Precious Child in the middle, trapped beneath that pesky onion, those masks and facades.

Hey, he went through Discovery, too! I'm so excited to find another program parent, I hurry to the stage at the break to ask him excitedly which facility his kid's in. He looks down at me, like four feet down at me, and says with amused disdain, "This technology has been around since the seventies. Everyone from IBM to tantric sex workshops uses it."

Uh, never mind, I mumble, my face burning. Now, Claire, I remind myself, humiliation is a choice, what are you making it mean, what are you choosing to feel?

I'm *choosing* to feel like he *chose* to be an arrogant asshole is what. Sometimes, being unenlightened feels so much better.

* * *

We see her sitting at the med counter, the new girl, Brooke. She's skinny, sweaty, and dirty as only a junkie can be and from her glaring expression and her leg shaking rapidly, she's already in withdrawal. Poor thing, I remember sitting there and it sucks.

We walk past her to the classroom and as we're about to cross in, Miss Zuza says, "Mia, Samantha, und Sunny, herausfallen, bitte (fall out of line)."

I hope I've been chosen to do an intake. When someone new comes, girls are always chosen to comb through their suitcase. When you've had the same schedule for three months, you do get excited at making a list of someone's contraband items. While she's taken to be deloused, I set aside her toothbrush and then make a list of things that include condoms, a Circle Jerks shirt that has been cut up and safety-pinned back together, and cigarettes, which I have a hard time not ripping open and smoking.

She comes back halfway through our intake, freshly showered. Her silky black Uma Thurman "Pulp Fiction" haircut and full lips haven't been missed by Sunny, who feigns interest in her intake list. I've been dying to talk to Sunny about being gay, but I'm not sure how she'll react. Maybe she's not ready to come out, who knows, she could be in total denial.

"Find anything interesting?" Brooke asks foully.

She must think we're freaks, girls in these uniforms excitedly going through her things. She has no concept of how this place works, that privacy is nonexistent here; she probably thinks we enjoy doing this, just like I did when Miss Zuza did it to me.

So much has changed since then. I've become so close with some girls and staff it's hard to believe we've only been in each other's lives three months. I appreciate being here now and on some days actually like it. But I suddenly want to be my old self, show this new girl this isn't how I normally am. But isn't it? Isn't this the real me, who I am when the image is stripped away? So why do I suddenly feel so naked now, why am I dying to throw on my army pants and a Descendants CD?

I don't want her to see me as a matching nerd, I want her to know that I used to be part of that world, too. Not because I want to be part of it again, I'm much happier now, but so I can connect with her in a way she'll understand. As I used to, she's operating in the external world, a world where everyone's so disconnected from each other that physicality is all we have to go by, how we determine personality and character, who we think we can relate to.

Growing up is about growing away, about finding an identity distinct from your family. But few teens have a strong enough sense of self to stand alone. It's why friends are so important; together you form a collective identity from which you gather strength and a sense of belonging. And your clothes, music, and friends announce that identity.

Weeks after the seminar, I'm still mulling the "Where did I go blind" question while shopping at Ross Dress for Less. Without a second income now, we're doing Everything for Less. Mulling, however is free.

Probably the first time I remember going blind, I mull as I check the size of a sports bra to send Mia, was when I ignored Nick's drug use, before we even got married, then in countless ways after we did.

Just as troubling was going into such denial about Mia's old psychologist Ella's warning that I "forgot" it altogether. And I've only recently recalled that my mother warned me when Mia was still in grade school that something like this would happen. What he did hurt her deeply, something like that doesn't just go away, she told me.

What was the payoff? It obviously kept me in my cozy zone of being in control, being a good mother, with a good daughter. Most of all, I realize, is that it allowed me to maintain the lie that she was healed, that Nick hadn't permanently damaged her, that I'd truly saved her. Because if I did, if there was no lasting residue of him, it meant that the denial that kept me in the marriage long enough for him to hurt her didn't help create the situation she's in now.

The person who I worked hardest to keep safe seems to have been me.

I've finally decided to share in group about my old dad. Glenn came to support me, but I'm still nervous. Seminar was one thing, everyone was bawling in a darkened room. But here, in a bright, silent room, it's much less comfortable.

"I don't really remember much of it. I used to, but all I remember now is vague details and the nightmares. It's weird how something I barely remember runs me so much."

"What came up for you in seminar?" Glenn wants to cut to the chase.

I'm silent for a minute. I'm not sure where to start, how to word it.

"I didn't realize how hurt I was by him. I was aware of the anger, and of feeling different, but I never acknowledged being hurt, too."

"Why is that? What would acknowledging the pain mean?"

I knew coming in Glenn wouldn't let me slide by, but that's not making this any easier.

"I don't like being out of control, being weak. I hate that it hurts me, that twelve years later someone I don't even know makes me feel like shit. It bothers me that he never went to counseling. He could have had visitation with me, a relationship with me if he went to sex offender therapy, but he didn't. He just went on and had another family."

I stop for a second. I feel dumb saying that. Who would want to be wanted by a pedophile?

"And I feel really fucked up for wanting him to want me, I mean he's sick, so what does that make me for missing him?"

Glenn leans forward in her chair toward me, but she addresses all of us. "We all want to be wanted by our parents, no matter how shitty they were as parents. It's human nature. There's anger toward them, sure, but beneath that is always hurt, why did he do this to me? It doesn't make you weird or perverted for wanting your father's love. Do you hear me, Mia? There's nothing wrong with you."

She holds my gaze and says it again.

"There's nothing wrong with you."

I feel my chin start trembling and Glenn's face starts wavering as my eyes water. She keeps whispering, "There's nothing wrong with you," as I bury my head in her chest and start to cry.

When I look up, my family's surrounding me saying how proud they are of me and how much they love me. I feel a mixture of love and gratitude toward them and Glenn and relief at hearing her words, though it may take me awhile to fully believe them.

During a lunch meeting with a friend, I notice for the first time since Mia left five months ago that I have just gone a whole meal without thinking of her.

My days have finally begun to take on their own rhythm, one not dictated by Mia's needs and wants. For the first time, I'm not obsessing about her progress or her future.

I would have been thrilled if Morava had merely returned her to who she used to be. But she's transforming in a way I never imagined possible. She's made huge leaps in understanding herself, in learning to communicate honestly and effectively. Most important, she's grown to love herself, the quality a teenager most needs to stay safe.

After lunch, I pick up a few ingredients for a small dinner party I'm giving on the weekend. I'm digging in my purse for my keys on the way to my car when I look up and see a pretty teenage girl and her slender, dark-haired mother come around the corner. The mother has her arm around her daughter and they're laughing.

The noise of the street drops off and tears spring into my eyes unexpectedly. I quickly duck my head and I look back into my purse as they pass me.

I don't just miss her, I miss *us*.

We've crossed out to go to lunch but the boys aren't finished eating yet, so we face the wall and wait in silence. As I wait, it occurs to me that I'm no longer bothered by the quiet. I actually enjoy it at times. It makes me realize how excessively we talk. We talk to fill the silence because it's easier than being with ourselves.

We're stripped to the bare essentials here, physically and emotionally. We eat, use the bathroom, sleep, exercise, and attend school, but all on silence. Talking becomes important only when it's a need, not a want, when someone needs to get something off their chest or say something important. I feel more in tune with my real needs versus wants now, both mental and physical.

I feel much healthier now, too. The drugs are out of my system, I've gained some weight, I don't get light-headed like I used to. It sounds dumb, but feeling good feels good.

Morava now has fifty kids, and most of the parents have gotten to know each other by email. There's a resilience and sense of humor common to the Morava parents. I guess you'd have to be a combination of tough and not a little crazy to send your kid to a brand-new program in a former Soviet faux chalet near the Slovak border to face the wall when the opposite sex passes and remain silent for most of the day.

I'm looking forward to meeting some of them and some of the girls that are now part of Mia's journey. The opportunity will come sooner than I expect.

19.

I'm in the second day of Focus, the seminar following Discovery, and the past two days have been harrowing, rewarding, and plain old exhausting. It's a smaller group, a handful of boys, including Jared and Robbie, as well as Sunny, Katrina, Roxanne. We've gone through another towel process, we've re-rediscovered our magical children, we've shared, we've sobbed. We've taken everything we did in Discovery to the next level, delving even deeper into what's holding us back. For me, it's how ugly and worthless the abuse made me feel.

Instead of David, we have Lou, a very little lady with a very big voice, who right now is asking us to vote ourselves and everyone else as a Giver or Taker. We tally our votes and line up in the order of the Giver votes, most to least. At least I won't get reamed in this process; compared to everyone else, I have a decent number of Giver votes.

"Mia!"

I jump at hearing my name. Glenn whispers something in Lou's ear. Why was I singled out? I'm not even at the Taker end of the line.

"Everyone who gave Mia a taker vote sit down. Of those of you standing, why did you vote the way you did?"

Roxanne volunteers, "I think Mia's a Giver because she's really unselfish, she's always willing to listen to people and talks one on one with a lot of us."

Sunny offers that I give really good feedback and am a good listener, and the rest of the girls basically reiterate what they said.

"Well, isn't that interesting?" Lou muses, pacing back and forth. Then she stops about a foot in front of me and stares me straight in the eye.

"The feedback I'm hearing has nothing to do with you, Mia. So far I've heard nothing about what you give to others, just what you take from them. You listen? How is that giving, that's taking in other people's words, other people's experiences. How often do you share in group, Mia?"

"I've made an effort since Discovery to open up in group."

I see Glenn stand up in the back—this can't be good.

"That effort consisted of sharing four times, Mia. You were real, you didn't small talk, but considering we have group every day, I wouldn't call that much of an effort."

"Neither would I, neither would I," Lou mutters. "It's sad, Mia, because you take away from others the experience of sharing yourself with them. And that's not what Focus is about. It's about risk, it's about standing powerfully as the gift that you are and the difference that you make. Your results don't seem to indicate you want to be here."

I swallow hard, resisting the urge to shout, "That's not fair!" I have been trying lately, I've been curbing my attitude and making relationships. I raise my hand.

"It's true, I have a harder time sharing in groups, but I've been working through my issues through letters to my parents or talking one on one with people. I don't think it's fair to base my progress only on group."

Lou asks my family for feedback about this and they're all very supportive. Maybe this will help sway her.

"Mia, notice how you create situations where others have to jump in to save you. Your family seems more eager for you to graduate from this training than you do. I experience you as being very selective about who you're with because it gives you the illusion of control. That's operating from a place of fear, which isn't control, it's cowardice. Young lady, you're on thin ice. I want to see you get real and open up or you're out, is that clear?"

I nod and sit down shakily. As she moves on to others, I think about what she said and start getting mad. Why is everything here based on sharing, like if you don't publicize your life you're not dealing? I hate how this place has this cookie-cutter idea of what change looks like. If you're too quiet, you're not showing up enough, if you talk too much, you're playing show up games. You just can't win.

Still, I'm so relieved to have not chosen out, I keep this last thought to myself.

Our final process is called our Stretch, and I'd rather face a charging bull. I have to put on glittery makeup and twirl around like a butterfly to Mariah Carey. Being Surfer Barbie would be less humiliating. It's meant to get us out of our comfort zones by taking on the persona of the part of us we avoid most. I don't see how making a total jackass out of myself will help me "grow."

Jared seems equally thrilled by the idea of donning a tutu and exploring his *feminine side as a ballerina, and Katrina's hyperventilating at having to clod around as a sumo wrestler. Watching pounds of fake flesh jiggle has got to be a nightmare for someone who panics at eating more than a piece of lettuce.*

We've spent the last two hours creating costumes from scratch, practicing moves, and making ourselves up. The center of the floor is cleared as a stage.

Samantha starts it off as Bananarama's "Venus." My jaw drops when I see our dark and moody Samantha dancing and twirling around in a costume of colored paper, streamers, and face paint as she lip-syncs. She looks radiant and I cheer loudly when she dances past me, trying to get her to hear my voice over Sunny's whooping and clapping.

When her song finishes, we watch three guys shimmy and shout as the Pointer Sisters. They were so pissed when they found out their Stretch, the only reason the words homo or fag didn't come out of their mouths was because they knew they'd get dropped. But something must have happened in the last few hours, because right now they'd put drag queens to shame!

Then the tone changes. An ethereal melody begins to play and the lights dim. Fabric rustles in the darkness. As low lights rise, Jared and two other boys begin to move slowly around the room to the "Nutcracker Suite." It's unbelievable to watch, it's not Jared in front of me in a pink tutu, but some otherworldly creature moving slowly, surely, with grace and strength. They're all beautiful. Not in a feminine way, in a powerful, peaceful way.

Any thought of their looking ridiculous has completely dissipated. Laughing at them would be like laughing at unicorns or angels. When they glide out, there's not a dry eye in the room.

Just as Katrina begins to sumo wrestle her way around the floor to our applause and laughter, Sasha taps me from behind and whispers for me to get ready. I'm so nervous I think that releasing all the butterflies inside would be a more entertaining Stretch than watching me pretend to be one.

Covered in a brown potato sack, I sit under two chairs pushed together (my cocoon) and wait for the music. When I hear the first few notes of the song, I take a deep breath and start wiggling my way from under the chairs and out of the sack. Sasha did my hair and makeup earlier with sparkling green eye shadow, blush, and lip gloss. Under the potato sack I wear tights, a long billowing shirt, and I tied the ends of a shimmering scarf to each of my hands. When I let the sack fall I feel naked, almost how I did that morning I woke up on Derek's sofa.

I try to remember the steps I planned out but I draw a blank and start to freeze up. Fuck it, I already feel dumb. Slowly, I start twirling around, circling the scarves around me and feeling completely idiotic. Then, I start to let loose and move to the music's beat, and suddenly, I'm having fun as my body takes the lead. I'm dancing like I used to when my parents left the house and I'd closed all the blinds. I spin, I stag leap, I twirl.

I feel weightless and angelic. When I reach Sunny, I see tears in her eyes. Being a girl always made me feel weak; I equated femininity with violation. But this feeling of female beauty and grace is awesome, empowering. The song ends, the lights dim, and I'm told to close my eyes. I hear feet rustling up to me and I'm told to let myself fall back. When I do, I fall into hands that lift me high into the air and hold me there.

". . . She's a sparrow, but she's an eagle when she flies . . ." I listen to Dolly Parton with my eyes closed, allowing myself to feel the support of everyone's hands. As it winds down, I feel myself lowered and open my eyes to meet those of everyone else smiling down at me.

Everything I wanted, love, belonging, feeling beautiful, feeling wanted, it's all here, enveloped in the arms of eighteen people I met barely four months ago.

I'm guided to the "Oasis," a chair in the corner with a plate of fruit next to it and a wash basin on the floor. I look down and see Roxanne smiling gently at me as she puts my feet into the warm, bubbly water. Her Stretch is to serve others, which is perfect for someone who is used to being waited on hand and foot. I tilt my head back, reach for some grapes, and enjoy a foot massage.

I feel as if a new me is awakening. Or perhaps reawakening. Initially, I found my Stretch fitting in that it helped me embrace femininity as a strength, rather than a source of pain. A butterfly is able to fly precisely because it's so delicate.

On a deeper level, though, it signified a transformation I've been undergoing. Just as a caterpillar cocoons itself away for protection, I began to shield myself from the world a long time ago. But, I had become so comfortable in it that, rather than protect me, I let it define me, stifle me. I became the shield, not the butterfly. Literally and metaphorically, my Stretch was about the shedding of a self that no longer serves me. One I'm now glad to see go.

20.

"We're being raided." It's Glenn, early on a Friday morning.

I'm sure I've heard wrong. "You're what?"

"Someone said we're abusing the kids, Claire. The police are taking them and strip-searching them. I'm going to need help."

My hand shot up with everyone else's as soon as Glenn asked for kids to be interviewed about Morava and now ten of us are on our way to the police station. Where did they get the idea that they starve and torture us? It's so preposterous, we had a good laugh until the look on Glenn's face told us she wasn't joking.

When our van pulls up to the station, a lady from the American embassy has us wait outside. She says they're still interviewing the previous group of kids.

"Still?" Jared exclaims.

"What are they doing in there for so long?" Roxanne asks.

We murmur in agreement, but the woman just shrugs before going back inside. Hours pass. We're freezing, hungry, and getting really worried, but there's also an anxious excitement in the air—the sudden change in schedule, unsupervised conversations with boys, just being outside in the world, much less riding to a police station in a foreign country.

A man loitering watches us with a cigarette dangling from his mouth. The smell is making us drool. Robbie gives in and bums one; the man gives us a handful out of pity. Everything about the day is so crazy, and we're all so nervous, what the hell.

The embassy woman comes back out and says they won't be interviewing us after all, so back we go. When we rejoin our families back at Morava, several girls who were in the station before us are crying. They were strip-searched and photographed, with men in the room and the door open. And they accuse Glenn of abuse? What the fuck is wrong with these people!

* * *

Ten hours after Glenn's call, I'm leaving the Prague airport in a rental car with two other mothers and a stepdad. We're anxious and uncertain, but confident we'll fix whatever's wrong. We're Americans, we're hardwired to think everything's possible.

We piece together what we know on the four-hour drive to Morava: a Czech employee angry over being fired for poor performance told police that kids who went to OP—Observational Placement, program-speak for time out—were physically abused.

The police showed up yesterday unannounced and hauled in the kids who had been in OP, offered them coffee, cigarettes, and plane tickets home, then interviewed and strip-searched them for signs of abuse. None was found but eight of them said they were abused (handcuffed, tied up, forced to defecate on the floor, given limited food and water). Three of these kids asked for tickets home; the other five wanted to return to Morava. The police took the eight kids to spend the night in what they said was an "orphanage."

They brought the remaining fifty kids in, made the same offers, and started strip-searching them until the American Embassy made them stop. Police refused to interview any of them because they wouldn't corroborate any abuse and accused the eight of lying. One group of boys was so upset at not being able to speak that they broke and threw things in the station until police finally interviewed several to pacify them. When their case manager, Dusana, pointed out that police deliberately mistranslated the kids' words, she was threatened with arrest and forbidden any further contact with students.

On the way, we're to meet the detective in charge of the investigation, Karel, at a McDonald's to pick up the kids who spent the night in the orphanage. As we reach the tiny golden arches attached to an ancient building, he calls to tell us that the kids went to Morava this morning. He apparently found it amusing to send us on a wild-goose chase to the quintessential symbol of American capitalism. This is prophetic.

"Mothers! Oh, mother hug!" hits us the second we walk in Morava's doors as fifty weepy, hyper boys and girls surround us. A few staff who speak no English move about, but the kids seem in charge of themselves. The teens range from fourteen to nearly eighteen, but in their distress they seem like small children. Some cling and cry, others are tense and withdrawn, all are angry, saying some version of, "They listened to a few kids say they were abused instead of fifty other kids who said they were lying!"

Mia isn't in the group, so a boy starts down the girls' hallway to get her. A tall young man chastises him, "That's a Cat 3, Off Area." He's obviously a senior boy, but the student doing the most to comfort everyone is a diminutive boy with huge dark eyes, who rotates holding and reassuring whoever's crying. He pulls on my sleeve.

Charles speaks slowly, sometimes struggling for words. "They tried to arrest Dusana she couldn't stop crying I had to hold her I was her only support Miss Fontaine!"

He blinks back tears, then turns to comfort a kid a foot taller than he is. A chubby Husky puppy charges out of a hallway. Gizmo! The kids race around after him. Barking, crying, hugging, reporting, it's pandemonium.

"Mommy!"

I turn and my little monkey runs into my arms. She had no idea I was coming.

"I can't believe you're here! I love you! Are you going to help Glenn and Steve?"

I have a million questions, but I'm content just to hold her and listen to her voice. Her eyes sparkle again!

I recognize her voice first, but it's when I see the mass of hair that I gasp. My mom's here! She turns at my voice, her eyes light up, and she has just enough warning to brace herself as I practically bowl her over in my excitement.

Her smell! When I bury my face in her sweater, it's the familiar mix of baby powder and Fracas that makes me tear up.

"Mommy, I missed you so much!" I whisper. I close my eyes so my senses can take everything in and I temporarily forget that, considering the state of things, parents showing up can't be good. Does this mean I'm going home?

"He promised to punish Morava for firing him," Peter says, shaking his head.

We've regrouped in the main office where Peter, the Czech head of staff for the boys, sits amid ringing phones and disarray. The police confiscated the kids' files and all but two computers. He looks much older than the sweet-faced young man I met at the airport last summer.

He waves at the ringing phones. "Leave them, it's just shitty journalists, pardon my word." He fills us in, lowering his voice because we can hear the muffled sound of the kids listening outside the door.

The fired worker didn't go to local police, who are very familiar with Morava and support it; he went to the state police, a more powerful, often corrupt, entity. Peter says most are ex-KGB, "Who have no more jobs spying on Czechs and who hate Americans. Of course, they find no marks from abuse, which is problem for them because now it's on the news everywhere about how they exposed American torture school."

State police apparently alerted the media ahead of time. Peter's friends at the Santon Hotel told him that reporters spent the night there before the raid, "waiting like hungry dogs."

The dogs will be hungry all week. We'll be besieged around the clock by reporters and news cameras from all over the globe, by state police, immigration officials, local gawkers. It's the beginning of a tragedy, and the vultures have begun circling already.

Glenn and Steve return and slip into their wing. They're under house arrest, a gag order, and forbidden contact with the kids. What's happening is already etched on Glenn's beautiful face. She's devastated and very grateful we've come.

We'll soon see why. The owners will send only a single consultant, a personable man named Roger, who will be gone with officials and lawyers most of the time. Which is staggering given the following: There's no one really running the facility, all six people who directly supervise the kids, their "parents" here, are forbidden contact with them—Glenn, Steve, Peter, Zuza, Eva, Dusana (Tyna had quit two weeks earlier); a lot of the Czech staff has already fled because they fear the state police; reporters are traumatizing the kids by crawling through bushes to film in their bedroom windows; and no one is responding to the outright lies in the press.

The company hasn't spoken to the teens, they have no idea who was stripped, who was sent home, or that the "orphanage" turns out to be a halfway house where addicts offered them drugs. Some of the kids had sex, one with a Czech heroin addict, and the head of the investigation, Karel, stayed in a bedroom with some of them, clad only in his red underwear.

"And they weren't boxers, either, Miss Fontaine, it was so gross!"

The company apparently hasn't spoken to parents yet, either. Our second day there, a furious parent calls asking how the hell it's possible his kid is calling him from the skies above his own home. We'll be on phones 24/7 for the next week with parents, trying to inform them, console them, calm them.

The company does begin to call parents, but their information is often outdated or incorrect. For some reason, they won't call us for correct information and they avoid our calls to them. In fact, they're clearly annoyed we're here and the owner is "unreachable." This is mystifying given that we are now running their school and seeing to the emotional well-being of over fifty kids whose lack of it landed them there to begin with—kids whose lives are in their care, and whose parents are paying dearly for that care.

We're worried their cavalier response means they've already decided Morava's a lost cause. Not if we can help it. This is the first place that's helped our kids and, despite our current dismay, we're going to do whatever we can to save it.

Three more mothers arrive and we immediately divide up duties: re-creating student files; property patrol (press and gawkers trespass continually); photographing kids and facility for documentation; police liaison; media monitor; ticketing and packing up kids already transferring to stateside facilities. Thank God one of us is an experienced travel agent, because we're afraid it's going to come in handy. In the next eight days, none of us will get more than ten to twelve hours' sleep total.

We work round-the-clock trying to arrange calls between parents and kids, to reassure both of them. Most difficult for us is figuring what to say to the kids whose parents won't talk to them, either out of indifference or because they're still too angry at their kids. One boy keeps asking if his parents are back from vacation yet.

A fragile Asian girl whose father won't speak to her begs me to convince him how sorry she is. He hasn't written her once since she arrived a few months ago. She sinks to the floor, clutching my ankles, sobbing, "I know I've shamed my family! I want him to forgive me!" I understand now why Duane nearly blew us out of our seats for doubting their guilt. And how terrible my silence must have felt to Mia.

We have very little time to spend with our own kids, though I observe Mia from a distance as much as I can. She cries less than the others, and then only for a moment. She often observes rather than participates, and she seems reflective, knowing. This is a Mia I have not seen before, perhaps one she is growing into.

"Are you open to some feedback?"

Sunny and I have cornered my mother for a talk. I wasn't going to say anything but after asking Sunny to give her some papers, the look on her face changed my mind.

"Are you crazy? She'll bite my head off!"

We steer my mom to the bottom of a staircase, away from the chaos. She looks both exasperated and amused, as if to say, I'll go, but is this really necessary?

"Okay, Sunny, tell her what you told me."

Her eyes bug out, then she takes a breath. "Hi, Ms. Fontaine. I'm sure you're just the nicest person in the world, I was just a little afraid is all."

"Sunny was completely intimidated by you, Mom!" I interrupt. "Granted, some of that's her, but you make yourself pretty unapproachable."

"Yeah, I can really see where Mia gets her stuff from!" Sunny exclaims before bashfully clapping her hand over her mouth.

My mom laughs. "It's okay, Sunny, I really appreciate this. I heard similar things in Discovery and obviously they haven't sunk in! What 'stuff' did you notice?"

Wow, that came out of left field. I'd made a whole game plan for how to approach her with the assumption that she'd get defensive and argumentative.

"Mostly, how much you avoid emotion," Sunny goes on more boldly. "I know whenever Mia's in pain, she goes into action mode to avoid it."

"Sound familiar, Mom? Remember during the big earthquake when Paul and I ran outside freaking out and you were on your hands and knees looking for our shoes?"

"I'm doing it now, aren't I?" she interrupts.

We look at each other a minute. She's smiling ever so slightly and I can feel pride radiating from her, though I'm the one that's proud of her.

Each of us gets a group of kids to "parent." I have eight boys who are absolutely charming. I'm surprised to find that the boys are more tenderhearted than the girls. They cry more openly and when they find out I still sing Mia lullabies, they want them, too.

One boy, David, gravitates to me. He's dark-haired and handsome, gawky-tall the way boys that age are. His family emigrated to the United States from Russia a few years back. David is the school's biggest run risk. He's told Steve he's going to run and no one doubts him—he can speak passing Czech and hasn't formed close relationships with other students. He's the least upset or angry of all the kids, because he has no illusions.

"State police are the same in Russia. You guys are wasting your time, they're laughing at us."

My mother says almost the same thing when I call her.

"Take Mia and get the hell out of there before they throw you all in jail."

"But we haven't done anything wrong, Mom."

"You think that matters? You think everybody loves Americans?"

The teachers stay on and classes are loosely maintained. The threat of arrest has kept Zuza and Dusana away for a few days, but the kids think Glenn's returning means we've saved the day. They're so excited, they put on a show for us in the lobby. The girls do a dance number, swinging their arms and ponytails. The boys do a rap number, with lyrics about their "Morava brothers" and their "magical child." A few boys and girls eye each other, but there's little typical teen mating behavior. They laugh and goof around in their dorky clothes like fifth-graders and keep asking parents to watch them do some trick or dance step. They're playing, they're happy. Such a simple thing, really. But, for us, a miracle.

We parents exchange glances with each other as we watch them. We feel as if we've been allowed entrance to someplace precious and rare. We're also secretly heartbroken, because we're afraid all of this is going to vanish overnight. And they have no idea.

Lupe's going home. Glenn just came to us with a list of kids being pulled by their parents. Glenn stands as a rock as Lupe falls apart in her arms. We all cry with her. Everyone knows she's not ready. Ricky will know she's home within a week, and one of two things will happen—she'll go back to him willingly, or she'll go back by force.

Is this what the media wants? The government? A week ago, everything in my life was falling into place. My mom forgave me, I'd finally reached Level 3, I was really beginning to feel happy.

Now, I feel like my whole world is ending. They keep saying this will blow over, that everything's fine, but it's not! Girls who've become like sisters to me are leaving, Glenn has to sneak out of her room just to see us for a few minutes, and we haven't seen Miss Zuza in days. We aren't just crying for Lupe, we're crying for ourselves.

We call a press conference to counter the increasingly ridiculous news reports. Overnight, their little puppy Gizmo has become a vicious dog kept inside to menace the kids. The company tells us not to let the media inside. We'd ignore them, but we're afraid they won't take our own kids in their other schools if Morava closes.

Everyone agrees it's best to let the kids make statements rather than be interviewed. They're afraid of being hammered by journalists; they've already seen them in action. Before we go out, I realize it might have been a good idea to let the kids wear street clothes, a bit of makeup. Mia's complaints about the food were justified—all the kids have the same pasty, pimply complexions. The girls haven't had haircuts in months and it looks like it.

At the appointed time, we walk outside and we're swarmed by media from the United Kingdom, Europe, and the United States. We haven't said a word, but already most of them are looking at the parents as if we're child abusers. They're annoyed that they can't directly question the kids.

"They don't trust you. You've lied about people they love. You've also trespassed and been generally uncivilized."

"Hey!" A journalist yells from the side of the building. "Come see this beast!" Half of them rush over with their cameras to where the tracking dog's yard is. Ify is a beautiful, sweet-natured German shepherd. He's void of aggression by training and breeding and will bark only when he makes a find.

The poor thing cowers as they taunt him and poke a stick through the fence in a fruitless attempt to make him bark for cameras. A British reporter looks at me with complete disgust. Her colleagues are terrorizing a caged dog whose sole purpose is to save lives, and she's looking askance at *me*?

With little exception, they taunt the kids almost as much as they did the dog and are downright contemptuous of the parents. Most of them simply refuse to believe what the kids are saying; they hardly let them speak. Despite being asked to simply let the kids make statements, they grill them knowing that kids can't help but answer. Many are rude and aggressive, even as tears stream down the kids' faces. At one point the parents try to stop the journalists but the kids insist on talking to them in the hopes they'll listen.

Our kids behave remarkably. These once angry, self-destructive drug addicts and delinquents are confident and polite, honest and respectful. This has elicited the very best in them.

I can't believe these people call themselves professionals! Several of us came out to talk about Morava, but unless we're discussing some minor flaw, like the food or the uniforms, they keep cutting us off. I listen to Sunny try to stammer out her story.

"The food's not the greatest but—"

"Do they withhold food as punishment?"

"No, I never said—"

"But you're not satisfied with your diet, right? Do they lock you in rooms by yourself? Why aren't you allowed outside? Have you ever been tied up?"

This is what they focus on after Sunny told them how long she's been clean for, how she no longer has the desire to self-mutilate, how amazing Glenn is? Why aren't they listening to us? It's humiliating.

I'm shaking by the time Miss Olga ushers us back inside. This could have been the difference between Morava staying open or not, but they already have their minds made up, their stories written.

Ruza knows how upsetting this has all been. She's waiting for us with our favorite meal, pancakes, and is doling out extra jelly and sugar. We jump at the sound of a dropped fork. It's Miss Olga, she's crying.

"Don't cry, Miss Olga!" we chorus. "You're not leaving, are you?"

"Of course not!" she cries, opening her arms to let in fourteen panicked girls. "I'm here still, girls, I'm always here."

I don't know what we'd do if she left. Over the past few months we've become as close with her as we are with Miss Zuza. It's horrifying that the very people who helped change my life might be going to jail for it, to see the people who gave us strength and support break down from exhaustion and fear.

"They're shutting Morava down for good."

Glenn's called us into her room. "They have no evidence, the kids all admitted lying. But after all this media, the state police will never admit publicly they were wrong. They're charging us with cruelty and abuse anyway. Karel told me flat out he'll dig till he finds something to hang it on."

She starts to cry. "They're charging Zuza and Peter, too."

Karel's on a real roll. Because by the end of the day we're told he's going to try to charge *us*, too, the parents. For violating a law they dug up that makes it illegal to leave our kids in their country against their will, something the owners never informed parents of.

It also turns out that it's illegal for children under the age of eighteen to be isolated for any reason here. And OP is considered isolation, even though it's supervised. Something else the owners either didn't know or never told Glenn. The law isn't hard to understand in theory; for a former communist satellite, "time out" often meant you never came home again.

Now, they have their grounds.

We collect the kids in the cafeteria to tell them. There's a sharp, collective yell of disbelief, followed by a wall of crying and boys shouting angry threats. Little Charles sits in a pile crying, barely able to be his only support. The wailing in the room comes in waves I can actually feel in my body.

Glenn and Steve don't hide their grief from the kids who crowd around them. They've devoted their lives to creating this haven for them, and they're losing it, and them, all at once.

Mia hasn't cried in my lap in years, and it's only a brief privilege. She stops quickly, wipes her eyes on her sweatshirt, then joins the other girls trying to comfort each other.

Some calm is restored when they stand up one at a time to express their feelings. One boy brings his guitar and sings for the kids; it is a tonic. The kids begin filing out quietly in buddy teams to begin gathering their belongings from around the facility. They don't get far.

Two police officers enter the school and arrest Steve right in front of their eyes.

Morava's closing. On some level, I sensed this coming, but hearing the words is devastating. The next few minutes unfold in slow motion. Sunny's wailing, Katrina's pacing back and forth, dazed, the normally composed Roxanne can't stop crying.

What's going to happen to us? There's not a day that's passed that I haven't thought about home, but now it's a possibility, I'm terrified. I've become so used to the sheltered world of Morava, I haven't been around "normal" teenagers in so long, I wonder how long it'll be before I'm strung out in the back of a van. I'm not ready.

And does this mean the staff are definitely going to jail, Glenn, Zuza, Olga? I feel sick, literally sick. In one week, the authorities have managed to destroy everything we've come to call normal and take from us the only people we trust enough to help us. Why?

Glenn takes a few spare moments to talk to me about Mia.

"I can't tell you how grateful I am for what you've done with Mia. She's a different girl, Glenn."

"No, she's not, Claire, not yet. Mia's come a long way, but she's got a long way to go. She's built up years of pain and confusion and anger about her father. What you're seeing is a new awareness. But it takes a long time for knowledge to be internalized to where it changes behavior. She needs enough time in a controlled environment to get strong in the person she's becoming, so it can survive outside in the world."

"I'm worried about what's happening now, how it's going to affect her progress."

"Knowing Mia, she'll shut down for a while, I think a lot of the kids will. This has been such a shock." She blinks back tears, unable to finish. I sit beside her and put my arms around her.

Mia and the kids will go on to other facilities. Glenn has no idea where she and her husband will go. If the police here let them go anywhere.

We've got three days to shut down an entire school and get forty kids ticketed, packed, and escorted out of the country to several different locations without having any runaways. What little sleep we've gotten in the last five days will have to last us. Roger stays inside, working nonstop, too, boxing up textbooks, doing whatever he can.

Against police orders, Peter, Zuza, Olga, and Dusana return to spend the last few days with the kids, providing much needed stability for them. And no little love. Peter and Zuza's tireless devotion to the kids, in spite of their bitterness at the baseless charges against them, is remarkable and heartbreaking. This wasn't just a job for them or the others.

Glenn ignores the order to stay in her room to be with the kids and to help assign them to new facilities. The girls interrupt their frantic packing to be with her as much as possible. Seeing her interact with the kids has made me realize how intimidated we are by our teens. They love her for what we don't give them anymore, individually as parents or collectively as a society. She doesn't care if they like her, and they love her. She's not afraid to discipline them, and they respect her. Even in the midst of chaos, I watched her hold them accountable for every little action, and it created not resentment, but trust.

Mia told me that when she came back from the police station, she went straight to Glenn to tell her she smoked, and that she never would have done that with me.

"Because Glenn simply held me accountable, consequented me, asked what my new declaration was, and had faith that I meant it."

This faith, I think, is the gift Glenn leaves these kids with. Her trust in them has created a space where they can begin to trust themselves.

Professional escorts work two adults per one teen. The four parents left will be one sleep-deprived adult per three kids, many high run risks. One is Mia, though I don't tell her this. Glenn and I agree the risk is mild, but I'm still a nervous wreck.

The biggest run risk is David. I ask him if, as one of the eldest and most mature, he'll help me look after my group. He shrugs a nonchalant agreement, but I can see he's pleased. Everyone, including Glenn and Steve, are sure he'll run anyway.

Not only will David not run, he will not let me carry a single bag nor open a single door through three airports. Even his posture will change—he'll stand erect and dignified, an example not only to the kids but to every man we'll pass.

His composure will be all the more remarkable given the way he and the others will be gawked at in every airport—eleven wide-eyed, huddled American teens wearing identical jean sweatpants and bright red shirts. The boys in white socks, sandals, and crew-cuts, the girls in shocking pink fur slippers and straggly hair.

At the Prague airport, they'll be recognized as the poor, tortured kids on the news and us as their lousy, irresponsible parents. The last image we will leave them with will probably confirm the accusations. Because one of the parents will pull a pair of scissors from I don't know where and proceed to cut the girls' hair. Right in the middle of the airport. The girls will giggle and blush as hair piles up at their feet. I'll tactfully suggest doing it in the bathroom as I scoop up handfuls and carry it to the trash.

"There isn't time, the planes are about to leave and the girls look terrible," she insists. "Besides, after what this country did to these kids, let them clean it up!"

I stand with my mother in front of Morava, just as we did six months ago when she dropped me off. I remember seeing this building with such a sense of dread and fury it's hard to reconcile that with the feeling inside me now.

Morava now stands only as a shell. It's empty of boys and girls walking in lines, of death-defying soccer tournaments, of dancing butterflies and ballerinas, of pseudo-German-speaking American teens trying to figure out their past and future selves.

Morava's essence is now carried inside sixty teenagers who call themselves a family, who are all painfully aware that a chapter of our life is ending. It's a chapter that is an indescribable mix of a Utopian environment and pure hell. We've all despised Morava, we've all loved it, we've all been thankful for it, but above all we've all loved each other. We've seen sides of people that they rarely show and grown together in ways that outsiders will likely never understand.

"Mia!"

I turn as Glenn grabs me tightly. We look at each other and both start to cry. It hurts to see this strong woman cry, this woman who helped so many of us find that same strength within ourselves. It's not right, Glenn's not supposed to cry.

"Be strong, Mia," she whispers fiercely. "For yourself, for the girls. Don't let them slide back into old patterns, Katrina's anorexia, Sunny's self-mutilation. Don't withdraw, don't shut down! Don't use this as an excuse to call everything you did here bullshit. The work you've done here is real. Take what you've learned and grow. Take it and fly."

"But what about you, Miss Zuza—"

"We'll be fine, sweetie. You have to go now, go . . ."

I stumble to the van, climb in and turn around to face her, pressing my hand against the rear window. I know this image will never leave me, seeing Glenn crying in the snow, watching her once powerful figure become smaller and smaller until it's finally swallowed up by the silence that was Morava. The silence where I listened for myself, and for the first time, really heard.

* * *

Glenn's reading of Mia is accurate. Whatever illusions I still had that Mia was almost fixed are dispelled by the time we get to Prague, the night before we fly out. Mia's mood and behavior had been subtly shifting as the situation at Morava worsened. I noticed her picking up Gizmo often, as a way to comfort herself. As the days passed, she no longer appeared reflective but withdrawn. Her face grew silent.

I remember that face. And I haven't forgotten that there can be another Mia behind Mia.

I see this other Mia emerge at dinner tonight, our last night together in Prague. We're in a cavernous, groin-vaulted restaurant lit only by candles. She's brimming with enthusiasm about what Morava taught her, and about being able to eat a rack of lamb.

"Every day we choose our life," she bubbles as she starts eating, "which means you choose the consequences, too. Oh, my God, this sauce! The whole atmosphere there is designed to help us learn who we really are and love that person. That's a choice, too."

I'm so impressed by her maturity and insight. Then she suddenly stands up, saying she has to go to the bathroom. I get up to go with her and she looks at me, hurt.

"Mia, I can't let you go by yourself, you're still under rules."

She rebels instantly, firing off, "Thanks for the confidence, like I'm going to run away or what, steal a cigarette from some guy at the bar?"

Well, yeah, I want to say. She's gone right back to the same verbal aggression and sharp, machine-gun delivery I used to dread. Like a nice little kitty whose claws are merely retracted, not gone.

I don't know why, but I decide to trust her. I hold my breath until she returns. But the Mia that returns is different; the sparkle is gone. She's pulled strands of hair to fall over her face and is doing her affected slink-walk as she passes a guy at the bar. The tentative peace of mind I've come to feel as Mia became a loving, honest daughter again completely disintegrates. Replaced again with that mushy-sick-stomach fear.

Mia and many of the others will be transferred to a sister facility, Spring Creek Lodge in Montana. It's on a secluded mountain far from a city. It has the reputation as being one of their most successful schools.

It has no tracking dog. It has no fence. It's why I didn't send her there to begin with.

partfour

21.

It's dead quiet in the van save a static-y country song twanging on the radio. It's odd enough hearing music besides Beethoven, but "She Thinks My Tractor's Sexy" at 1 a.m. with an eight-hour time difference is too much.

I'm beat, the kind of tired that comes after tears. We just learned that Sasha won't be coming to Spring Creek, as we'd been told. I never got to say good-bye. Only Sunny, Roxanne, Katrina, and Samantha remain, along with several newer girls, including Brooke.

The driver, Mr. Jim, said we couldn't sleep in the van, so we sit like zombies, staring out at the night scenery. Even in the darkness, Montana's beautiful, with pine tree silhouettes and an enormous yellow moon low in the sky. The freeway narrows to a two-lane road with "Watch for fallen rock" and "Bighorn sheep crossing" signs.

Someone coughs. Mr. Jim jumps and turns around.

"Y'all are still awake?! I thought you'da been passed out by now!"

"You said we couldn't sleep," Katrina responds politely.

He starts laughing so hard he about spits out his soda. "And you believed me? Aww, I feel awful now, I was only joking with ya. Go on and catch some shut-eye."

It's hard to imagine any of the Morava staff joking with us. I wonder how else this place will be different, but the last thing I remember being conscious of is that big yellow moon. Until Prague, I hadn't seen the moon in six months.

Waking up at Spring Creek Lodge proves no less disorienting. I'm in a giant, barren rectangular room with twenty bunk beds lining the walls. Two chests rest in the gaps between bunks, and I vaguely remember having to lock our shoes up in them when I came in last night with Samantha and Roxanne. They promised to keep all the Morava girls together, but until they build our cabin, we divide up into different cabins each night.

Strange girls rub sleep from their eyes and give us curious glances. I assume we're on silence because no one talks, though they smile briefly at us. A tall blond woman in a parka opens the door, letting in a freezing draft.

"Morava girls, I'll be back in ten minutes, please be ready and lined up."

We rise and head to the bathroom—it's blinding! Polished chrome reflects bright white walls, spotless sinks, and shining linoleum. Gone are Morava's buckets of water so you can flush down what the toilet couldn't and, to my great delight, in their place sit glistening, new American toilets.

Samantha jabs me and points—there are mirrors here! In a flash, she's looking for blackheads and Roxanne's admiring her hair as if she'd never seen it before. I head right for a stall because we can't pop zits in the program, it's considered self-injury, and until I can shave, I have no desire to see a fat, hairy version of myself.

The woman returns and we follow her up a narrow dirt path to yet another log cabin. Except for the silence and walking in line, this place doesn't feel like a program. We're high on a snowy mountain slope thick with evergreens, in the middle of nowhere. A cluster of about ten red-roofed log cabins so perfect they seem fake peep from between the trees and deer eye us calmly as we walk right beside them.

I suddenly realize that we'll have to walk outside every time we change activities. Which means that unless there's an electrified fence hidden in the trees, there's nothing between me and freedom but a very long hike down.

We stop in front of a long, low cabin called the Hungry Horse, where the other Morava girls are waiting. Katrina and Sunny reach out and squeeze my hand as we line up behind them to go inside.

On the way in, I notice a teeny, tiny cabin across the path. Several students wait on the porch, hopping from one foot to another to keep warm, and I wonder what they're waiting for.

The cafeteria's full of girls already seated with our first familiar sight— watery, gray oatmeal. Heads turn but few smile. Several girls walk around in full makeup, junior staff no doubt. But, nobody, upper or lower level, wears a uniform! Even more surprising is that the people in the kitchen are students!

There are no fences and *students are allowed access to fire and knives? I can see why my mother sent me overseas.*

We eat, cross out, and stand freezing as staff pats us down to be sure no one pocketed food or utensils. As I lift my arms and spread my legs, I hear engines gunning in the distance. Zooming toward us are identical, burly, blond twins riding identical four-wheelers. They smile and wave as they zip by.

"That's Cameron and Chaffin. They'll be by your cabin this afternoon."

"This afternoon" turns to evening as dusk settles around the cabin we've spent the last five hours in. Cameron, the Glenn of Spring Creek, came by after group. Because the police took all our records, he asked us to assign ourselves levels—and he wasn't joking.

Katrina, Roxanne, and I rated ourselves fairly, asking for Level 3, and he agreed. But now he's agreeing when the newest girls ask for the same thing! He sees our expressions and laughs.

"Where did you all just choose to go? Anger? Jealousy? Smug, because you think I'm clueless?"

D—all of the above, especially the last one.

"And I'm sure your reaction stems from genuine concern for your peers, right?" He laughs again. "Gimme a break! You're jealous because they had the guts to ask for what they didn't deserve and you didn't have the courage to demand what you do."

He looks at Sunny and Samantha, who realize they screwed themselves by asking for too little.

"I know it seems like I just changed the whole program, but this is just an exercise, a chance to learn something about yourself. Your own behavior will drop or raise every one of you to exactly where you're really at in no time, I guarantee it. You can't disguise the truth, girls."

Spring Creek is beginning to feel like Morava Light.

It takes me three days to sleep off last week. I feel so bereft about the loss of Morava, more than what should be reasonable, and it's a while before I realize why. It was the first time I felt a real connection to my mother's family. My ancestors lived nearby for centuries, which makes it the closest thing to a home I've ever had. It felt almost fitting that my daughter would heal in the place where my mother was born.

I'm somewhat worried that Mia will run from Spring Creek, but I am more concerned that the conditions that elicited her amazing growth were specific to Morava—Glenn, the foreign location, the Czech staff, the girls there, many of whom didn't go to Spring Creek. There was a sweet, innocent quality to the place that was utterly unique.

We don't have a family rep yet (their version of a case manager), so I express my concerns about Mia's behavior to whoever will listen, a supervisor, the school counselor, a secretary.

I finally reach Chaffin, Spring Creek's codirector, who assures me that he's aware that a lot of the Morava kids have gone back to old patterns. Unlike me, however, he sees this as a positive.

"Events like this are a tremendous opportunity for growth. It's a chance for these kids to learn to handle a major setback in a safe place. It's also a chance for you parents to see where you go with yourselves."

Fear and control, my favorite destination, it seems. As usual, there are as many lessons for me in this as for Mia.

"You went across country by yourself? And did speedballs?" A girl from our cabin named Jessie stares at me.

"So, we've all done stuff like that," Samantha defends. "Why are you here?"

"I just smoked a lot of pot and skipped class."

"That's it? You must hate your parents! Are all the kids here like you?"

"Most did more drugs, but kids from overseas are usually worse."

"Jessie," interrupts a junior staff, "showers started five minutes ago, self-correct your late consequence?"

Jessie grumbles a self-correct, then flips her off when she turns away. I smile to myself. I was the same way to Sasha at first. I really miss her. I hear she's already practically running the facility she was sent to, some new school in the South. I wish junior staff here were more like her. There are about forty of them and they're like the Spring Creek mafia.

The general attitude toward them is a mixture of respect, admiration, fear, and hatred. Some of them are so confident and powerful it's hard to imagine why they're here. The rest of them you wish weren't.

Jessie emerges from the bathroom and joins some girls in the corner. I may have bitched about Morava feeling like kindergarten, but I prefer that to high school, which is what this feels like. The Spring Creek girls are in various cliques in the cabin and their stares are unnerving and unwelcoming. In Morava, every new girl was subject to a loving interrogation her first night, but Jessie was the first one to come and talk to us in almost a week.

They've finally finished our cabin and we're so excited to all be back together it's all we can do to keep silence as we move in. We've named ourselves the Harmony family, and their goal is for us to assimilate into Spring Creek.

Because the staff here discourages it, we talk about Morava as little as possible. I think about it, however, constantly, and can tell the other girls do, too. Roxanne is quieter, in school she gets distracted easily and I know whenever she's doodling, her mind's in Brno. Samantha's nails are gnawed to the quick and Katrina's been given a bathroom buddy to prevent her from purging. It's never brought up, but we're all worried about Glenn and Miss Zuza going to jail.

I'm sweet sixteen today, or bittersweet rather. My family woke me up singing happy birthday and gave me a paper tiara along with ingeniously made gifts. We can't use scissors, so Katrina tore paper into small squares, hole punched them, and threaded a ribbon to make me a small diary. Sunny sketched me a butterfly in honor of my Stretch.

But it's still mildly depressing. There's nothing like handing over gifts to staff (keeping my cards would be considered note-passing) to remind you that you're locked up.

They let me keep the best gift, though. Growing up, my favorite question to ask adults was, "What was your Most Embarrassing Moment?" I would die laughing hearing about adults making total fools of themselves. My parents had friends and family members write down their stories. The whole cabin's been hysterical over them.

I miss my parents so much, especially after just seeing my mom. Walking with her in Prague on the Charles Bridge that night was pure magic. It was a storybook perfect setting, a sky full of stars, a layer of snow coating the statues on the bridge. Everything was so still, it felt timeless, and we stood there, hand in hand, listening to a musician play "Ode to Joy" on water glasses.

Even so, there was always an edge. When I got up to go to the bathroom at dinner, there was that split-second panic in her eyes. It's painfully obvious how little she trusts me, how scared she is I'm faking it.

Still, it's touching how she rests her hopes on the small chance that I've *changed, that bit of faith that her baby girl is still in me. That part of me loves how she and Paul still take the time to make me feel special. As far back as I can remember, my mom could always think of a reason to come home with my favorite pastry or take me on a surprise visit to the Getty. She'd leave notes inside lunch bags that Paul drew calligraphic M's on. I cringe when I think about how many beautiful lunch bags ended up in the Dumpster of my elementary school.*

It's funny how care becomes a source of embarrassment. When puberty strikes, you start acting like you were hatched from some egg and dropped off in a random house. You're on a sudden mission to prove you're parentless. Mom, don't kiss me in front of everyone! Paul, stop decorating my lunch bags!

And now, we get excited over even just a letter from them.

MUDDER'S MOST EMBARRASSING MOMENT

The day before I left Brno, a Czech staff member, Ivan, took me to tour a nearby castle. On the way there, I bought my first Czech candy bar, which I happily consumed as we drove past sleepy villages.

When we reached the mountaintop castle, I stuck the candy wrapper in my purse before joining a group of elegant Europeans. Once inside its cool, stone walls, Ivan politely pointed to my rear end. A hunk of chocolate must have fallen onto the passenger seat and melted. There was a big brown splotch on the seat of my nice linen shorts.

Great. In an effort to blend, I'd slicked my hair into a French twist, worn my black Italian loafers, and I now looked like I had diarrhea and the Depends weren't up to the challenge.

I'd already cried through all my Kleenex, so I carried folded toilet paper in my purse. I tore off a few sheets, backed up to a shadowy corner and discreetly wiped off as much as I could. Which wasn't much. Ivan assured me with, "Don't worry, Ms. Fontaine, everyone is interested in the castle, not your bottom, they will be looking up not down."

He's probably right, I thought, I'll just stay at the back of the line. When we came to a very narrow staircase, I lagged and went last. Halfway up, there was a rush of squeaking soles behind me, then a sudden gasp right below my butt. I froze—it was the aloof couple in Mephistos. Looking up.

There were murmurs of disgust beneath me, my translator was nowhere to be seen, and it was too narrow to let the couple pass. So, I turned, pointed to my butt and said as graciously as I could—

"Chocolate—it is cho-co-late," as if they were third-graders, "caan-dy?"

They looked at me as if I were mentally ill. Worse, mentally ill and trapping them on the stairs to speak of things fecal. Quick, Claire, show them the candy wrapper! I jammed my hand into my purse—and whipped out a wad of brown-smeared toilet paper.

I could hear those Mephistos tripping over themselves all the way down.

22.

Cameron's speech was prophetic. The new girls are already back to Level 1. Except Brooke, the girl whose intake I did in Morava.

Once the heroin finally left her system, it was hard to believe it was ever there. In less than three months she's become a bright-eyed, feedback-giving machine. Between being molested as a child, addiction, street life, and having an abortion, she had plenty to deal with and wasted no time getting down and dirty with her issues.

As she shares today, there's a giant, fair-haired man in jeans and cowboy boots sitting cross-legged next to her, his head cocked in concentration. He leans his elbows on his knees, as if he doesn't know what to do with his huge top half. He's probably in his thirties, but he's got a friendly-looking boy's face with an upturned nose. His name's Mike Linderman, and I've seen him around the school during the week. The way kids run after him and try to monopolize him, I thought he was a PE coach or some local cowboy. He's the last person I expected to be the therapist Brooke's been raving about. Oh, well, nothing else is remotely normal about this place.

We've all heard Brooke speak about her molestation before, but never like this. She's not just crying or angry, she's talking about how it translates into her everyday life, how it affects her relationships, her ability to feel feminine, her ability to feel at all.

I think about those things all the time! I never know if not liking girly clothes is a personal preference or my way of avoiding sexual attention; or if always feeling nervous, like something really bad's about to happen, is about my old dad or just the way I am. I want what she has, to understand myself like she does, to not feel so out of control.

We end group and Mike starts to head for the door. Without thinking, I leap up and tap his back. He turns around. Shit, what am I doing?

"I'm like Brooke," I blurt out. "I mean, that happened to me, too, and I don't know how to deal with it."

It pops out more coherently than I anticipated. He crinkles up his green eyes and smiles.

"I might be able to help you out with that."

The teensy cabin where kids are always waiting on the porch turns out to be Mike's office. The staff escorting me there is overweight and out of shape. It'd be a cinch to just take off. I've been thinking of running and it's not even because I want to, just because I can. I think part of the reason I liked my old lifestyle was the challenge of it. Always having to find your next fix, being on the run, was exhilarating. I never thought like this at Morava and it bothers me that I think it here. Sometimes I worry that I can't do well outside of Morava, that it was a magical place and the me that existed there can only exist there. Like a cake in the oven, if even one ingredient is missing, the entire recipe is ruined. Seeing Mike's red roof snaps me out of my daydream. I thank staff and walk inside. Immediately, I feel claustrophobic. What are you doing, Mia? You hate shrinks.

He's on the phone but smiles and motions to the chair in the corner. The walls are full of photos of students, their poems and drawings.

"Where do you think your son gets that pattern from, Tina?" Mike says into the phone. "You create the same dynamic with your husband."

It's hard to tell if the mom's in therapy or the son. I try unsuccessfully to picture Colleen giving my mom marital advice. As he wraps up, I notice a framed desk photo of a blond woman hugging three small children, his family I'm guessing.

When he hangs up, he grins at me, leans way back in his swivel chair, and kicks his feet up on his desk.

"So, let's talk, Mia."

I look at his mud-covered cowboy boots, shitkickers. Everything about him is so untherapeutic, I'm not sure whether to talk about myself, ask for tips on riding, or just shoot the breeze. Not to mention it's only now sinking in that I'm in a male therapist's office. I've never seen a male shrink—a male anything for that matter.

"About what?"

"Oh, this is my session, I didn't realize that. Well, let's see, I birthed a calf yesterday, there's a new Chevy blazer I've been eyeing. This what you had in mind, dear?"

I laugh, but still can't think of an opening line besides "No."

"You came to me, girl, you had to have something in mind, something, say, like sexual abuse, maybe?"

Shit. He doesn't waste any time.

"That term make you uneasy?" he asks.

I nod.

"It's a common reaction, Mia. Those words make people squirm who've never even been abused. It's not a popular topic, it's un-com-for-ta-ble. And that's what I'm all about, diggin' up the dirt. That's what we'll do in here if you choose, pull up the rug and see what you've been sweeping under it. And it's not always fun, but you must have realized that something about the way you've been dealing with it isn't working for you, or you wouldn't have come up to me."

Part of me wishes I hadn't, because I am un-com-for-ta-ble.

"Why don't we start with the facts, what happened, who, how long."

I go over the part I could recite in my sleep. Molested, biological father, two or three. It's the other parts that I omit. The becoming terrified for no reason, the urges to scratch off my skin, to rid myself of any part of me that can be touched. I leave out feeling like no guy will ever want me and hating myself for wanting one in the first place.

"You're voting up today, or I WILL drop you to Level 1. You've earned it, everyone supports you, and I'm done convincing you to trust in yourself."

Miss Kim is our new family mother and yet another one of the brick walls my mom is so happy this program is full of. She's as tough as Miss Zuza, but less formal. She's half Native American, with delicate features and black eyes and already feels like she's been with our family much longer than a few weeks.

"This is so unfair! I'm not ready to be junior staff and I'm irritable and they're going to sense my bad attitude and no one's going to vote me up."

She gives me a look, the look, where she raises her eyebrows, tilts her head and, poof, you know you're screwed.

"Then change your attitude," she replies, walking away.

The remaining hour of class goes by way too quickly. Before I know it, the door flies open.

"Girls going to junior staff group, line up!"

Sunny, Roxanne, and I rise, all looking less than thrilled. Advancing on the lower levels is easy, you just need points. For upper levels, you need points and your peers' approval.

Their group's outside today, great. It's about forty degrees and the wind's blowing, so I have to vote up with my teeth chattering while trying to project my voice.

"Everyone voting up today, stand up," Miss Marcy shouts to the group. She's a tiny, energetic woman in charge of junior staff.

I rise. Most of the others are smiling, excited. I feel like a case of dysentery is setting in.

Roxanne's vote-up takes all of two seconds. A natural leader, she only has three people stand in lack of support. She's smiling ear to ear as everyone claps and cheers. Sunny, who threw a bigger hissy fit than I did, looks positively miserable. Like sharks to blood, the junior staff instantly pick up on her insecurities, and Sunny disappears into the ring of people standing up around her.

Her face falls, and my heart along with it. She's so easily affected by things, it will be hard for her to get the confidence to vote back up. I saw this coming, though. She still hasn't come out about being gay and even if they haven't guessed it, they sense something's not ringing true.

It's my turn. I feel nauseous and I'm praying words come out of my mouth instead of vomit.

"Hi, I'm Mia. I'm voting up for Level 4 today. Everyone who doesn't support me, please stand."

I hold my breath.

Two, four, eight, eleven, fourteen people out of forty. I call on the closest kid.

"Mia, you give awesome feedback, people look up to you, but in my experience you still hold back when it comes to your emotions and that sets a poor example."

"DITTO!" is echoed by the group.

Max Silvers goes next. He's a stocky redhead, one of the most powerful males on the facility and he knows it. The fact that he doesn't support me isn't good; staff tend to respect his opinion.

"Mia, in my experience you could be one of the most powerful kids in this facility, but you're stubborn. You know what you need to do to change, and the fact that you don't is what bugs me. I experience you as relying on your potential to get you through the program. I feel a lot of the support you get isn't what people see you doing, but what they think you can be doing and that's just not enough for me right now."

Great, he basically just told everyone supporting me they shouldn't be. I half listen to the rest of my feedback, while picturing Max dangling from a cliff, one hand clawing the edge while I look down at him and he pleads for his life.

While the other kids finish, the junior staff have been talking among themselves.

"Mia, congratulations, you just earned Level 4."

The kids cheer and Roxanne rushes over to hug me. Sunny smiles weakly, and I feel awful for her. I spot Mike mouthing "good job." I hadn't noticed him standing outside the circle.

"But," Miss Marcy continues, "we agree with Max's feedback. You aren't living up to your potential and until you do, consider yourself on thin ice. We really need to see you run with this, got it?"

Got it. I don't care if she just stipulated I can't breathe the entire time I'm up there—I'm Level 4!

"He's not your typical shrink, that's for sure. I half expect him to arrive on a horse," Mia tells me on our monthly call. "He actually birthed a calf the other day, yuck."

"I hope his therapy is just as atypical."

"Well, if you call putting muddy cowboy boots on his desk during therapy atypical, it is. I like him though, he doesn't BS." She pauses, then adds, "You're still going to Focus next week, aren't you? I really want you to go, mom."

I can hear the hope in her voice. Because, unlike Discovery, which is primarily about awareness, Focus demands real change based on an even more unsparing look at yourself. Which means a lot of parents avoid it, including Paul.

This is going to disappoint her. "I was getting to that. Jordana got a director for *All Good Children*, and we're going to London for rewrite meetings with him."

Jordana is a close friend and the producer of a screenplay I adapted from Marianne Wiggins's transcendent novel, *John Dollar*.

"Really? I'm so happy for you!" A pause. "But you'll still do the seminar, right?"

"As soon as I get back, monkey, I promise."

23.

EXT. RANGOON HARBOR 1919 MORNING ESTABLISHING

Steamships, freighters, and native fishing boats crowd the harbor. Docks SWARM with Burmese fishermen in sarongs, Chinese coolies, Europeans in white linen. Rice mills belch filthy smoke. ELEPHANTS stack teak logs with their trunks.

A dozen turbaned SIKHS swim to a barge, put the tow ropes in their mouths, turn and swim back, pulling the barge in by their teeth. Beyond them, a huge golden spire towers over Rangoon, the Shwedagon Pagoda.

ANGLE ON A STEAMSHIP—*THE VICEROY OF INDIA*

A milky-skinned young woman with sea-colored eyes, CHARLOTTE LEWES, stands at the bow, entranced by all she sees. Her fingers rest on a small metal military kit balanced on the rails. The kit is stamped *Lt. Harry Lewes*. Without lowering her eyes, her fingers appear to move slightly. The kit slips down and sinks into the cloudy water below. It might have been an accident.

She turns and walks around a group of wilted ENGLISHWOMEN in pale silk dresses already clinging with sweat. She continues toward the gangplank as it's lowered.

Charlotte walks unaided down the narrow plank. Into the sweating humanity, the shimmering heat, the unearthly sounds and colors. Into Burma.

* * *

"That's the moment, Claire. She wouldn't turn back even if she knew, would she?"

"She might walk faster," I reply with a smile.

Marshall is gregarious, witty, a perfect director for the screenplay. Jordana and I are sitting with him in our small rented flat in Sloane Square. I'm excited to be taking meetings in London, a city as delightful as Brno was depressing. A city where I'm not as depressed. For the first time in ages, I'm not an anxious, terrified mother—Mia's on level four and she's *asked* to see a therapist. What more could I ask for? I'm like any other professional woman doing what she's passionate about—I'm writing again!

Like the script I'd been writing last year, this is also a period drama about a woman who goes to a foreign land and is forever changed. However, Charlotte, a British WWI war widow, doesn't lose a child, she gains one, and a lover, sailor John Dollar. The book is about a group of British colonials who are swept away in a tsunami off the coast of Burma in 1919. Only Charlotte's students survive, a handful of schoolgirls who unwittingly create a microcosm of their parents' imperialist world, at once touching and brutal, a bit like *Lord of the Flies*. John and Charlotte's unexpected survival and appearance both destroys and saves them. The moral center of the story is a ten-year-old girl named, coincidentally, Monkey.

Our goal is to expand John's role to attract an A-list actor and intensify the love story, which means I must create histories for them that don't currently exist.

It strikes me that, again, my work and life are mirroring the same recurring themes: children, loss, a new life built in a new world after the destruction of the old.

"Roxanne, come on! I need to shower!"

Not having timed showers on the upper levels isn't always a blessing. She's been in there at least an hour. Still, living in the junior staff cabin is paradise. It's like a real house—there's no silence, we're allowed to decorate, girls chase each other around with rollers in their hair.

I wrote my parents asking for a razor for the Amazon that's become my legs;

the rest of my list consisted entirely of food, starting with Trader Joe's chocolate raspberry sticks. Roxanne's consisted almost entirely of cosmetics.

She finally walks out of the bathroom with two rainbows of eye shadow and foundation caked on so thick you could carve a relief on her cheek.

"I know you're trying to make up for lost time, Roxanne, but you don't have to do it all at once! They're gonna think you're trying to rub your level in their face."

She bends over, flips her hair back, and smiles.

"That's their problem."

Not entirely. Cameron comes into junior staff group, takes one look at Roxanne, and bursts out laughing.

"Who thinks this calls for the pond?" he shouts with a grin.

"The pond! Yeah, throw her in the pond!"

The pond isn't a pond, it's a cesspool. Algae covers the top of it, and it's more mud than water. Roxanne crosses her arms defiantly over her chest and gives Cameron a death look.

He moves toward her and she tries to dodge, but he's too quick. He throws her kicking and screaming over his shoulder, and we all follow him outside laughing and shouting as he races over to the pond.

"Let me down, Cameron! I'm gonna sue your fat ass!" she screams.

We laugh hysterically as Roxanne flounders, splashing and swearing up a storm. She makes her way to the edge and emerges like the swamp creature, hair dripping and black eye makeup streaking her face. Needless to say, the next day mascara and lip gloss seemed adequate.

My first shift as junior staff is in the library. I dust and catalog books, making mental notes of must-reads, and as the clock hits the hour, I walk over to let the girls lining up outside the door cross in.

It's Harmony family, and they all raise their hands, excited to see me. I'm excited to see them, too, and it's a few seconds before it sinks in that they can't speak until I call on them.

I look around at all the faces, at Katrina's crooked smile, at Brooke's aggressively questioning eyes, at Sunny's half-moons. Then I notice three brand-new faces in the family, and it hits me how assimilated the Morava girls have become.

Our first few months here, all we heard was how we needed to integrate, but it was impossible then. But now, with our old ugly uniforms long gone; two of us on the upper levels; Samantha, Katrina, and Sunny soon to follow; and three unfamiliar girls who've probably never heard of Brno, it saddens me to see how deeply Morava's getting buried.

I've always been fascinated with war. Few things could make me happier than sitting under the cupola of the Imperial War Museum, waiting for a bespectacled librarian to haul up dusty boxes of documents from the bowels of the building.

I spend two days reading the copious and touching correspondence of a British soldier on the frontlines in World War I France and his young wife in London. I'm so engrossed in their lives that by the time I untie the faded ribbon on the last bundle, the red K.I.A. stamped on the envelopes catches me completely off guard. Killed In Action. A dozen of them arrived in her mailbox after he died.

Having gained a deeper understanding of the world Charlotte left behind, I hit the British Library to conjure up John's past. Edwardian England, the Raj, smuggling, colonial opium dens. I'm ecstatic as only a nerd in the stacks can be. Even if for no other reason than I'm not in L.A. thinking about Mia, points and levels, and what to make for dinner.

"So how's it feel?" Mike asks at our next session.

"Awesome! I really didn't think I was gonna get it, Mike."

"Oh, I know how that feels. I meant how's it feel getting called on your shit?"

I stop smiling and stare at him.

"Are you talking about Max?" I demand.

"Girl, you about shot fire from your eyes at him!"

"Cuz he's an arrogant asshole! It's fine for him not to support me, but he didn't have to imply that other people are idiots by voting me up!"

"See, that's funny," he says, "because I agreed with just about everything he said."

I glare at him. What the hell was I thinking voluntarily entering therapy?

"And I think you do, too."

"What!" I explode. "That's bullshit, Mike. You know I deserve this!"

"Do you, Mia? You're a great leader in some ways, but how honest have you been with your family? You know everything about them, but do they even know you were raped?"

He might as well have shot a cannon at me. Last week, he asked me to write him a letter about issues I wanted to cover. I, stupidly, included Derek.

"You asked me for those papers so we could work through things, not so you could use them against me!"

"Mia," he says, unruffled, *"this can't work if you're not honest or if you hide out emotionally. I asked for those so we could build a relationship, and you knew that. I've observed you for a while and you're so used to using yourself as leverage against other people, rewarding and punishing others by how much you share with them, you probably can't remember what an even-footed relationship feels like."*

He sits, waiting for my response. I cross my arms and slouch down into my chair. He can try to pry information out of me until his precious cows come home—I'm never talking to him again.

A minute passes in silence. He sits patiently, his growing annoyance barely perceptible. Another minute. Swinging his feet down from his desk, Mike walks to his door and opens it.

"Get out."

"What?"

"Get the hell out."

"Fine!" I say, storming past him and slamming the door.

"It's sad that I care more about you than you do right now!" he yells out to me. Fucking shrinks.

"She got *what?*"

I've called Paul from London.

"You heard me, thrown out," Paul says.

"Great," I sigh, "here we go again. She probably had it coming."

"I'm sure she did. Kim also said that Mia just *happened* to mention in passing that she sniffed paint dust to get high in Morava."

"Paint from the wall?"

"Yep, when she was in worksheets. Can you believe she'd be that stupid?"

"*Would* be? You mean *will* be. That paint's full of lead."

I try to put this out of my mind as Jordana and I get ready to meet the director for dinner. Over dessert, he proudly shares the accomplishments of his older kids, who are in college or apprenticing in creative fields. Your kid's interning with a curator, how impressive! Mine? Oh, she's busy finding new and exciting uses for pulverized paint.

* * *

I look up at the clock on the library wall.

"Girls, start putting your things away, please," I say. "You have one minute to be in line."

The room becomes noisy as papers rustle and books are slid onto shelves. The girls I'm in charge of walk past me, eyeing me warily.

Being disciplined by someone your own age is hard enough. Being disciplined by someone your own age who has privileges you can only dream of, and who is a lot closer to home than you are, plain sucks, and lower levels spare no expense demonstrating this to us.

One girl shuffles into line late. Sonia's one of those people you never forget. She's so aggravating and endearing she seems more like a caricature than a human being. A petite, doll-faced Amerasian bombshell, nobody was surprised to learn she used to be a stripper. You can tell by the way she moves, slow, deliberate, almost snakelike, that she revels in the attention her body commands. Even after being raped by a customer.

She's had one of the more sordid pasts in here and is perfectly comfortable talking about it. In our first conversation, she told me about having to use her feet and toes to shoot up once other veins collapsed. She and her boyfriend dealt heroin and had several near-death encounters with dealers for not paying up on time, the money no doubt already in their veins. She's so forthcoming you'd think she'd be a program poster child, until you notice she talks about it a little too eagerly.

"Sonia, do you wanna self-correct?"

"I know you're just dying to dish out the consequences, but isn't it typical to explain what it's for before handing it out?"

Like you don't know, you dumb bitch, almost slips out of my mouth. Profanities seem to be doing that a lot lately.

"It's also typical to remember the rules after you've been here over a year."

She glares at me with a disdain as blatant as mine must have been toward my mother. As an authority figure, I find myself wavering between callousness and caring. Half the time they throw attitude, I remember being in their shoes and try to be patient with them.

Then there are days like today when I'm homesick and don't feel like putting up with some little shit's attitude over a rule she deliberately broke. Days I feel like laughing at this pathetic girl who's too stupid to realize she's just keeping herself here longer while I can go off-shift, shave my legs, and eat chocolate-covered raspberry sticks.

* * *

My new scenes are a jumble in my head, and it's so damp in the flat that my scene cards won't stick to the wall. I'm in a lousy mood anyway, so I bundle up to take a walk. It begins to rain and I think of my foolish daughter as I dodge puddles. Hello, up there—not to trouble You or anything, but I couldn't have gotten a regular teenager with regular teenage problems?

I've been walking so fast and furious, I suddenly realize I'm completely lost, I'm soaked through and freezing, and my neck is so tense from anger, my scalp's pulled two sizes tighter than my skull.

I duck out of a downpour into St. Paul's Cathedral, and while I'm dripping in the vestibule, it hits me. I'm not angry at Mia. I'm angry at Nick. Thirteen years later, he's still making my life hell. And I'm not just angry for what he did to Mia. He didn't just steal her innocence, her psychological well-being, he damaged me, too. He stole my youth. Years I'll never have back. My twenties, my thirties. With Mia's problems, now my forties.

And what if this isn't just a phase, what if she's always a screw-up, because his filthy hands have made her hate herself into that identity? What if the rest of my life I'll feel bad whenever I think of my daughter?

I'm in the right place to pray, but this anger feels much more powerful than faith. Certainly more logical. I must have been crazy—one answer to a prayer to find Mia and suddenly I believe? If that's the case, then losing Mia means losing faith. Which means that belief is nothing more than a willful delusion born of either desperation or gratitude.

"Ready to try this again, bucko?"

I jump. It's Mike whispering in my ear in the middle of class. Where the hell did he come from?

"Shouldn't you be asking yourself that?" I hiss back. "You're the one that kicked me out. Bucko."

He looks at me calmly, waiting for a real answer. I roll my eyes, grab my jacket, and wordlessly follow him outside.

"Boy, have I missed your attitude, girl!" he says once we're outside. "After a week of peace, I just couldn't take it anymore and had to come getcha."

I trudge behind him in silence, scowling every time he cheerily waves to passing students. He stops on his porch before going in.

"Mia, look at me."

I look up. Way up, Jesus, I always forget how tall he is.

"I'm glad you got Level 4, dear, I really am."

I breeze past him and sit down. He follows me in and sits in his chair, facing me with his elbows on his knees.

"I'm also still glad Max gave you that feedback. We both know you're operating at a fraction of your potential. How are people supposed to help you grow if you withhold from them? Oh . . . wait, that's right, they can't!"

He leans in toward me and I press back against my chair.

"Mia, when I look at you, I see a beautiful, bright young woman who's too scared and stubborn to admit she's stuck."

He pauses, lowers his voice, "You think you've dealt with your rape, with your old dad . . . then why do you freeze whenever a male comes within a foot of you?"

The faces of past students on his wall seem to be pressing in toward me, too. I put my feet on the chair with my knees under my chin and stare out the window with my jaw clenched tight.

"I want to see you happy, Mia. I want to see you put on a dress without worrying about the attention it's going to bring. You're still so run by what happened thirteen years ago that you don't even feel comfortable in your own skin," he says softly.

Then he doesn't say anything. He watches me watching the trees. I'm so frustrated—doesn't he think I want those things, too? That I wouldn't give anything to enjoy hugs without feeling claustrophobic and squeamish? To wear makeup without feeling like looking pretty is asking for trouble? I want that more than anything, but I just can't, so what does he want from me? I hate this, I hate Mike, I hate my old dad. I hate that every other memory has a me in it that he touched. I hate that some days I wish I wasn't me.

They come of their own accord, big rolling drops down my cheeks. I wipe them away silently, but they keep coming.

"Do you want me to help you, Mia?"

I nod. I've never cried in front of a man before. I hardly cry, period. I'm terrified of intimacy, of vulnerability.

"Then let me in. I can't help you if it's always on your terms. You're going to have to get a little vulnerable, feel a little out of control sometimes. That's why I kicked you out of my office. You weren't being emotionally honest."

I still can't bring myself to look at Mike. I look up to reach for a tissue on the filing cabinet and catch his eye as he watches me from his desk. He smiles at me. His eyes are moist.

"Mia," he says gently, "I know how hard that was for you. I'm real proud of ya', girl."

I nod as I wipe my eyes. It caught me off guard, seeing his eyes like that.

Cat 2, major horseplay. One overly rough tussle and it's back to Level 3. I don't fucking believe this. I was on sickbed with another girl and by afternoon we were feeling better and started horsing around. I tossed her a rock, but she missed it and it nailed her near her eye.

"But, she wasn't hurt and I'm really sorry, Chaffin," I protest on the way back to Harmony cabin with my arms full of my stuff.

"If a lower level did that, wouldn't you consequent them? Here, give me some things," he says, helping me. "Half an inch lower and you could have blinded her."

"I know. But, I worked so hard to get to Level 4 and it was an accident!"

"That's life. You break a rule, you pay the consequence. You were in a position of authority, a role model for others, and it's time you started acting like the young lady you are and not some hooligan."

I suppose he has a point, though if I hear about how I need to start acting ladylike one more time, I'll scream.

"That's a good size buck," Mike says, pointing to a big horned deer nibbling grass on the trail ahead of us. There's a boy on a parent call in his office, so we're doing my session while walking a fire road above the facility. The buck chews and watches us.

"You hunt?" I ask, somewhat surprised.

Mike's blunt, but he's also soft-spoken, gentle. Not the type I picture proudly strapping an openmouthed carcass to his bumper.

"Girl, I grew up dirt poor. I was putting food on the table by the time I was ten. I was fighting in the Gulf when I was the same age as some of the boys here so the service would pay for university."

We turn down the fork that leads back to the facility below us and the buck bounds away, his white tail flapping up and down.

"When you said you were a star football player, straight A's, volunteer fire-fighter," I say, "I assumed you had this perfect, carefree childhood."

"I did. We didn't have any money and we lived in a tiny farmhouse, but

I don't think it's possible to have had a better childhood than I did. My parents were awesome."

The second we reach the facility drive, kids outside are yelling his name already. Kids who've said fuck you to three hundred dollar an hour shrinks clamor for Mike's attention and time, calling out to him even on silence or making desperate gestures.

I think part of it's physical. He's got a broad, welcoming face and an expression that's curious, interested but not intrusive. Then there's his sheer size, which says don't-fuck-with-me and at the same time feels big and fatherly.

I think it's also because he's not just honest about you, but about himself. He's not afraid to talk about his own childhood, about a lousy weekend, losing a calf, hammering his thumb while pounding in a fence post. There's nothing clinical about him, no condescending doctor–patient relationship.

"Mike!" a boy makes a slam dunk on the court and comes running over. "You HAVE to make time for me tomorrow!"

"First appointment in the morning is yours, Mark."

I remind Mike that tomorrow morning's Harmony's group and he said he'd come.

"I didn't forget, Mia—you think I want you bitching at me about it next week? Now, so I don't have to tell your folks they're paying me to talk about myself, how's life on the lower levels the second time around?"

24.

As if dropping wasn't bad enough, I'm waiting for results of an AIDS test and Hepatitis C. I doubt Derek used a condom that night, and the type of people he shared needles with have cost me four nights' sleep.

My family's outside for PE, but nobody feels like exercising. I look up from my book. Montana really is big sky country, this place feels like it's in the clouds sometimes. I think just being out in nature is half the success of these programs. Suddenly, I hear an angry Chaffin.

"What is this? Why are you not exercising?" He looks over at me. "And you? When you were junior staff you had everyone doing pyramids like champs, what the heck's this?"

Right then, a junior staff boy passes by the court and Chaffin waves absently at him. Suddenly, his hand freezes midwave.

"Hey, come over here!"

Damn! Of all boys to walk by at this moment, it happens to be Max.

"Silvers, what does a normal fitness look like for the boys?"

Max shrugs. "Maybe 10 pyramids, 100 push-ups, some laps."

"Harmony family, listen up. Max will be your junior staff until I feel you're all out of your crap. Max, I'm giving you free reign to whip this family into shape, I mean black and white on rules, getting involved in group. Got it?"

This is just fucking great. One of the cockiest guys on the entire facility has just been given carte blanche to make our lives hell.

"Get down and gimme twenty!" Max yells. "Now! Last one on the ground takes two laps. Go! Go! Go!"

Everyone flies to the ground but me, I never signed up for the fucking army.

"Mia, two laps, go!"

"Fuck you," I scream back at him.

I hate Max, I hate everything about guys in general. The way they walk, the way they smell, the way they shovel food down like starving pigs.

"Two laps, Mia, or you have a Cat 2, blatant disrespect."

"What part about barking orders at us like a bunch of dogs should I respect? The power tripping part, or kissing Chaffin's ass part?"

"How about the your family is full of BS right now part and one of their oldest leaders isn't helping by copping the attitude of a Level 1. Two laps, go."

"Fuck you! You can't tell me what to do."

How original, I only said the quintessential self-righteous teenager phrase. Nice work, Mia, your big mouth just got you a day in worksheets. I haven't been to worksheets since Morava, but I'm sure it's the same dumb tapes and microscopic room.

"First, let's clear two things up," Mike says. After another round with Max, Miss Kim radioed Mike. "The AIDS test is bringing up issues, so you're in a man-hating groove from the get-go. Add to this a guy who's in a position of control over you, and that equals one nervous and defensive Mia. And what does Mia do when she feels vulnerable or out of control?"

I shrug, still annoyed.

"How does acting out or shutting down sound? Question—who's typically the prominent male authority figure in a kid's life?

"My dad," I sigh, hating how everything comes back to him.

"So, it's not about Max being controlling, that's his assignment per Chaffin. Your attitude and that irritated, shitty feeling you get whenever you're around guys is about you, about your current inability to put the past behind you and not see every guy as your dad. Or Derek."

Turns out, it's not just me. Come group, Mike shows up at the cabin with a red-eyed Brooke, who listlessly plunks down next to me in the circle. When she starts to share, her voice is monotone, exhausted, but it doesn't take long for her to get back into the emotional state she was obviously in before she came.

"Talk to Max, Brooke," Mike says. "Look him in the eye."

"I hate when you tell me what to do," she sobs. "I can't listen to you without remembering the times he told me to do things."

Brooke displays her emotions so rawly it's almost more powerful to watch her than to listen. She cries with her whole body. I want to breathe in her anger and pain, I want to use her emotions to ignite my own, steal her memories to replace the ones I can't call up in my own mind.

"To this day if I ever walk by that house, I'll vomit on the spot."

As Brooke goes over the details of her abuse, I can't sit here anymore, my skin's twitching. I drop out of the circle and go to the bathroom as quietly as I can.

As soon as I shut the stall door I slide to the floor, shaky. How awful for Brooke to remember all that! She was six when her abuse started and it lasted for three years, so she remembers a lot more than I do. How does she do it, how can she sit in her own skin, think with a brain that holds all those memories, all those touches, all . . .

Sets of feet are pattering around me, to the stalls to my right and left. And then directly in front of the stall come two mud-covered cowboy boots.

I can't put into words how I'm feeling and I don't even try. I just sit there and cry. Mike waits until he hears my breathing steady again to speak.

"Was listening to Brooke getting to be too much?"

"Yeah, I'm sorry, Brooke. I don't want you to feel bad about sharing, this is all my shit, it doesn't have anything to do with you."

A hand slides under my stall and squeezes mine, hard.

"I know, Mia," she whispers.

I start sharing, first about my talk with Mike, but then it all starts tumbling out.

". . . it pisses me off! It's like he never goes away! Knowing's a double-edged sword, Brooke. I can see how shitty it is for you to have to live with those memories, but at least you know what you're dealing with. It drives me nuts that I'm being affected by something I hardly remember! It makes me feel crazy."

"Do you remember anything?" she asks softly.

"Yeah, weird things, details. A fuzzy pink toilet seat cover, tile patterns. I remember the bathroom was to the left of a long, dark hallway. I used to remember everything real clearly when I was younger, but now I mostly remember remembering; and the nightmares—the clowns poking me, the spiked jacket, a blond, curly wig."

I've calmed down now, so I open the stall door. My whole family's crammed in the bathroom, smiling at me. We sit in a circle on the floor and finish up right there in the bathroom.

"Let me ask you this, Mia," Mike says, "would knowing make it any easier? Would remembering make it more real for you, help you let things go?"

I've asked myself this a million times.

"I'm not sure, but it might help. I just feel like a living secret sometimes, you know? He has other kids now. Sometimes, I think I want to talk to them, but what if they don't know about me? If he never abused them, I'd kill their image of their dad. I couldn't do that. But, I have so many questions. I want to get over him for good but it's hard to get over something when I'm not even sure what exactly it is I'm supposed to be recovering from."

I think I just talked for twenty minutes straight. I look up and notice Max. He has tears in his eyes and is quiet for once. I go over and hug him. Neither of us says anything but I know we've made our peace.

Dear Mom,

I'm going to write my dad a closure letter that I can burn. But before I do, I want to know everything. All the gritty little details. What did he do to me, what exactly happened? Did he ever beat you? Did he sleep around? What drugs did he take? Do you have any photos of him, do I look like him? I want to know everything so I can let it go. I know how hard this will be for you, Mom . . . I'm here for you if things come up for you while you write this to me.

Mia's request for documents will be easier to put together than she realizes. Spread across my desk are all the old court papers ready to be copied.

I'm suing Nick. He's the reason she's in the program, he should pay for it.

25.

"When this is over you're going to have a lot more than a headache to worry about."

Nick hasn't changed a bit. This time it's my new lawyer he's threatening, right in the courthouse. Probably because his letters telling her that her actions on my behalf will haunt her conscience and condemn her to eternal hell didn't have enough of an effect.

Mia's glad we're suing him. She's told Mike she feels it empowers both of us. And that if she's being held accountable for everything she's done, he should be, too.

"I know she's glad, but I'm sure it's bringing up a lot of issues for her," I say.

"Oh, it is," Mike answers. "But those issues will come up anyway. They will for anyone who's been sexually abused, only most folks never deal with it. Mia is doing a lot of hard work most adults either never get the chance to do or are afraid to do. You should be very proud of her."

Only in this sense has Nick paid any price for what he did, and it is a steep one. He'll never get to be proud of Mia, a punishment of his own choosing.

"How 'bout it?" Mike asks before I can sit down.

"How 'bout what?"

I'm already not liking the way this session's headed.

"How 'bout we walk over to Unity after this session?"

"What?" He said something about this last time but I thought he was joking!

"You're not really going to stick me in a boys' family—you can't!"

"I've already cleared it with Cameron."

This bites! Unity's one of the most notorious boys' families on the facility. Whenever you hear someone radioing for backup, it's almost always Unity family. He stands up.

"Right now?"

"Right now, kiddo."

I reluctantly follow him to the Hungry Horse. We walk in and a roomful of boys all turn around to stare at me. I wheel around to walk back out but Mike grabs me by the shoulders and half leads, half drags me over to a tall, tan man in his thirties with a scruffy beard. Mike explains the situation to him, two weeks of joining the family from 7:30 a.m. to 7:30 p.m., then two days a week from then on. I stuff my hands in my pockets and stare at the ground.

"Boys, listen up," Mr. Greg announces. "This is Mia, she'll be joining our family."

Their names come in a whirl, Brad, Sean, Jeff, Aaron. They give the same introductions as girls do, name, age, where from, why here. The drugs and dropping out are similar but there's a lot more gangs and violence.

When I get back, I'm hit with questions: what do their cabins look like, do they have the same rules, what's fitness like with them? It's not until I'm about halfway through that it hits me. Brooke, Samantha, and Katrina are all missing.

"Where is everyone?"

"They got Level 4 today."

"All of them?"

I instinctively seek out Sunny, whose expression and presence tells me she didn't get voted up. Again.

"Katrina and Samantha I saw coming," I tell her, "but Brooke's only been here seven months!"

"Yup, and we shining examples are still Level 3 after a whole year, isn't that just faaabulous!"

Boys smell. They shower, they shave, they do laundry once a week, but their cabin still stinks of sweat and socks. They're louder during fitness and quieter during group.

There's so much snow on the court today, fitness turns into a snowball fight. They tackle one another, rubbing snow in each other's faces. It looks like fun but they're so aggressive, I'd probably get massacred.

I walk over to talk to Mr. Greg and ask about his weekend.

"Oh, it was great, I went to the Testicle Festival."

"The what?"

"Testicle Festival," he says, as if every town had one.

"Right. And I suppose come fall, there's the Pussy Parade."

He laughs. "Bull balls, Mia, not people's!" He's practically smacking his lips. "Got down ten of those bad boys this year."

Only in Montana. I'm grimacing and trying to imagine testicle festivities when Thwack! A snowball slams into the back of my head. I turn to see blond frizz taking off. I ball up a handful of snow and chuck it back at Zeke. It hits him squarely in the back. He turns around and we both start laughing. Before I know it, I'm snowball fighting with Zeke and ducking attacks from the others. Paul was always proud that I could throw a baseball like a boy, and the skill is coming in handy because they aren't cutting me any slack for being a girl!

Every week I feel less like an outsider. I've made a few friends and feel comfortable with the whole group in general.

I'm in the middle of helping Aaron with a math problem when we hear a loud pounding. It's Sean. A minute ago he was quietly reading a letter but he's livid now, slamming his fists into the table as he yells, "That bitch!"

Mr. Greg rushes over and grabs his arms. Sean wrestles free and slams his fist into the wall. Mr. Greg grabs him again. "Michael, radio staff central and tell them we need backup here NOW!"

"Fuck you!" Sean screams while trying to punch Mr. Greg. Suddenly, he buries his face in his chest.

"She lied to me, Mr. Greg," he sobs. He makes one more fist, then drops it.

"She lied, she was never pregnant."

Sean's girlfriend was two months pregnant when he came into the program. She was due this month. Or so we thought. Turns out she was worried Sean would leave her and faked the pregnancy. Poor thing, he was so excited to be a dad.

Women don't have a monopoly on being abused, I think, as I watch Mr. Greg cradle Sean. I've listened to guys share about being beaten by drunken dads, cheated on by girlfriends, one was even molested by an aunt, another by an uncle. I'd been so busy seeing the world through my own experiences, I didn't think to view it through anyone else's.

"I'm not wearing a dress."

Mike's putting me on a challenge by making me wear girl clothes for a week. "A skirt, then."

"N-O."

"Mia, what don't you like about being a girl?"

"Nothing," I lie.

"Hmm, musta been another client who made that long list of all the things wrong with it. Let me think . . . I believe you said you don't like walking down the street and being catcalled at, you feel that guys enjoy sex more—that whole fucking versus getting fucked—you don't like being physically smaller than guys. And, my personal favorite, you can't pee in the woods standing up."

"Just because I don't like being a girl doesn't mean I want to be a guy."

"That's why I think it's a good idea to get you more comfortable with being a girl, so you can embrace it rather than let it be a source of frustration and pain for you. The rest of this week, you're going to dress like a girl, and I mean makeup, hair, the works."

"Even when I'm in the boys' family?"

"Especially when you're in the boys' family."

It takes three days of walking around in a skirt for me to break down. A new boy came into the family and he's been eyeing me all day. Then I got so frustrated during PE because I can't do anything in these stupid clothes, I yelled "fuck" and Mr. Greg made everyone circle up. Of course, as soon as we do, who happens to walk by but Mike.

"I was wondering when this would happen."

"You wanted this to happen? Everyone's staring at me like I'm a freak or a piece of ass and I can't do anything in these stupid clothes!"

"Guys, if you weren't in the program and you saw Mia walking down the street, how many of you would say, damn, that's a good-looking woman?"

All their hands go up. I'm on the verge of tears.

"Okay, then what would you have done?" Mike asks me. "Actually, don't answer that. Mia, I want you to guess who would have responded in which way."

I look around at the guys. "Micah and Jason definitely would have catcalled, Sean would have waited for me to approach him, Aaron would have come up and been very respectful, Zeke would have said some jackass pickup line."

"Now go around the circle and tell me what each of these guys' biggest issues are."

"Micah was adopted and has big abandonment issues, so does Jason, though he's more afraid of rejection. Zeke's ridiculous pickup line makes sense, he always uses humor to mask being nervous or scared."

By the time I finish the circle, Mike's point is obvious. People's reactions are always about themselves, their own insecurities and fears.

"Mia, if I thought you genuinely hated dressing like a girl, I wouldn't have done this. But I see how you look at other girls. I know you want to do certain things but don't because you're scared of the attention it might bring. This was to help you get more comfortable with that attention, to teach you how to handle it appropriately."

Micah raises his hand.

"Guys aren't all just after sex, Mia. I know we talk about it a lot and you've had some bad experiences, but half the reason I would have wanted to hit on you is because you're cool. I'm not saying sex isn't a factor, but give us some credit."

"Yeah," Zeke says, "and how you dress makes a difference too. Sure, if we see some girl with tight-ass pants and a thong showing we're gonna want to hit it. But if you see a woman who dresses nice, honest to God, sex isn't the first thing we think of, it's more like damn, that woman's beautiful, she's never gonna go for a dude like me. So we make some retarded pickup line when all we really want to do is just ask you out."

"Mia, what did we do today?" Mike asks.

"We tortured me."

"Well, maybe," he laughs. "We made you face your fears. Now tell me you don't feel a little bit better?"

I smile reluctantly. The bastard, as usual, has a point.

26.

Good God, that voice. High, sharp, nasal, and LOUD.

"It's great, isn't it?" Lou Dozier says of her voice, grinning. "Men who have issues with their mothers just love it."

She's a tiny, pixie-faced ball of energy who will be our Duane for Focus. She's in her mid-forties, agile. Her body speaks as expressively as her voice, her movements are fluid and gestural.

"Focus is about being 100 percent responsible for your life, about opening yourself up to new possibilities. I'd like you to step forward in any order and introduce yourselves."

A tall young woman steps forward. She says she works for the company and came because she wants to better herself and her marriage. Her voice is familiar.

"You're Priscilla from Utah! I'm Claire, from Morava!" I blurt emotionally. "You were the only person in the whole company who would talk to us—"

"VICTIM!!" Lou yells.

My jaw drops and it's like a thousand-watt bulb went off in my brain, *instantly*.

"I said introduce your *selves*, not your stories and drama!" she says. "Next!"

"No, wait! You're right!" I sputter. "You're right! That's exactly what I'm doing! I'm whining like a . . . I *hate* whiners!"

Lou walks up to me.

"No, you don't, Claire, because you've always gotten something out of it. I get that you've been whining and angry and righteous for years—ooh, they did it to me, look what he did to me! Always fighting or blaming some bad guy, aren't you?"

"Yes! That's exactly—"

"How's it been working for you, Claire?" Lou cuts me off. "What were the payoffs?"

"It feels awful, I'm always stressed. The payoffs? I don't know," I say, flummoxed.

She addresses the group, "Being a victim gives you an excuse for not being accountable for your own life. Blame is a wedge against feeling powerless. Claire," she looks at me, "I get that what went on at Morava was tough on everyone. Looking back from a place of accountability, what did you create for yourself there? Resentment? Chaos?"

"Yeah, I did."

"Keep going."

"Exhaustion, umm, fear . . ."

"Sympathy, approval, control!" she belts out. "You got to be *right*. A victim always gets to be right. If they're the bad guys, then you must be the poor good guy. It's a covert way of controlling. Can you see that?"

It's true, I could have done the exact same things I did that week with an entirely different attitude. My attitude was, indeed, that what the police, the company, and the press were doing was wrong, which made me, of course, right. My anger upset me, it upset Mia, it added to the anger and hostility already there. It didn't control people, it further polarized them. As if anger ever really controls anyone's behavior.

Like your child's. Another Bing! moment for Ms. Fontaine. The worse Mia got, the angrier I got. On some level, I thought that if I just got mad enough, I'd scare her into line. I just made us both miserable, and she just got better at pretending.

Touching knees with a few people in a tight circle is not my idea of a good time. I like personal space. A member of the service team, Annie, joins my small group, telling us no kid talk, just what's been working and not working in our own lives since Discovery.

"Transformation will not tolerate mediocrity, it will not tolerate fear," was what Lou left us with, and Debbie Norum is taking that last one seriously. She's a pretty, pale blonde in her thirties with the kind of bright blue eyes that look even brighter when they're shining with tears. Good thing, because I'm going to be seeing a lot of them.

"I am so tired of feeling guilty and angry!" she exclaims, bursting into tears. "My son got his only student of the month award and I was lying in a hospital bed with tubes down my throat because I tried to kill myself, how fucked up was that? But I can't take it back, I can't take back the drinking. I've done everything I can to make amends, but he can't get over it—"

"You mean, he *won't* get over it," Annie reminds her.

"No, he won't, and I'm sick of buying into his letters home about what a lousy mom I was! I'm just so sick of being sick of things, mainly of being sick of myself. I don't want to feel this way anymore!"

I feel like I'm witnessing open-heart surgery, hello group, here's my heart, eat of it. Her version of sharing is paralyzing, it's making me sweat and I haven't said a word.

John Dean's a big man in his late forties, with dark eyes, intense and intimidating. He's guarded, says little, and when he does, it's usually sarcastic, judgmental, or sly. It's obvious he isn't going until last, so I start. I talk about losing my dream job when Mia went down the tubes, about my new job, about my ex.

"Lou really nailed me. I want honest feedback if you see me being a victim or overreacting."

"I get it," John says dryly, "'Group, I'll tell you how I'm going to screw up, so you can be ready for it, and I can be ready with my response,'" John says, mocking me. "There's certainly no risk in that, Claire F."

"There was no risk in telling Debbie that all men aren't jerks, either, John D," I shoot back.

"Aren't we a pair?" he grins. "Hey, let's make this all about Debbie." We laugh and he feels less intimidating to me.

"How about let's not," Debbie suggests. "Claire, you just spent ten minutes on 'stuff.' I didn't get anything about how you feel."

John pushes up his glasses, sits back in his chair. Defensive position, I think to myself. Debbie intimidates him.

"Open body, John," Debbie reminds him.

He leans forward and says, "My experience of both of you is of two very sad and worn-out women."

* * *

Around 9 p.m., Lou asks the entire group to come up with a purpose for our weekend. Drafting a new constitution would be easier.

There have been a few men who've gone head to head with Lou. Big guys who have issues with women, little Napoleons with authority issues, run-of-the-mill boneheads who have issues with women in authority. One brave man didn't come back after lunch. Of course, these are the first guys at the easel. I think I'm about to witness grown men fight over a marker.

Not that the rest of the room is much better. We're all arguing in no time. We've even gotten anal about "the," "it," and just whose purpose is it, anyway. Tempers flare and pettiness reigns. John sits against the wall, muttering biting but funny remarks. Debbie keeps jumping up, crying, "Why can't we all just come together as a team, my God, look at us!"

By 1:30 a.m., we finally agree to disagree on: "Our purpose is to create growth and joy in an exciting, caring environment." So far, only "exciting" applies.

"You took four hours to do this," a staffer says. "Know how long the kids take?"

"They're probably here till morning," our Napoleon-in-chief says smugly.

"Twenty to thirty minutes."

The word "horseshoe" takes on a whole new meaning in the world of seminars. Especially when it's got a solitary stool in the middle of it. Today, it's an opportunity to get a look at the Grand Canyon between how we think we are perceived and how we really are, the latter, at our worst, being called "our number." We "run our number" when under stress or when we go unconscious about our behavior. We're being given new names that reflect "our old number." "Old" because the weekend is about moving past those beliefs and behaviors.

"Morticia?" I practically fall off the stool. "But I'm one of the most cheerful, optimistic people I know!"

"Are you nuts, Claire?" Debbie practically yells, suddenly deciding Lou needs an assistant. "All you wear is black turtlenecks, your face has no color, you don't let anyone in—you're like the walking dead!"

"Ditto!" calls out someone else, probably Rebel Without a Clue, who has to stick his two cents in everything.

I don't get me as Morticia at all, but they do and I guess that's the point. We have to wear new name tags with our old number names, which I find exceedingly annoying. Debbie didn't argue when it was her turn, in fact, she came up with her own, DOORMAT—Men, Come Shit All Over Me. Lou coached her that doormat was just the symptom, the belief behind it was Not Good Enough. Which sets Debbie to weeping again as she plasters on her new name tag.

"So, John," Lou asks when he's on the stool, "who made you feel so small and weak when you were a kid?"

From the look on his face, she hit the bull's-eye.

"Fate did," he says, half-facetiously. "I was a very sick child, I was small and could die at any time."

"Fate, huh?" Lou says, unconvinced. "You look pretty hearty to me, when did you start looking like that?"

"After I left home, I gained forty-five pounds."

"Gee, there's a surprise."

"What are you gonna do, call me Mama's Boy?" he says sarcastically.

"Why, do you like that name?"

"Hell, no, it doesn't—"

"Mama's Boy!" she calls to the back table. They're nodding in agreement as one of them scribbles a new name tag.

"Are you open to some feedback, Debbie?" I ask her in this morning's small group.

"Of course," she says brightly.

"My experience of you is that you don't realize how controlling you are."

"When did that come up for you, Claire?" Annie asks me.

"Suggesting the group work as a team last night is one thing. But crying and judging everyone for not doing it was trying to control the experience of sixty people. And acting victimized when you couldn't."

"Oh. Huh," Debbie says, frowning, "welllll, I've got to think about that."

"Comforting Aging Barbie, I mean Deana, when she got that name, was about controlling someone's experience, too." I'm on a roll. "It says you think she's too weak to handle it herself; it's like saying: I think you're needy and the person you need right now is me. Which made it about you."

Deana is a sexy little blonde in tight jeans and a high-collar blouse bursting with bosom. She's super feminine, with bleached blond bangs hanging low on her forehead and a lot of mascara. She says she hates her forehead and obsesses about her weight.

"But, it seemed so mean," Debbie protests, "I hated to see her cry."

"The whole point was finding the name that pushed her buttons. Getting old and losing her beauty is her biggest fear in life. Of course, she's going to cry, what's the big deal?"

"Caretaking is never about the other person," Annie adds. "It's about wanting to feel needed because you're afraid you're not wanted. Debbie, can you see the connection between that behavior and the belief that you're not good enough?"

"Yeah, I need to look at that," she says thoughtfully.

"Need to?" Anne prompts gently.

"I *want* to look at that," Debbie corrects herself, then says to me, "Though I sure didn't expect to hear 'what's the big deal' about crying from you, Miss Stick Up Her Butt."

"You're in a rut in your life, just going through the motions," Lou speaks dreamily into the darkness around us as we lie on the floor. "And you get an opportunity to go on a four-day cruise. The sky is blue and the air is fresh and bracing . . ."

I see dolphins arc gracefully below me, waiters with trays of lemon tarts, chaises with silk cushions and ample shade . . .

"The burdens of your life appear and you do something unusual. You request assistance and people respond. They're excited that you're there, making a difference just by being who you really are, sans image, pretense, or mask."

I picture myself at the prow in lotus position, serene and content and the . . .

BANG!CRASH!BAMBAMBAMBAM!! thunders throughout the room, scaring the living daylights out of me.

"THERE'S AN EXPLOSION IN THE ENGINE ROOM!!" Lou

yells, "THE SHIP'S GOING DOWN FAST! You're 2,000 miles from shore, the radio's destroyed and there are sharks in the water! There's room for only SIX of you on the lifeboat! ONLY SIX OF YOU WILL LIVE, THE REST OF YOU WILL DIE!

It's dark and the banging and crashing keeps going and I feel genuine panic.

"THE ONLY WAY TO LIVE IS TO BE ON THE LIFEBOAT. YOU HAVE THIRTY SECONDS TO STATE YOUR NAME AND YOUR INTENTION OF WHETHER OR NOT YOU WILL BE ON THE LIFEBOAT AND WHY! GO!"

This feels so real! The dark room fills with the sound of people shouting for help and drowning. People start popping up right and left, vying to claim their place. There's desperation and panic in our voices as we try to save our lives in thirty seconds: I have small children! Their father is an addict, I'm all they have!

I hear John Dean call out, "I'm giving my seat to the youngest!"

They go on about the things they want to do, the amends they have to make, and oh, their children their children, as Lou calls TIME!

"My daughter needs me!" I jump up and cry out. "She's suffered so much already, she can't lose her mother! My own mother's lost enough family!"

I don't even know what else I'm saying when Time! is called and I sit on the floor, sobbing at the thought of never seeing Mia again. When it's all over, dim lights come up and we're given six little sticks. We have to go up to each person in the room, look them in the eye and say "You live" to the six we give a stick to and "You die" to the fifty we don't. It feels so dreadful to tell someone "You die," some of us are hysterical.

We finish and are asked to line up in order of how many sticks we have—just in case there are some of us who haven't fully scraped bottom yet. I only have four sticks. And one of them was my own.

The lucky six sit in an area designated as a lifeboat while the rest of us lie around them, sinking into oblivion. None of us can stop crying; the sickening feeling of near loss is still fresh in us.

"It's too late, you had your chance in life and now it's all over," Lou says quietly as she walks between our bodies. "You're sinking down into the darkness forever. Your loved ones will never see you smile again, hear your voice again, the world is going on without you. Because you didn't get on that lifeboat.

"This is not a popularity contest. It's about your awareness of yourself as a unique contribution. There is no one who can make the difference you can make. Your purpose and vision can only be fulfilled by YOU! And if you're lying on the bottom of the ocean, if you don't take a stand for your own life, it ain't gonna happen."

The service team comes out and calls our names one by one.

Poor Debbie gave away all her sticks, and it felt like another suicide attempt. The service team hardly has to prompt her. She gets it, loudly and wetly—she's still giving herself a you-die vote.

"Mama's Boy!" a thin young woman on the service team calls out. She graduated from Spring Creek a year ago. I see his silhouette rise as she walks up to him, her voice ringing out.

"You sent your son away to save his life and you're not even willing to save your own! I just staffed your son's seminar and he did the same thing! He chose death, too!" Her voice breaks as she looks up at him. "Who do you think he learned this from?"

I can see his chest heaving as he sobs.

"Morticia!" Annie calls out and I stand up.

"She's had too much suffering . . . I've had so little joy!" she quotes me. "Claire, all you could think of was what you *didn't* want or what you *didn't* have! You're all about fear and doom and gloom! No wonder you got so few sticks, why would anyone think you'd create something different if given another chance?"

There are murmurs of agreement all around me.

"I'm not sure what you'd create if you got a second chance," Lou says to me quietly, "but you sure earned your name this time around, Morticia. Lest you doubt how you show up in life."

"Mommy, why are all your scripts and stories so depressing?"

Mia was always bothered by what I wrote. Also by what I wore. The physical world was like a person to her, and she wanted it to laugh. When she was five, she woke up from a nap and her eyes fixed on my black stockings. She said in the most despairing little voice, "Why do you have to have on black stockings? I wish you had happy hearts and flowers on your legs, Mudder."

I take out last night's homework. When asked to list the dates of the significant events in my life, I did not put a single happy event: 1962, cried when started kindergarten; 1964, wet my pants in second grade; 1966, moved to Michigan, sad leaving friends; 1974, broke up with boyfriend; 1980, marry ex, . . . right up to the dates of Mia's downward spiral.

A litany of tragedy. I'm always either looking back with regret and anger or looking forward with fear and doubt. Being alive in the moment, much less feeling joy in it, got left behind somewhere in a little yellow dress.

Once I grew up, I was sure that marriage was the ticket to happiness. Oh, it's gonna be smooth sailing now, I thought when I found Nick, I've finally boarded the right ship, the one with dancing and moonlight. Instead, I got the one with a hole hidden in the hull, the one that started sinking as soon as it lost sight of land. I've spent so much of my life paddling and holding Mia up to safety that I've forgotten there were any other kind of ships. Or that I could stop thrashing about and trust that the water would bear me up, because that is what water does, if you let it. And Mia could have learned to do the same by watching me. She could have learned ease, learned to trust, in herself and in the universe. She could have seen her mother know joy.

I suddenly realize that I know *exactly* what it was like for Mia to have a mother like me. When I was growing up my biggest fantasy was not to be a smoky-eyed secret agent or Ginger on *Gilligan's Island*. What I fantasized was this:

I'm in a fabulous department store, trying on pearls, in my hot pink Twiggy dress. I have stick-straight hair and no glasses. A beautiful, elegant woman in a pink pillbox hat, à la Jackie Kennedy, joins me at the counter and says, "I see you like pink, too."

I notice her accent is familiar. I ask her if she's from Hungary and she is! We get to chatting and more things sound familiar—she had a brother named Leo, too! And a big sister named Leah? Oh, my God! we both exclaim, raising our fingertips to our lips just like Audrey Hepburn in *Charade*—she's my mother's sister, the Nazis didn't kill her after all! She throws her arms around me and I'm overjoyed! I have a brand-new, glamorous aunt who likes me immediately and a lot! I run home and tell my mom I found her sister, she's right here, mom, look! She's alive, you have a sister again, Mommy, aren't you happy? Are you happy now, Mommy, are you happy?

I share last night's thoughts with Debbie and John. Debbie throws up her arms.

"God, Claire, you don't get it, do you?! We don't want your thoughts about the past, that's just a reporting of events! That's all you do! How the fuck do you *feel* about any of it?" she says passionately. "Can't you cut through all that blather and connect with me heart to heart?"

I feel like I'm being jabbed with a cattle prod. "What, just because I'm not crying, this isn't my heart? I'm not you, Debbie!"

"I'm crying because I'm letting go of a lot of shit! I think I intimidate the hell out of you because I'm strong enough to do it and you think you're not!" she challenges.

"Strong enough to do what, whine all over the place?"

"No. Strong enough to admit you feel like a failure. As a mother. Just like I do," she says bluntly. "You're too afraid to admit it, because you don't want to ruin your image. I've been sensing in my gut that you are full of shame from the first time I saw you."

I sit. And stare at my hands. The floor. Listen to myself breathe. Try to will myself out of here. I have a moment where I'm someone else watching a film of myself.

"Claire, the only way out is through," Annie says quietly.

A voice says so softly I can hardly hear it myself. "I failed three times. When she was little, when I told her about the visitation, and now. I can't even stand to see other mothers and daughters together. Mia's not the fuck-up. I am."

I don't know what I sound like, or look like, for the next twenty minutes. Letting go of "a lot of shit" can't be pretty. I don't care. And neither do they. I feel safe, I feel surrounded by love. It feels like hearts and flowers.

Today is Stretch Day. We're to inhabit a persona that is a part of us we deny and given a song that we're to create a performance around that embodies it.

"Aaarrrgghh!" John's just heard he's to be the Full Monty. He drops to the floor and goes fetal, only half mockingly. His mates, also very closed-off men, are nervous and up in arms—"Just how far are we supposed to take this?"

Debbie and her vocal group are to be mimes, silent for a full day.

Five really macho guys are to embody the beauty and elegance of the human soul. In tutus. Two are pissed and threatening to leave. The other two are asking them if they want their wives to tell their sons in the program that their dads wimped out.

A group of women with body issues will belly dance in full costume. Two are very heavy, two are very thin, all are in full panic.

"But, I'm very ladylike," I protest. "I wear dresses all the time!"

"Always an argument with this one," Lou muses. "Claire, being a Lady in Red is not about being "ladylike," that's external. It's about the very essence of feminine beauty and grace. And that's the last thing you project. I think if they still made chain mail, you'd wear it. You have no clue how much beauty and grace you're covering up. I assure you, you will remember this day for the rest of your life. Let go, my dear."

By noon, I'm standing in a darkened room, wearing a sexy red gown and red lipstick. The transformation of sixty people I will witness is miraculous.

Aging Barbie has slicked her hair off her forehead for the first time in years and projects a very different, powerful kind of sexy in a fabulous cone bra as Madonna.

By the time John and his gang are bumping and grinding to "You Can Leave Your Hat On," it's been a day unlike anything I could have imagined. I can't believe I'm watching the same dark, serious man lip-syncing and flinging his pants at us. His entire face has opened up, and for the first time I can see that he's a very handsome man.

I'm so paralyzed by stage fright that when our music starts to play, my brain is in lockdown. But my body isn't. It decides to leave my brain behind. My arms feel light as air and my body comes alive in a way I've never felt before.

I hear my neck and my back and my hips singing as I move around the room. Men. I'm suddenly aware of men watching me in a way that feels beautiful. Some are crying as I dance slowly past them. I feel myself as a gift.

* * *

While the last group is stretching, I start to feel uncomfortable, light-headed. I slip out to go to the ladies' room. I hurry into a stall and sit down, and being a Lady in Red becomes far too literal. I'm having a miscarriage.

27.

"Mia, come on in, I'll grab you in a second, Brooke."

Chaffin pulled us out of class and had us wait in the library. I'm back up on junior staff and have been doing great so I have no idea why. Samantha just left his office. Her eyes were red from crying and met mine for a second before darting away.

I sink into the oversize chair in his office.

"So, you can't even go two weeks on Level 4 without pulling some sort of crap?"

"What do you mean?"

"No inappropriate conversations lately?"

Ohhhh. Now, I understand Samantha's look. Two days ago we were all canoeing and inevitably, boys and sex came up. I didn't think much of it at the time, but now I remember how much trouble we could get in for that. Fuck! I just got back up here!

"That was nothing, Chaffin! We talked about boys and sex, but nothing that bad."

"Who'd be good in bed? Who's 'hung'? That's nothing bad? You hate when guys view you as a piece of meat and you're doing the same thing to them! Seems the boy's family was a bad idea if all you did was research who's hot enough to sleep with!"

"That's bullshit! I got a lot out of being in there, ask Mike. And I never thought about those boys like that, the people we talked about weren't even in Unity."

"Like it matters?"

"I hate it here! You want to take away normal thought and feelings, it's not human to never think about sex!"

"Of course you guys think about sex, that's normal. But you know you're not allowed to talk about it like that. Having integrity and respect means using self-control. How would you feel if a group of guys compared your chest to the other girls'?"

Like they don't. They're just smart enough not to get caught. I can't believe this, one stupid conversation.

"Samantha's the only one of you with any accountability. You're acting like you didn't even do anything wrong!"

"Fine, so what's happening to us? Are we getting dropped?"

"Well, Samantha's going home today—"

"Samantha's WHAT?" Why would she rat us out before she's leaving?

"Her mom came to pull her this morning. You and Brooke are both Level 1, zero points."

"You fat fuck!" explodes out of my mouth.

Chaffin takes a deep breath, no doubt to keep from swearing right back at me. I storm out of his office before I have to listen to any more of this shit.

"Mia. Mia! This just came for you," Miss Kim says, handing me a thick letter.

It's bothered me far more than I expected, losing this teensy almost-baby that wasn't meant to be. Part of me is relieved because I've finally come to enjoy having my time to myself for the first time in sixteen years. Most of me is sad, though, because even with everything I've been through with Mia, being a mother is nothing short of bliss. The things we're called upon to do for our children are not sacrifices, they're privileges. What else could make a person say, with gladness, "You mean to save my child's life all you want is my arm? Take it! My other arm? Where's the axe?" Space travel, the Sistine Chapel, splitting atoms? Small potatoes next to growing a life. I would have liked to do it again. And I would have liked to give a sibling to Mia.

I hadn't told Paul I was a month late because I wanted to be sure myself. I don't know if he's more bothered that I miscarried or by the fact that I didn't tell him I was pregnant, or both, but he's anything but supportive; he's withdrawn and testy. It doesn't help that Mia's so excited that I went to Focus that she's bugging him to go, too. Fat chance.

I could intervene and push him to go, but one of the biggest lessons I got from Focus was that control is an illusion. I watched Debbie try to control others, with good intentions, and I saw myself in her. He'll do what he's going to do, and Mia will handle it how she handles it.

Of course, all this is easier with support from Debbie and John in daily emails. Debbie's finally told her son to get over it. He's angry, she writes, because now it means he has to focus on himself. And now that John's opened up his heart to his son, his son's gotten off Level 1 for the first time in months.

Mia's just had a huge drop and fully expected me to be angry or give advice on how to improve, succeed, change. "Hmm, what did you learn from this experience?" totally threw her.

Till now, my emotions have been a function of her behavior. She succeeds and I fly; she drops, I plunge. I see now that my reactions have been her heaviest artillery. Which makes me both her target and the arms supplier.

One of the parents I read most on the Link, David Stoker, a psychologist whose son is in Samoa, has made me realize that my past reactions have had an even more insidious effect on Mia, something I think all parents are guilty of without realizing it. He recently wrote:

"My experience of these program kids is that every one of them is or was terrified of growing up and fearful that they would botch up their future. So they kept delaying the maturation process by remaining unaccountable, immature, and rebellious. When we parents collude with their low self-esteem by pointing out their shortcomings, criticizing their lack of progress, or in other ways invalidating them, we buy into their deep-seated fears about themselves, and they then hate us for seeing that side of them and focusing on it."

I wait several hours before opening the letter. It's a thick one from my mom, probably telling me all about college and the things she's excited to do together once I graduate. I just wasn't in the mood. Not that I am now because I don't see how it's humanly possible for me to ever leave this place. I open the letter:

Mia, I love you very much, no matter where you're choosing to be . . .
I love you beyond the circumstances, the choices, the image, the lies, the manipulations, the self-delusion, all that surface stuff you get stuck in.

Because who you are is not that. You need love at this point most of all . . .

This is what she writes me after hearing I dropped? She should be furious, dismayed that her daughter can't simply be good. She's actually asking what I learned from it—why is she being so supportive, so . . . neutral? It's great to not get bitched at, but it's making me nervous.

Coming home will be hell if my mom gets into the program hard-core, it'll be just like living here. I can just see it now, I'll pour too much cereal and she'll ask me how taking more than I can handle is a reflection of my life. What kind of idiot was I, pushing her to go to Focus?

But I keep reading and I think she's changed on a deeper level. Mail from my mom is always one of three things: educational, upbeat, or angry. But this is so real, it's like she accidentally sent a page of her journal.

I wish I had you here to become friends with, to feel support and truly unselfish love and empathy from you instead of me always being the giver . . . Sometimes I wouldn't share things with you because I was afraid of how it would affect you.

I know exactly how she feels. That was the main reason I pushed her and Paul away, though my silence hurt them more.

I'm going to share something with you. I had a miscarriage earlier this year.

She what?! She wants another kid? What happened to me? No wonder she's in no rush to have me home!! Hell, her life's gotten nothing but better since I came here! Her career's picked up, she's become a regular jet-setter, and now she'll have a clean shot at motherhood. She'll finally get her "normal" child.

And she said earlier this year—it's August! What was she waiting for? She bitched about me not being open with her before coming here—well, dear mother, where would I have possibly learned that from?

Jordana's getting antsy for the rewrite and, knowing my propensity for distraction, has asked me to Provence for the month to finish it. She spends August with her partner in a farmhouse in the Luberon, outside a tiny mountaintop village. Like Colette, I'll have no choice but to write. She's not giving me the car keys.

"Interesting you chose to see it that way, Mia."

She's obviously gotten my letter about the miscarriage. I couldn't decide if she'd be upset because she's always wanted a sibling or because she would have been jealous of one. I decided not to do what I've always done, assume she couldn't handle emotional challenges.

"What do you mean, 'interesting'?" she snips. "What's interesting is that the minute you put me in this hellhole to rot, presto, you decide to have another kid."

"Actually, what I figured is that being your mother has been such a joy, another child would be just as wonderful. We also wanted you to have a sibling, so when we're old, you won't have to wipe our drool all by yourself," I say, hoping to humor her. Right after I say it, I realize I've done it again—I tried to make her feel how I want her to, rather than accept whatever she really is feeling.

"Nice try, Mother."

"Mia, I can hear that you're hurt. You're making it mean we're rejecting or abandoning you. That's your stuff, not ours. I also recognize that my feelings about it are still tender, so I'm choosing not to talk to you about it until you're ready to be more respectful. You can be hurt or have fears without being rude."

"Fine!"

"*Au revoir, ma fille, je t'aime.*" (I love you, my daughter.)

"*Je t'aime aussi et bon voyage,*" she says sarcastically. (I love you, too, and have a great trip.)

28.

Each step outdoors in the Luberon valley is redolent with scent—thyme, lavender, honey. Provence smells like pleasure. It's a perfect place to write a love story.

And to continue discovering what began when I danced in a red dress—a genuine, visceral awareness of my physical presence in the world. Till that day, I wasn't really aware that I'd been walking around like a brain on a stick. I feel so physically present now, I can feel the air on my skin when I walk in the woods, my fingers notice my face when I wash it.

Of all the things I'm feeling blessed with in this beautiful place, what makes me happiest is that my voice returned. I sit on the deep window ledge and sing a lullaby out to the stars to carry to my girl in Montana who's struggling right now. I feel the kind of crazywild love for Mia now that I did when she was little.

The ancient farmhouse sits on a hill, with a plum orchard and old stone walls. I perch my laptop on my knees and work on the screenplay beneath a giant fig tree, and my pleasure infuses the work. John and Charlotte's scenes together now have a vibrance and intensity they lacked. You can feel their hunger for tenderness, their impatience for joy.

If I write enough hours in the morning, Jordana deigns to let me walk to the village, where I have as many mishaps and commit as many faux pas as I did in Brno. Only the French are much more vocal. Czechs stare; the French huff, argue, and publicly chastise. How am I supposed to know you don't squeeze your own tomatoes here or that you're supposed to jump in the roadside ditch to let a car pass? For a dog or a bicyclist they'll swerve fifty feet out of the way. A pedestrian? Forget it—*des animaux tués par les voitures* (roadkill).

When they're not yelling at you or ignoring you, however, they're very tender and sentimental, a national character I find familiar and endearing, not unlike my mother's.

I vary my route to town, discovering paths once walked by Romans and revolutionaries. Along the way, I often gather fruit, thyme, lavender. While I walk, I let my mind wander back to my childhood without Morticia's dark glasses and I'm rewarded with happy memories. One afternoon, as I stoop to pick up fallen plums, I see the veins on the back of my hands and think of my mother's hands in an old photo I have.

I had always thought my mother's lack of physical affection was because I looked just like my father, who turned out to be a rather less than ideal husband. In this photo, she's a slender, blue-eyed blond around thirty, holding a fat, squawky baby named Claire. You can see the veins in her hands, and that she's smiling. As I see my mother in my hands, I realize for the first time that, far from disliking me because I looked like my dad, whom she still loved then, I was a source of joy for her. I was the first new life in her arms after losing her family in the war.

I've spent so much time blaming and being angry at her for not telling me she loved me for forty years, I didn't see the most obvious thing, something that must have hurt her very much—that *I* waited forty years to tell *her*. Me, an expressive, modern woman, for whom saying I love you should have been no big deal, was mad at a woman who had no blueprint for such things.

Her mother was hardly warm and cuddly. She didn't have the luxury; she was dying of kidney failure while trying to raise four kids. She died when my mother was only twelve, a few years before the rest of her family was taken to the camps. My mother was on her own at thirteen and in hiding by sixteen, when she wasn't doing slave labor. Or passing as a Gentile without false papers, just guts and Aryan-looking beauty.

Whatever else I've learned about her history has taken my sisters and me thirty years of coaxing out. In this regard, survivors fall into two categories, those who never stop talking about the war, and those who never speak. Only a few years ago, out of the blue, my mother mentioned at lunch why she's never been a big fan of Raoul Wallenberg. She used to overhear Wallenberg and Eichmann making deals under the staircase in one of the buildings she was hiding in. "He only saved you if you had money, what are you ordering, Claire?"

My parents refuse to pull me, so there's no way I'm going home. Which means I have 18 months left in this hellhole because I refuse to work this program. I've learned what I'm going to and at this point it's just circus tricks, a game.

Ever since I dropped, Sunny's the only junior staff who doesn't treat me any differently, even though she probably gets reamed by other junior staff for "supporting me in my crap." Roxanne has totally avoided me. I love how in one conversation I've managed to do a one-eighty. Never mind anything else, she talked about sex, OH MY GOD, she's a terrible person.

This drop was the last straw. A favorite expression here is that the definition of insanity is doing the same thing over and over and expecting a different result. Well, I've been working the program for fourteen months and, obviously, I'm still not home.

Being out of control of your own time, of your own life, is the worst sensation. To know the world keeps on turning while I'm locked up makes me so frustrated, so furious, I dig my nails into my skin to keep from screaming at the top of my lungs. I feel like I'm rotting.

The past few months, I've divided my days between working in the kitchen to avoid my family and Miss Kim, and deliberately getting myself sent to worksheets when I accumulate enough points to move up.

I've thought about running, but there's no point. I couldn't go home, they'd just send me back and I don't want to live on the streets anymore. It's like they've destroyed my desire to do one thing without replacing it with another.

Five minutes to the end of group, thank God. Most of the girls who shared today were new and full of shit, all they do is bitch and blame and not actually deal with anything.

"Okay, girls, see you tomorrow," Miss Kim says as we line up.

"Wait!" Sunny cries.

We all turn, puzzled by her outburst. She looks like she's about to either laugh or cry. Then, she takes a deep breath, raises her head high, thrusts out her chest, and announces like Spartacus:

"I . . . AM . . . LESBIAN!"

Not I am gay, not I am A Lesbian, but I Am Lesbian, as in hear me roar. Only Sunny.

Roxanne rolls her eyes. "Tell me something I don't know."

Several girls ditto her, including Miss Kim. Sunny bursts into tears. "Oh, you guys, this is just faaabulous!"

"Time's up, kiddo."

Mike tosses me my coat and reaches to scoop up the pile of candy wrappers I left on his desk.

"I'll get those."

"Oh, I'm not cleaning up your mess, just counting it. Twenty-three, know what that means?"

"What—I'll soon be rich and famous?"

"You ate more than you spoke today."

"You have interesting ways of measuring productivity, Mike."

"You have interesting ways of justifying sitting on your ass."

I shove my arms through my jacket, annoyed.

"So, you're jumping on the bandwagon now, too? We both know you don't need to graduate to succeed. I've been through all the seminars, I've been almost every level there is to be in here, I'm done, I get it, this place is wasting my fucking life!"

"Then go home."

Is he not hearing me? I open my mouth to swear at him, but stop myself. Mike's the last person I need to be getting mad at now. I sit back down in the chair, frustrated.

"I almost cut myself the other day, Mike."

His eyebrows shoot up and his eyes flash surprise and hurt.

"I found a safety pin from when I was on the upper levels. I was in a stall, just pissed about being locked up, it was that same feeling of being out of control I felt whenever I cut myself back home. But it just seemed pointless and stupid. I don't want to hurt myself anymore.

"And that's the thing, Mike, I haven't wanted to do drugs or run away in eons. And everyone thinks I'm in my crap because I won't work the program, but they don't get why."

"Bull! Everyone thinks you're in your crap because you are. You're sabotaging yourself to prove a point. And this situation translated into the outside world scares the hell out of me. There's always a "man," there's always a system, and the sooner you get over it, the quicker you can get what you want. I don't particularly like paying taxes, I could say lock me up, I'm not giving you a dime. But, then I'd be missing my kids' birthdays while Bubba tries to bend me over. And I don't really like that idea.

"You know what you need to do to get what you want and the only thing stopping you is you."

"Hey, you have a minute?"

Roxanne's the last person I expect to hear this from.

"Yeah, one sec."

I grab my toiletries from out of the shower and sit next to her on my bunk. Without a word, she starts brushing my hair like old times.

"Your hair's grown a lot since the last time I did this! Remember how fried it was when you came in?"

"Yeah. I was jealous because you had this thick, shiny hair, but when you—"

"Mia, I'm going to the next PC2."

I turn around and we stare at each other for a minute in silence. PC2 is the final seminar, it means graduation. And just like that, it's like we never fought, like I never dropped, like we never left Morava. We both start apologizing, she for avoiding me, me for resenting her for doing what I wasn't.

"It's crazy," she says. "I've hated being here but I really think some of the best memories of my life came out of it."

"Yeah, remember when Lupe put on "Bohemian Rhapsody" during dinner?"

"And when you and Brooke had that chugging contest at Halloween with cranberry juice and you both puked gallons of pink vomit!"

"And das penis brot!"

The other girls in the cabin look over at us, they have no idea what we're talking about.

"I can't believe you're going home."

She reaches over to hug me and I feel two things: sadness at losing someone like a sister to me and frustration because I should be in her shoes.

A sudden shaking rouses me from a dream. My first groggy thought is that it's an earthquake. Then I hear Chaffin's booming voice, "Wake up! You have five seconds to get in line!" The shaking is fourteen girls jumping out of bunks to line up heel to toe.

"FIVE! Anybody talks and you're all back to Level 1! FOUR!"

We're marched along an icy road, slipping as we try to stay heel to toe. We finally stop at the edge of a huge crater full of mud, big rocks, and junior staff.

"Ladies, welcome to the Gravel Pit!"

We've all heard of this process, but don't know anything about it, just that it's "powerful," which can mean many things here at Spring Creek.

Chaffin starts shouting orders like some sinister ringmaster, and we're the circus animals. Our first performance is to move an enormous pile of rocks from one side of the pit to the other. The icy drizzle is turning to sleet. Our fingers are frozen so we keep dropping the rocks on our toes. Why is he doing this to us?

Junior Staff surrounds us, taunting and antagonizing.

"Come on, Mia!" Max yells, following me. "Your mom's not gonna come rescue you this time, hurry it up!"

We're ordered to freeze where we are and squat, then to walk in this position in a circle ten times. Like ducks! Brooke waddles in front of me, sniffling as she moves pieces of mud-covered hair from her eyes. Chaffin's yelling again, this time to go up the sides of the rocky pit and back down ten times. This is unbelievable! It's two in the morning, I'm frozen, and my knees are killing me from squatting. There's no possible reason for this! Nobody tried to run, no one stole meds or passed notes, no one did anything wrong!

Some girls are crying, others silently fuming for fear of losing points. Brooke's totally given up now and sits crying in a mud puddle at the bottom of the hill.

"Get up, Brooke!" a girl shouts at her. "This is just like the way you let guys shit all over you back home while you just sat there and cried."

Brooke slings a handful of mud in the girl's face before screaming and running up the hill. I follow the orders as long as I can until I feel my knees give. As

I start to fall, I feel a pair of strong arms reach out and lift me to the top where I'm given some water.

Chaffin blows his whistle and circles us up.

"All I said was move the rocks from here to there! I never said you each had to do it on your own! But you were all so busy being in your crap it didn't occur to you to stop and think, you all went right to the same patterns that landed you here! You could have made a line and passed the rocks hand to hand in no time!"

He continues yelling at us collectively, then he starts in on us one by one.

"Mia, do you think your parents knew what the hell was going on when you ran away? Did they know if you were ever coming back? If you were dead or alive?!"

He goes on and on till I get it, really get it. I had no idea what was going on tonight, it came out of nowhere. It seemed mean and pointless, I didn't deserve it, I was hurting, I was scared, I wanted it to end. All the things my parents felt every time I took off. For the first time I really, literally, felt how they did. Only, for them it wasn't over rocks and frozen fingers. It was over their daughter.

Then I think of my mom's miscarriage. The first time she opens up to me, I throw it in her face. I did exactly what she was scared I'd do.

Dear Mom,

I'm so sorry. I've been so selfish about your miscarriage that I understand if you never open up to me again . . . I was unsupportive and hostile. I just felt like you had moved on and left me behind, like the pregnancy was your way of making a fresh start at motherhood . . . I feel like I'm not your little girl anymore. I guess I haven't been for a long time now, it's just hard to admit. I still wish I could be five and grow up differently and have been a better kid . . .

I also realized you have your own life I'm not a part of; you've changed in ways I haven't been able to witness. When I read your letter I felt like you were a stranger . . . It made me feel really empty . . . that's why I've been so desperate and anxious to come home, I felt as though everyone was changing and I was getting left behind . . .

I'm realizing that you had a whole life before me, that you are your own person with her own hopes and fears and dreams, that there are sides of you I have no idea exist. I do want to know that woman . . . the you who isn't a wife or mother. And now I feel like I fucked up. I responded so cruelly and immaturely that you have no reason to let me in.

I am still very selfish in some aspects, I guess I still have some growing up to do. I don't know how to say all I want to, just know that I love you. Mia

29.

I've pulled myself out of my funk. I still refuse to move up levels, but my attitude's better—I just try to think of this as my permanent home. I've made a list of books to read, I've started playing basketball every day, I made a list of art projects. As long as I'm in here, I may as well be productive.

I still go to Unity family twice a week, though I almost don't need to be there anymore. I feel just as comfortable with guys as girls now. I'm about to eat my words.

During group, I tell them that we're suing my father and that I think it will help me get some closure.

I finish and Mr. Greg calls on Jason, a golden-haired guy who'd be considered handsome if his face wasn't covered in zits.

"I've been sort of pissed off since Mia came in the family. Not at her, I mean you, but just agitated. I haven't been around a chick in a long time and it's bringing up a lot of shit for me."

Dittos are murmured. I'm suddenly very self-conscious. Sometimes guys are slow to react. I've been with them for three months and I'm just now bringing up their issues?

"See, back home, I had this girlfriend. We were together like five months."

He stops and looks around the room, then back at his shoelace, which is now twisted in a gigantic knot.

"Well, I sort of raped her."

There's an awkward silence. There's rapists here?

"I raped her!" he repeats, almost frantically. "Me, I'm a rapist! She looked at me like I was a monster."

"How does Mia bring this up for you?" Mr. Greg asks gently.

"Every time she looks at me, I feel like she knows, it's like my old girlfriend looking at me. Just being around her makes me feel like shit."

He continues, beating himself up over and over. The fact that he watched his dad beat his mom growing up comes out, too, and explains the origins for the lack of respect for women.

"I'm just scared shitless I'm gonna end up like my dad. I always got in fights with him to protect my mom, I thought I was different, but then I did something like that!"

Eventually, anger turns to tears. It's strange, but the more he called himself a monster, the less I saw him as one. His actions were selfish and cruel, but seeing how strong his regret is, seeing that what he has to live with is its own torture, makes him painfully human.

After my dad, then Derek, I stopped seeing guys as human. They were like this alien species you could lock in a cage with peanuts and Playboy *and they'd be happy. How a father, or friend, could do the things they did was so illogical it seemed like a mistake. The only way I could understand it was by seeing guys as fundamentally different, by grouping them all together as assholes.*

"I was raped," I interrupt him.

I sit on my hands to keep them from shaking.

"My first reaction when you started talking was anger. I wanted to leave the room, I thought you were deranged and perverted, probably all the things you were scared I'd think. But the more you spoke, the more I felt myself wanting to say, it's okay, you didn't mean to, just because you're so miserable and guilty.

"And it's not okay, it's plain wrong. But you know that now and you need to stop beating yourself up and move on. Have you apologized or communicated with your girlfriend since then?"

He shakes his head. "She probably hopes I'm dead."

I touch his arm to prompt him to make eye contact with me, which he's avoided.

"She probably hopes you're sorry, Jason. When you were talking I found myself getting mad at the guy that raped me because I don't think he regrets it, or even feels like he did anything wrong. Same with my old dad. If he ever apologized, if he even just admitted what he did, it would have meant a lot to me. Not that I necessarily would forgive him, that's not why you apologize, but it would have meant something to me.

"She's probably just as hurt by your taking off and never talking to her again than by the rape itself. Half of what hurts is the violation of trust. For them to acknowledge they're just as horrified as you helps for some reason."

He looks at me and nods his head contritely, a little boy nod that reminds me of something Mike told me last session.

He said that some of his favorite cases are boys, but that they can be much harder to reach. They're like rocks, he said, they seem unemotional, they're hard to move. Most of the time you drop a rock and it just sits there. But every now and again, when you drop one, you look down and see a shining geode at your feet.

"P. BOY."

Tiny blue letters painted on little white ceramic cubes, strung together and tied to his newborn wrist. Nick wasn't always a violent, druggie husband, or a stoned, moody fiancé.

I came across his birth bracelet in a yellowed dossier while searching for documents needed for the lawsuit. He's refused to acknowledge any responsibility, financial or otherwise, for Mia's problems, so we're going to trial. I've spent months gathering statements, canceled checks, receipts, Mia's psychological records. Both Nick and I have been deposed, myself over the phone. He still denies that he ever abused her in the first place, which I expected.

I'm surprisingly relaxed at the prospect of seeing him in court. Focus was like having a demolitions expert detonate the charge of accumulated emotional garbage I'd been schlepping around for years. It gave me some new tools, then kicked my ass out into the world with them, where I could do the hard work of being awake and aware in my own life and conscious of my choices. Or I could keep doing what I've always done. Which would give me more of what I already had. No, thank you.

The stakes are too high, I don't get a do over, this is it. Going through the records of my life and Mia's really drives that home. Twenty years of my life is spread out on my living room floor, which is some mirror.

It's all spread out before me, tufts of brown carpet sticking up between stacks of papers. Mike feels I'm ready to read the packet my mom sent me about my old dad.

"She labeled everything," he says. "I've spread it out for you by type—court documents, various letters, reports. Do you want me to be here when you read them, leave and come back when you're done, leave and not bring it up until you do . . . how do you want to do this?"

"I think I'd like to read them alone. But can you come back when I'm done?"

"How about I go electroshock some people for the next couple hours and then swing back by?"

I smile, that works. I decide to start with the hard facts and reach for the court reports when an envelope marked Do Not Bend *catches my eye. I've never seen a picture of my father. My heart pounds lightly as I slide it out and stare at it for a few minutes. He looks so nice and safe. I study the soft brown eyes and shiny, light hair. He looks like the type of dad any little girl would want; I'm surprised to see he's not the seismic force of evil I'd always envisioned.*

I scan the photo for any resemblance. There's some, but I'm definitely more my mom's child, which is comforting. One by one, I go through all the documents. My mom's written a history of our life and hours pass as I catch up on the Chicago years. Before I know it, Mike's peering through the door.

"Still need more time, kiddo?"

"No, you can come in, I was just finishing up."

I read for a minute more and then we sit in silence for a while. I feel like I should be crying or raging, but I'm calm. After another minute, I look up.

"I'm not really that upset, Mike, is that normal?"

"It's not normal, it's not abnormal, it's yours."

I nod. Mike's comfortable prodding if I'm not talking, but he's silent now. I have to do this one on my own.

"It's weird, like reading about someone else. It's just details, you know. They almost seem irrelevant now. It didn't change how I feel about myself or my old dad. It helped me see those events as . . . just events, not anything that necessarily defines me anymore."

Mike smiles. "And that's a good place to be, Mia. I have to remind kids constantly that no one's touching you now, no one has for years. It's the beliefs you form about yourself based on those events, it's what's going on in your own head that's paralyzing you."

I nod and grab a Tootsie Roll.

"My mom's stuff was hardest. The court reports were tough, but in a physical way. It made me feel squirmy because it's gross, but it didn't screw with my head too much. Reading about her tying me to her waist and sleeping on the beach—that was hard."

I always thought of my mom as fragile, emotionally. But she was rock solid. She was just a few years older than me when all this happened. I couldn't do what she did—the death threats, the not being believed, being a single mom in college, it's amazing, she's amazing. And I'm amazingly lucky.

In going through my family history, I was looking for closure. And I guess it did close the door with my dad to a degree, but what I didn't expect is that it opened an even bigger one with Paul.

I always subconsciously figured that if my first dad abandoned me, Paul could, too. Also, something about knowing another dad of mine was floating around out there was just weird and until I had completely laid him to rest, it was hard for me to fully let Paul in. As hurt as I was, I wasn't ready to let my old dad go.

I wasn't ready to let go of my anger at him, or my secret hope that he would apologize. The hardest thing to let go of though, was the fear. It controlled me for so long, it made me feel so weak and small, it just seemed like it was part of who I was.

But after reading about how drugged up he always was, how dysfunctional his family was, he shrank from a towering, terrifying presence to a cowardly, wretched little man that, poof, I can just blow away.

30.

Nick looks like a dimmed version of himself. He's paler and his voice is thinned, higher, he sounds squeezed. Even his familiar combination of arrogance and menace is watered down. One thing hasn't changed. His eyes are still bloodshot.

He sits across the room from me and his presence doesn't upset or intimidate me anymore, nor does it elicit any hatred or anger. I look at my first husband and feel two things: sadness and pity.

His first tactic in the case was to refuse any responsibility to pay for psychological care related to the abuse, as court ordered, because he never abused Mia in the first place. Sorry, Mr. P, that case has already been tried and the judgments stand.

His next position was that he wasn't obligated to pay for treatment because no one ever informed in all these years that Mia ever had any problems at all related to him.

"Is this your handwriting, Mr. P?" my attorney asked in deposition.

Ooopsie. Claire kept your letter asking her to stop writing to you about Mia's emotional difficulties. I'd kept him very well informed since the divorce, and sent bills for Ella and Colleen, which he never paid. By the time Mia was twelve, well, he'd just heard enough of Mia's "problems and therapy."

Okay, then, he doesn't have to pay because he was never contacted by *professionals*. But the order never stipulated that, Mr. P; your wife's notification wasn't enough?

Claire could be lying. She could have made up all those invoices.

But there are canceled checks, Mr. P, going back years.

It's still a possibility these bills aren't legitimate, he claimed.

Then he argued he shouldn't have to pay because Claire found some-place too costly. He's read about teenagers in state institutions that are doing pretty darn well.

State institutions are for indigent people, Mr. P. Are you saying Mia's indigent?

Well, he doesn't exactly like the word "indigent."

Then, he tried saying he was never notified that Mia had any problems *recently*.

But, Mr. P, we're all here because you received notification six months ago.

But he had no clue in the world that all those dates and names of doc-tors and psychologists and institutions and treatments meant that Mia was getting treated for anything.

You're telling me that you don't know what the phrase "medical and psychological expenses for Mia Fontaine" means, Mr. P?

It's a falsehood, he announced, there is no Mia Fontaine. (She hasn't used his name since the divorce.)

Round and round we go. "The girl's" problems had nothing to do with him. It's not a treatment program, it's just a private school.

I cannot force him to apologize to Mia. Nor can I force him to pay, even if we win the case. Because, as I expected, his financial affidavit shows a man with no assets except a pension fund. And that's untouch-able. Because our government feels that no child, abused, unsupported, or otherwise neglected, should afflict a man's golden years.

But I can ask the court to hold him responsible *and* accountable. Even if all he pays is a dollar a month, that dollar will remind him of his crime every month. A judgment would say that you, Mr. Nicolas P, are accountable for the pain and shame Mia's felt, for the nightmares and self-loathing and fears.

There's a synagogue nearby that I stop in for a moment before meeting old friends for dinner. I pray for Mia to be safe and know happiness, for God to watch over Paul, my mother, all my loved ones, over children everywhere. That last one's always a sticking point. How could God cre-ate a world where children suffer so much?

God doesn't create suffering, Claire, we do. We make the world and then we break it. It occurs to me for the first time that I don't think you pray to change the world, you pray to change yourself. That *you* may change the world.

I remember something I read in Samantha Dunn's moving memoir of her spiritual awakening after her horse nearly severed her leg. She wrote that when God wants your attention, first He throws feathers. After that, He starts throwing bricks.

I obviously missed the feathers, God. But, let me make of these hard clay lessons not a wall but a staircase to climb, to lift me out of blindness, anger, judgment, ego. To see more clearly and deeply, within myself and others, so that I may live what I've repeated in a hundred yoga classes, *Namaste*: the God in me sees the God in you.

And, so, before I leave, I pray for Nick, too, that he may know peace.

I'm picturing my father in court, a man I know nothing of but his own personal demons, and I see a haunted man. The feelings he instilled in me, self-hatred, anxiety, sadness, he must feel these every waking moment. And having lived and felt as he must—and then had the chance to change—I feel sorry for him. Sorry that he was too weak to face himself and change, that his pain was so great it poisoned him and he chose lies instead of me. Sorry that the only legacy he left with me with was one so dark.

And it hurts all the more because I understand it. Because I know how it feels to only be able to operate from the shadowy part of you that feeds off pain, because it's familiar and it makes itself available in such abundance.

Sometimes I wonder if I was attracted to the streets, to those darker places, as a way of getting to know him, of feeling some connection with the man who half put me on this earth. I knew nothing of him but that black hole he left inside of me. There were times I would wake up in so much pain it felt like the world was crying in my ear as I slept. It was a sadness I wasn't equipped to handle and I did it the only way I knew how. Maybe diving in was my way out. Maybe this is what I had to understand to let him go.

I spend the next day driving around the places we lived. I drive by the complex where I rented my first apartment with Mia. Where a policeman sat in my pink velvet chair and forgot the English language.

I walk around the university in a light rain, enveloped by the smell of wet sidewalks, the quality of the light, the heaviness in the air. All at once, the sense of it floods me. Of my life here, of the craziness of being in the system, of him whispering threats in the courthouse elevator; and of the memory of Mia behind me on our bike, giggling as her red helmet bobbed up and down with the bumps, of the hours in the library while she slept in her stroller, of singing in our campus apartment in the dark, of the anticipation on her face at the word "beach."

The sky clears as I drive there, to where we built sandcastles and she made me chase her in the sand, saying catch me, Mudder, catch me! I can see the image of us running along the water's edge and it almost takes my breath away—how young I was! Barely six years older than Mia is now. I see my young face and I feel such tenderness for that girl. She did the best she could with what she knew at the time. And I wonder: what if in looking back no one were to say bad Mommy, bad Claire? What if *I* didn't? What if I forgave myself completely and saw her smile back at me?

I walk until I find the place I slept with Mia on a hot day under an umbrella. With her tied to my waist so she couldn't run away while I slept. In the end, she did run away, when I was asleep in my own life, when I wasn't looking because I didn't want to see. She untied the knot between us and ran as far and fast as she could. Because, I now believe, she knew, she always knew in her heart, that her mudder would catch her, still.

31.

"You don't think we should at least consider it?"

"Come on, Paul. It's the same manipulation and control we saw before."

Mia's doing well, particularly in her progress with Mike. But, in terms of certain behaviors, there's more work to be done. The reasons she gives for not needing to graduate—I'm different, I'm special, I don't need to do what everyone else has to do to succeed—are the same reasons she gave for doing what she did last year.

"That's the way the world works, Paul, you have to jump through hoops to accomplish something—getting a degree, a promotion, getting anything. She'll sabotage herself with this same attitude when she comes home and justify it every step of the way down."

"I'm just afraid she's going to get discouraged, it's been such a long time. Don't you remember being sixteen, Claire?"

"If it's such hell, then why doesn't she do what she needs to do to come home? All twelfth-graders are sick of school, but they finish that last semester, they do whatever's necessary to graduate—why should she be different? I'm not taking the bait this time. I'm not sending the message that all she has to do is dig her heels in and we cave. I also think she's had enough failure; it's about time she create some success. She needs to have a sense of solid accomplishment."

"Mia's right," Cameron tells us on a phone call. "She has gotten all the tools she can get from us. She's just not using them. She's afraid to shine, she's a leader who won't lead. She calls it 'show-up games'—a lot of it is, so is life, that's the point! What she doesn't see is that she's playing her own show-up game—how to show up empty-handed. It's never about the levels, it's about growth. This 'waste of time,' as she calls it, is her biggest mirror, it's her biggest opportunity to grow."

"So, what do we do now? She's not budging, and she knows we aren't either."

"I think Mia's lost her desire because she doesn't see the light at the end of the tunnel. Not because it's too long, she could be out of here in two months tops, but because she's filled the path with obstacles. I want to give her a jump start, something to motivate her."

32.

"You don't know what it's like. I haven't seen Paul in over a year!" Mia complains on our phone call.

We can hear Kim in the background telling Mia to wrap up.

"Don't worry, Mia, you'll be seeing us before you know it," I assure her.

Like in two minutes. We're on the phone in the visitor's trailer at Spring Creek, where we've come for a surprise visit. Cameron felt *we* were the motivation she needed. We hurry outside into the snow and run to the building where Kim told us to wait.

The door opens and I clutch Paul's arm. Mia's looking down as she and Kim walk outside toward us. Kim grins at us. Mia finally looks up and freezes.

"Mommmm!!! Paaaaull!" She runs at us full speed, flies into my arms, and sends me flat on my back, then she jumps up and leaps up into Paul's arms the way she did when she was little.

"My little monkey!" Paul says as he spins her around in the air.

It's all Paul and I can do to muffle smiles as we watch Mia with the menu. We've taken her to a restaurant overlooking the Clark Fork River and her eyes are practically bugging out of her head as she agonizes over what kind of steak to order.

"What?" she says, noticing us. "I haven't had good food or been out in the real world in ages!"

She eats enough for two, with the same relish she did in Prague. The meal, the scenery, catching up on everything back home, is all so enjoyable we don't want to spoil it by broaching the subject of her being stuck.

Kids are forbidden to speak of the seminars in front of anyone who hasn't done them, so as soon as Paul gets up to use the men's room, we talk about Focus.

"I noticed a huge difference in the way you relate to me since you've taken it, Mom."

"I agree, monkey. There's a difference in the way I relate to everyone."

"See, better living through delinquency," she quips. "Was getting cradled the most amazing thing? That was such a high for me."

"I know! When Dolly Parton sang the 'sparrow when she's broken' part, I couldn't stop cry—"

Mia's fork stops in midair. "That was my song, too!"

"You're kidding! How funny they saw us the same way, Mia."

"No it's not, Mom. Mike's been saying we're just alike since the first time he got off the phone with you!"

I get to stay with my parents at their hotel, which means a hot bath! I still have no idea why they've come, I'm not at a level it's allowed, but they're avoiding the subject, so I figure I better wait for them to say something first. I slip into the new PJs they brought me and go outside to where Paul's stargazing. He turns when he sees me.

"You're lucky to look up to this every night."

"You're lucky you don't have to!" We laugh and a he gives me a hug.

"Dad," I suddenly ask, I can't help it, "are you guys taking me home?"

He looks at me carefully for a minute.

"No, sweetie, we're not. I won't lie, I've wanted to, but we agree that it'll be good for you to have a sense of accomplishment. And to know there are some situations you can't manipulate out of."

Paul calling me on manipulating is unexpected. His calling me on anything *is.*

"I know it's hard, Mia."

"You have no idea," I sigh.

"What's the worst part?"

"Missing out on real life. It's not what we do in here that makes it hard, it's what we don't do. Hilary just wrote me saying what she and my old friends have been up to lately. They're all doing such fun things, traveling to Europe, touring colleges, I feel like I'm wasting my life in here."

We're quiet for a minute. When I look up Paul has tears in his eyes.

"I'm sorry, Paul! I didn't mean anything . . . ."

"No, no," he says, "it's good, Mia. It's good to hear you have aspirations now besides drinking and speedballing with creeps. Just hearing you talk like this makes me glad that we're doing what we're doing."

I should have kept my mouth shut! I'm glad he's happy about what I said, but, shit, I want to go home!

We're spending part of the day on the facility and everywhere we walk we draw looks that are curious, excited, and wistful. I've watched other girls flaunt their parents around the facility and now it's my turn.

Our first stop is the Morava boys' cabin. My mom wants to see the boys she looked after and deliver some gifts she brought for them.

"They're going to be so excited to see you, Mom. What'd you get them?" she asks.

"Just some bath stuff they raved to me about when I was in Morava."

The boys are tickled to see me, hugging me and sharing their progress or disappointments. Little Charles hangs on to me, rattling on. David is taller and quieter. A few of them monopolize Paul for man talk.

"I brought you some presents! I remembered how much you guys loved the scented lotions your moms sent you in Morava."

Mia's eyes grow wide as I start pulling out an assortment of body lotions in different scents, cucumber, marine, peach. The boys are fighting over them already.

"I got some for you, too, Mia, don't worry."

This doesn't change her expression.

How do I break this to her?

"Mom, come here," I hiss, trying to get her off to the side.

"One second, honey. Oh, here, Elliot, I remember how much you liked Pearberry."

By now my face is crimson, but she's in her own world, having a ball feeling like the Jewish Santa.

"Mom, do you have any idea what you just did?" I whisper the minute we're out the door.

She looks at me, puzzled.

"You just lubricated half the boy's facility."

"I what?"

"Why do think they're so excited? Cameron banned lotion from the boy's facility months ago because the staff was getting sick of finding cum rags."

"Finding WHAT?" She stops in her tracks.

"The socks that they you-know-what into. They like those lotions because they smell like a girl, so when they . . . you know . . . it reminds them."

I omit the incident that broke the camel's back, a boy throwing a "used" sock in the face of another. And it's not just the boys. We had one girl confront another because her bottom bunk would shake so much she couldn't get to sleep.

She stares at me a minute, her mouth agape.

"Boys wanting a girl's beauty item didn't seem weird?" I ask.

She starts laughing so hard she actually plunks down in the snow. For being so smart, some of the things she does amaze me.

Paul and I hike with Mia on the cliffs overlooking the Clark Fork River. Copper deposits make the wide river a surprising jade color. Mia climbs up the rocky trail ahead of us chattering about the girls in her cabin.

Paul catches up to her and they look out over miles of river and mountains, pointing things out to each other. Sometimes it's hard to imagine they're not biologically related. She's got a gentle, more observant side like his. I watch her lean her head against him and say a little thank you prayer for Paul. There has never been anything "step" about his fathering.

Later on, Mia and Paul toss a football while Chaffin shows me around the school. He and Cameron look like twin surfers, but their personalities differ. Cameron's sensitive, easier on the kids, "a real pushover," Chaffin says affectionately.

"They go to Cameron when they want to be 'special cased.' I'm the rule enforcer."

"I figured as much. Otherwise, Mia wouldn't butt heads with you so much."

He walks me down the main road past the staff trailer to a path leading into the woods. The path drops down toward a huge barn-type building.

"Mia makes things a lot harder than she needs to. She does the same thing with people. She's mistrusting, so she makes people into rocks she has to push up a hill. And I'm the rock she can't push. It's one of the biggest differences I see between you two. If you each had to get a piano in a building, you'd sit down and plan, figure out a way to do it without damaging it. She'd ignore your advice and smash it into pieces to get it in there as quickly as possible."

"Yeah, but one of us would have music and the other would have firewood."

"Mia would make it look like that's what she wanted, or she'd say her way was more exciting. She'll bang her head against a wall before she'll listen to anyone tell her where the door is."

Chaffin opens the door to the big building and a chorus of disapproval greets us from a darkened, stinky room.

"Sorry!" he calls inside before shutting the door. "I forgot it was Level 3 activity today. They're watching *The Wizard of Oz*, they love that movie. It's a perfect metaphor for what the kids go through in here."

"Oh, hey, is this where Duane does the kids' seminars? He said it stunk."

"Hah! Yeah, it gets intense. We have to replace the carpet all the time. You've gotta come staff some kids' seminars, gives you a whole new perspective on your kid."

He starts us back up the trail to the cabins.

"Mia hates to admit it," I tell him, "but she has a lot of respect for you. Not many people stand up to her."

He laughs and shakes his head. "A lot of these kids think I'm the devil, just because I'm willing to stand up to them. For most of them, this program is the first time they've been held accountable for anything. So many parents today are afraid of their own kids. They don't want to be seen as uncool, or, get this, like their own parents. But if you take a look at where kids are at today, our own parents did a much better job! Our society doesn't even teach them that right or wrong is a black-and-white thing anymore, today everything's 'relative.' We're afraid to let kids feel pain or disappointment—they don't even allow scorekeeping at my son's school! But life *has* hurt, it *has* pain, there are winners and losers, rich and poor."

An older staff member walks past us with a glowering boy toward a tiny log cabin.

"Is that the Hobbit?"

"Yeah," he pauses. "See, what kids don't get till there here for a while is that consequences are not about making them wrong or making them suffer. I want them to learn something about themselves. When Mia got dropped the first time, I could have put her in the Hobbit—"

"Are you kidding? It would have been a reward."

"Exactly! Being a loner is her comfort zone, she wouldn't have learned anything. I made her look into someone's eyes for thirty minutes every day for a week."

"Oooh, yeah, she told me she hated that."

"I know! Because it was about connection and love, which she avoids. But you know what? By the end of the week her whole expression changed, it was relaxed and glowing. It was more trusting. I'm sure it was a lot more like the face she had as a child."

I picture Mia's little four-year-old face and feel like smiling and crying at once. He stops before we get to the playing courts where Mia and Paul are chasing each other around, laughing and pitching snowballs. Chaffin points at them.

"See that? That joyful quality, that freedom? That's what we're all about. When kids are little, they believe in their own power so much that they get back on their feet no matter how many times they fall. They're so sure of their own goodness that even in the face of things that are vulgar, disrespectful, or unfair, they're pure and positive. Kids come here closed off and paralyzed with fear. But we can see through all that to that little kid, to the heart of who they are. I want them to remember what they knew about themselves when they were little."

"Hey, how about this one?" I ask.

My parents took me shopping for some things I need and I just spotted a cute beanie.

My mom raises her eyebrows. "It looks like something you would have bought before you came here."

"It is something I might have bought. It's a beanie, Mom, millions of people buy them. I drank milk before the program, too; if I buy that, are you going to assume I also want to shoot heroin?"

I'm overreacting and being bitchy. But, I hate how she reads into every little thing because she's scared I haven't changed.

"I don't respond well to sarcasm, Mia."

"Well, if you weren't so paranoid, I wouldn't be sarcastic."

"*You're being really disrespectful.*"

"*Girls,*" *Paul cuts in.* "*I'm sure you can find one you both agree on.*"

"*That's not the fucking point—*"

"*Mia, stop swearing—*"

A store clerk walks by, asking if we need help with anything. We all stop arguing long enough to smile sweetly and say no thanks. I wonder how much of this she gets, with Spring Creek families being their main livelihood.

"*I haven't seen any other kids here with beanies. Why do you always have to be different?*"

"*Why do you always have to see it that way?*"

"*Why don't we find something we both agree on.*"

"*Because something we agree on means something you want.*"

Paul throws up his hands and walks out.

"*She always assumes it's me trying to be different instead of maybe considering the novel idea that I just want to keep my ears warm!*"

Mike assumes the position, leaning back in his chair, shitkickers on his desk, smiling, amused at the three clueless people before him.

"*So, what I just heard is that Mia's concerned her mom's never going to get over the past, Claire's wanting Mia to be more understanding of why she's having a hard time trusting her, and Paul just wants everyone to get along.*"

Yeah, that about sums it up.

"First of all, I think we both overreacted because we're leaving today and we're all on edge. Second, I'm upset because of all the hats in the store, you chose one that's the epitome of street grunge."

"It's a fucking hat, Mom. Do you even have to control what I put on my head?"

"Look, I don't think it signals heroin on the horizon. It's a visual reminder for me, Mia, can't you get that? And what you wear *is* a statement about who you are, it attracts certain people and repels others. And I asked you to stop swearing, it's trashy."

"Mia, can you see why Mom would be upset?" Paul says gently.

"Oh, I think she can see," I interrupt, irritated.

"Sounds like you're telling me that Mia's as controlling as you are," Mike says.

Bing, Ms. Fontaine, another flashbulb moment.

"She *is* . . . isn't she?" I say slowly as it sinks in. Talk about slow on the draw.

"What, Mia controlling? Hell, yeah!" Mike says.

"And I thought you did things because you couldn't help it, because you were *out* of control. But you knew exactly how I'd react, and how everyone would react to me."

I look at Mia and she shrugs sheepishly in agreement. "But it wasn't just that, Mom; it was also the only way I felt any power in our relationship."

"I don't know about that, you seem to have had plenty."

"Mom, please, you could verbally demolish me. I felt powerless. Trying to get you to understand me, much less stop controlling me, would have been pointless."

"But I was controlling for good reasons, the things I wanted for you were normal things. The things you wanted were *terrible* things. You actually thought the way you wanted to live was a good thing."

"To me, what I wanted made perfect sense! *You* were the one who didn't get it," she says, frustrated. She thinks a moment. "Okay, look—you wanted me to be an apple, just like all the other apples. And it was *good* to be an apple. But, *I* knew I wasn't an apple. I was an orange. It wasn't an opinion, it was a just a fact—they're apples, I'm an orange. What made no sense to me was that you kept trying to applify me, you were trying to do something that was so impossible it was almost funny."

"And Johnny Rotten was no doubt an orange," I say dryly.

"Yes! Do you know how excited I was to find out there were other oranges in the world, people who were as fucked up as I knew I was? It was like the answer to a prayer! All I had to do was find some oranges and go live with them. It's fucked up, I know, but it's how I felt. The drugs just gave me courage to act on it."

She pauses. "You know, Mom," she says, shifting tone, "you were so hung up on the fact that I wasn't 'normal,' well, you're not exactly a Golden Delicious yourself."

Mike's face says he's been waiting for this.

"Do you have any idea how hard you are to live with sometimes?"

She's really animated now, skinny arms waving, eyes flashing, brows going up and down. "You're this insane mix of Morticia and Lucille Ball, half of your ideas are brilliant and half are featherbrained. In second grade I had to go to school reeking of garlic because you read some article about how good garlic pills were for you. During the lice scare, you put so much perfume on my hair, it gave the teacher headaches!"

"You were one of the only kids who didn't get lice."

"Mo-om, I just wanted you to be normal sometimes! Everybody else has cereal for breakfast, you have tomatoes with garlic and olives. And the boobs hanging in the hallway? *You* try explaining angry lesbian art to your friends when you're ten years old!"

"Mary is an acclaimed artist and everyone loves them. Would you prefer china plates from the Franklin Mint?" I turn to Mike. "They're three clear, acrylic busts, you know the kind that display bras in Sears? One is filled with metal toy soldiers and an image of Queen Elizabeth; one with money, dice, and playing cards; and one with blue marbles and little fish. They're provocative and powerful."

Mike looks at Paul, who rolls his eyes my way as if to say, see what I've been telling you, Claire, they're weird. I roll my eyes back at him.

"Look, Mom, I love you to death but sometimes the same things that make me admire you also make me want to shoot you! Can you understand that?"

I can see Paul and Mike expecting me to react, to go on autopilot and "run my old number." Not Mia. We're looking into each other's eyes and she doesn't doubt me for a minute. She knows I hear her now.

"Yes, I do, Mia. I know I have a strong personality and that I wasn't always easy to talk to, and I'm hearing how frustrating it was for you. Maybe it still is."

She smiles at me and grabs my hand and leans against me and we're the same Mommy and Mia we've always been. Before all this.

"I promise I'll be more conscious of it when you come home," I say. "What would that look like to you?"

"Listen more, don't jump to conclusions. Let me make some mistakes."

"I promise. And you must be open to knowing that, given your track record, much will depend on what kind of mistakes you want to make."

"You know what I mean, Mom."

"Mia's trying to be realistic about making normal teenage mistakes," Mike says.

"Normal we can deal with," Paul says. "Normal is good."

I want to say that there's nothing normal about Mia. Mia is extraordinary, she's spectacular. She's Queenie Princess Arosia.

A bridge was crossed with our visit. Mia has come out of the woods and met us at the clearing. The mossy darkness is behind her but only just; it still beckons. It's little things that tell me this. Mia and I both know that a beanie is never just a beanie. Just as a book was never just a book and red cheeks weren't just red cheeks. I can feel this knowledge beneath our held hands and smiles and our great, great love.

Tonight I dream I am in Berlin after the bombing. I am sitting at a dinner table with Mike, Paul, and Mia, surrounded by a neighborhood reduced to smoking rubble. Mia lays her head on the table. She looks sad and I'm afraid she wants to leave us. We lean in and try to encourage her, convince her of something.

Two girls pick their way over the smoldering ruins toward us. They're dressed in filthy tatters and have big metal rings in their noses. When Mia sees them, she sits up and smiles. The girls stop several yards away on a heap of bricks and wait for Mia without saying anything. Mia stands up and kisses me, then Paul.

"I'm sorry, I love you both, but I live with them now." She smiles sadly at us.

Mike tries to stop her, but she hugs him and walks away with the girls. I wake up crying and tell Paul about the dream. It's been over a year since we laid in bed at night crying over Mia. But, it feels the same, like no time passed at all.

33.

To be so completely immersed in a world of broken and healing teens and then come home to Los Angeles, where most teen culture is generated, is a disturbing jolt. It's impossible not to see these teens as miners' canaries. I pass billboards, watch movies, TV, I peruse the newsstand, and it feels like we're all fiddling like Nero while our fifth-graders wear thong underwear and learn the difference between oral, anal, and vaginal sex before afternoon recess.

Don't designers get that "heroin chic" should be a contradiction in terms? That the drug-eyed postcoital teens in those "hip" seventies basement ads are irresistible to teens who live and die by how much they look and act like models? Doesn't Matt Groening find it disingenuous to denounce censorship a few years after apologizing to parents once he had his own kids? Why don't we want to acknowledge that the biggest parent of all is the culture?

Our generation has no problem with censorship when it suits them. We censor a man if he wants to comment on a coworker's chest size. We deny him his right of free speech because we acknowledge the damage it does. But we won't limit the "free speech" that surrounds our kids even though it damages them. Are we really too stupid, or too profit-minded, to see the connection between what they grow up seeing, hearing, and imitating and the fact that they can't build schools like Spring Creek fast enough?

I used to dread feeling like I didn't belong. Before this happened, I would keep my opinions to myself at meetings or dinner parties for fear of being seen as uncool. What's uncool to me now is the greed and arrogance of those who want to create, or defend, teen culture and deny its effects, who think they've come so very far from the era of children being seen as chattel.

Children are still chattel to them—they're just chattel with a disposable income. Not to mention perky breasts and bee-stung lips.

Even my little corner of the world looks different to me now. I can see how unconscious I've been about what I've surrounded Mia with in her own home. She's right, it is severe, there's little color, and those breasts. They may be culturally relevant and provocative, but they're also angry. Abuse of power, greed, male violence, and misogyny are important themes for artists, but perhaps not in Mia's home right now.

Even my refrigerator poetry magnets are a mirror for me. "I am a bitter goddess, Beneath my whispering petals, Lies a crushing tongue." "I want languid red dreams, But my dreaming apparatus is rusty, And so, My dreams are pink." They're the depressed mother's version of cheesy, angst-ridden teenage poetry.

My home reflects a state of mind I'm not in anymore. I want the feeling of our home to be one of happiness. White walls become buttercup, pale olive, sunshine yellow. I hang Mia's pastels, childhood photos of all of us. I want Mia to return to a home as transformed as we are.

My relationship with God has evolved as well. I no longer rail or beg or sass back. I was standing on a bluff over the ocean the other day and suddenly laughed out loud as I realized what an illusion that was, what an impossibility. That would assume a relationship between a "me" and an "Other," a separation. There is no otherness; to be separate from God is to be separate from myself, from life itself. What I've been looking *for*, I'm looking *with*.

Well, I'm back in the saddle, I think, looking around at the seminar room. Two days on junior staff and I'm already staffing Discovery. Cameron and Chaffin offered me back my Level 5 status after my parents left—and this time I took it. I wasted enough time. Plus, I'll get a home visit in time for my seventeenth birthday!

It's my first time on a staffing team and I had no idea how many hours you work preparing and getting coached. If I thought David was intimidating before, he's twice as hard on the staff team. We're about to do the first release process, and he's going over our duties.

"I want the kids to come in to dim lighting and 'Cristofori's Dream,' that's CD 12, song 3." He nods to the people in charge of lights and music. "Small

group leaders, I want you already seated in their circles. It's critical you're on top of your duties or the mood will break. Half of what gets these kids to open up in these processes is trust. The other half is the separation of this atmosphere from their normal lives, where they avoid dealing with things. Your job as a staffer is to help create that environment."

Sonia's one of the kids in my group. When it's her turn to share, she rises slowly and smiles coyly before speaking. She's perfected the art of captivating an audience, knowing exactly when to pause and stare woefully at the ground, when to lower her voice to barely audible, bringing listeners to the edge of their seats.

But I've heard her stories before, and while stripping, being raped, and dealing drugs were no doubt formative experiences, I suspect those she leaves out were more so.

"What about your parents, Sonia?"

"What about them? I don't appreciate you interrupting me when I was sharing about my fucking issues," she snaps.

I remind myself not to react, to remember how easy it is to get defensive when someone's trying to break through your walls.

"I'm not saying what you're sharing isn't important, but I've heard it enough times to say it myself. I also don't think these things are that hard for you to share."

"Yeah, rape's a real easy topic."

How do I explain this without sounding like a bitch?

"I'm not saying it isn't. I just have a feeling that whatever came before it was worse."

She stares at me for a few seconds, a cat deciding whether to play with her prey, or just pounce.

"Okay, if, as you say, I omit what's painful, why wouldn't I just refuse to talk?"

She's playing. The fact that she's speaking almost flirtatiously tells me she's acknowledging I hit a chord. Now that I've won a few points, she's testing me to see how well I know her, which, unfortunately for her, is better than she's about to like.

"Attention," I answer. "You equate it with power and control, you've said yourself that's why you liked stripping. Good work on changing the subject, by the way."

"Thanks," she smiles at me.

"You're so aggravating, Sonia!" I suddenly exclaim. "You're so used to wrapping people around your little finger, you don't even know when someone's try-

ing to help you. I'm not asking you this shit to amuse myself —I'm asking be-cause the reason you're so manipulative is to keep people at arm's length so they won't see how miserable you really are. You act stronger than you feel, and I know because I've been you."

Her amused expression changes to one of wariness. I need to watch my tone.

"Look," I say, more calmly. "We all have our secrets, it's okay to keep some. But, like I said, I know nothing else about you. Tell us about your life, I mean, were you a good student, did you have a happy childhood, anything?"

"Off and on, my childhood was happy, I guess."

"You don't sound very convincing," I say gingerly. I'm afraid to push her too much or she'll clam up, but I also want to get past the bullshit.

"We moved around a lot, but my parents were happily married. I got along with my siblings."

"Who were you closest to?"

"Probably my sister, my mom, too, though."

"What about your dad?"

"What about him?"

She's getting defensive again. I hit another chord. She senses my train of thought and changes her demeanor, flashing a quick smile.

"My dad's almost sixty, so I never related to him much, but we get along fine."

Something's not adding up, nobody from such a "happy" background does what she did. And I get a weird feeling when she mentions her dad.

"Did your dad abuse you?" I ask softly.

I don't know what makes me ask this, maybe it's seeing something of myself in her, her refusal to create intimacy, her need for control. It would explain her running away, the stripping and heroin, she might have been trying to blot her father out.

"Physically, no," she answers. The look in her eyes is a mixture of dread and desire, of wanting to expose him while still fearing it.

"Sexually?"

With that one word something in her dies. Her eyes go vacant, her face blank. Her mouth opens a couple of times, but nothing comes out. After a minute, she nods ever so slightly before dropping her head. It comes out in whispers.

"When I turned thirteen. It went on until I ran away when I was almost fifteen. You know the rest."

As she says this last part, she looks up from the floor at me. I've never seen anything so vulnerable in all my life.

"I've never said that out loud before."

On impulse, I take her hand and squeeze it.

"Me, too, by my dad."

There's a lot more I want to tell her, things that she's probably going to face in the future, patterns I noticed that stem from the abuse, but for now, I'm just glad she acknowledged it happened and that I have the chance to connect with her.

I hear David telling the kids to stack their chairs on the side of the room and find a space on the floor.

"I can't say anything else, but what you're about to do might help," I whisper to her, as I move toward the staff table.

It's time for the towel process. Barf bags are stationed in each corner of the room and we've all memorized the location of the first aid kit. Slight rug burn from an overly enthusiastic hitter is generally the worst that happens. The kids will have their eyes closed, so it's our job to make sure no one's about to bush-whack someone else.

David begins and I listen to the familiar dialogue, the imagining your father's face, calling up the unpleasant memories. When it comes time for them to begin hitting, I brace myself. He starts the count and with three, it's like waking sleeping dragons. It's darkened so all you can see is their silhouettes, like a machine, arms rising and falling, rising and falling. The sheer energy is breathtaking, it's pure emotion, unfiltered.

Whish! A towel whizzes by my face. *"FUCK YOU!!"* a girl to my right screams over and over, hitting the floor with such gusto I stand behind her to be sure she doesn't hit the boy to her left. It goes on for at least fifteen minutes. When it's time for them to rest before beginning to imagine their mom, David whispers to us to go out and soothe the kids however they feel comfortable, rocking them, putting a hand on their back.

I go to Sonia first. She's not crying anymore, just breathing heavily, her hair clinging to the sides of her face, wet from sweat and tears. I kneel beside her and lift her head into my lap, stroking her hair and cradling her lightly. She opens her eyes for a second and stares up at me, smiling softly before shutting them again.

I kiss the top of her head before moving on to the next person, who happens to be Sean. I can make out Jason farther down and I see Zeke's blond curls in the distance. My wall-punching, snow-slinging boys are curled up in the fetal position, rocking themselves and sniffling. And in comforting them and giving them someone to rock with as Sasha did to me, I feel something I haven't felt before.

The last time I felt an emotion so intensely was in this same process, the freeing of a little red demon my father left and I secretly nurtured. But this is entirely different. It's not anger or pain I feel, but love. It surprises me to find I have love, not just insight, inside me in such abundance.

And in letting myself love them, I see for the first time the gift I gave to my mom. And why she fought so hard to keep me.

34.

Cameron's instinct was a good one. Mia's finally becoming the leader everyone knew she could be, but what's new is that she's actually liking it. Not just the doing-ness of leadership, the *being*-ness of it. I can hear it in her voice, even on the phone.

This is possibly the most crucial time in her healing process. Stopping the pain of a troubled child, and the behavior it elicits, is only half the journey. Because it's one thing for them to finally know what they *don't* deserve—to be molested, addicted, or in jail. It's another entirely for them to know what they *do* deserve, for them to fully embrace success, to dream big and achieve, the true mark of self-worth.

This is what I want Mia to get from this last phase. That she's worthy of being looked up to, worthy of the self-respect, confidence, and distinction that comes of great accomplishment, hard earned. And what she's achieved so far is an accomplishment few of even the most stalwart adults could.

This is becoming a familiar scene for us—Mia running into my arms and bowling me over, while Paul stands nearby with tears in his eyes. We're at LAX picking her up for a ten-day home visit. She's been in the program a year and five months and hasn't been home for twenty-one months.

Just how isolated Mia's been, and for how long, becomes apparent on the freeway going home. She's clutching my arm and staring around like a scared bunny, flinching whenever a car goes by. "I forgot about traffic," she whispers to me nervously.

We stop at Whole Foods on the way home. Mia's agog at three whole shelves of cereal; she takes half an hour deciding on Ben and Jerry's, and practically swoons in the produce section.

"Mangos and persimmons and kiwis! All we ever had were oranges, apples, and bananas!"

The program has cost us a small fortune, but she's come home a really cheap date.

It takes being away from home for a long time to be able to actually smell your house. I stand in the doorway, inhaling that delightful mix of clean laundry and simmering pasta sauce until my mom, eager for me to see the house, steers me away.

I wander through each room, soaking up every last detail, familiar and new. The house looks a lot brighter. Gone are the breasts in the hallway and in their place are pastels I did when I was younger. My room is almost empty, but the color! It's the most vibrant shade of pear green.

"We can decorate it together when you come back. I've been saving—"

I stop her mid-sentence with a crushing hug. My parents, my home! I've been gone so long, everything I'm seeing doesn't feel like reality yet. I'm afraid I'll go to bed tonight and wake up staring at the bars of the bunk bed above mine.

If Mia continues to do well, she'll be home in a few months, just in time for the spring semester at Santa Monica College, which we've all agreed will be a good transition to university. We scheduled this home visit to coincide with registration for spring classes, which starts today. She must have changed ten times, finally settling on jeans and a roomy yellow fleece top.

It feels strange seeing her write "Spring Creek Academy, Montana" on the enrollment forms. Stranger still is how clingy she's being. She holds me close in the crush of the registration lines and refuses to hold our place while I go to the ladies' room.

I expected the opposite, especially around people her age. She stares at the students like they're another race. There are thousands of them, speaking a cacophony of languages. Has she grown so used to the mountain quiet, walking heel to toe in silence and knowing every face? Or is she simply disoriented and scared because she has no real experience of herself in this world? The last time she was in the big-city world of teenagers she was almost always high. With each day home, a truer picture emerges of what the possible long-term effects of being gone in a program so long might be.

I watch her among the kids in the packed cafeteria, looking like just another student, and I almost have to pinch myself—Mia's going to college, Mia's home, Mia is *alive*!

"There won't be anywhere near this many students when you go to classes," I whisper to her. "It's only this crowded because everyone's here to register."

"I hope so," she whispers back.

"You'll adapt in no time. Really, Mia, could it possibly be harder than the Gravel Pit?"

I can't believe I'll be going to school here. Alone.

The fleece my friends envied in Montana now seems atrociously earthy. The girls are all in really low hip-huggers or miniskirts. Kids I would have once considered cool now look like deliberately crafted projections of personality rather than their real selves.

My mom sits in the grass and pores over the course catalog.

"Mom, can't we do this in the car?" I whisper, dying to leave.

"If you don't register today, you'll be locked out of the classes you want."

"I can register by phone, I checked. Can we go now?"

I look around the campus and wonder how hard coming home is going to be. As much as I've hated the program, I've loved it, too. People are vulnerable and honest, I've formed deeper friendships there than I ever had before, and there's no temptation in terms of drugs or sex.

In the real world, if I have an issue come up or I'm just having a bad day, I won't have fifteen girls or Mike or Chaffin to talk to me at the drop of a hat. I won't have anyone there to call emergency bathroom therapy sessions.

It almost seems wrong to have you change and mature in an artificial reality. They strip you of any facade, teach you to be totally open with your thoughts and feelings, and then send you into a world where it's impossible to live without a label, where people smile when they're sad.

I used to know how to operate in this world. I had a skin thick enough to withstand the harshness of it, but I feel like I'll be re-entering it virtually naked.

"You can't take just three academics. And you can't hold my arm while I drive."

"So, just drive with your left hand. And I'm taking four classes."

"Sculpture is not a class. You've missed two years of the academics you would have gotten at Hopkins. You're at a disadvantage for admissions when you transfer to begin with."

"Mo-ther, I'm not even home yet and already you've got my next year of school planned. You're taking charge as if I'm incompetent. And why am I at a disadvantage? I plan on getting all A's. It's not like I want to transfer to a shitty school."

"Mia, please don't swear, it sounds trashy."

We drive most of the way home from the school in silence. It feels miserable. She stops me before we get out of the car.

"What are you so scared of, Mommy?"

"What do you mean?"

"It's not about the classes. Control's always about fear, you know that."

She's right, Claire, stop, what you're doing isn't working. My inner Debbie is practically shouting "Get outta' your damn head and be emotionally present for your daughter!"

"I'm afraid you'll get bored."

"What would happen if I got bored?"

"You might decide you don't like college."

"And if that happens?"

"You might cut classes or quit."

"I'll cut to the chase, Mom. If I cut classes, I might flunk and end up working as a janitor for life. Or start partying with the other class-cutters and, voilà, I'm addicted to heroin all because I didn't take enough academics."

"Well, I didn't consciously take it that far, exactly."

"That's worse, Mom. If you go unconscious with letting your fears run you, you'll be exactly where you used to be two years ago and we are going to seriously butt heads."

She's right again. I'm avoiding my feelings by pretending they're not there. But knowing this isn't enough. I have to live what I've learned—right here, right now I have an opportunity to create a stronger relationship with Mia.

"I'm afraid of what you'll do with your spare time. Actually, I'm terrified. So, I want you too busy with school to have any."

"If I'm going to screw up, I'll do it if I'm taking ten classes. You can't control it, only I can. I know I have to earn your trust back little by little, but it would feel nice to know I started out with *some*. You know, you sent me all the way to Morava basically so I could learn to let go of what my old dad did to me. Well, the things *I* did to me are part of my history, too, and *you* have to learn to let go of that."

Mia needn't have worried about coming home to a "program parent." *I'm* the one who should be worried.

Halfway through opening the pastry box with Mia's birthday cake, I realize that I'm doing it again. I'm afraid the top of it got smashed on the ride home. I'm afraid I won't have time to iron the napkins or put on lipstick. I didn't push my cuticles back after my shower, the street's full and her friends won't find parking, why aren't my inner thighs responding to exercise, what if Jordana doesn't find financing, what if Mia comes home and tanks, what do I do with the rest of my life?

And that's just in the space of two minutes.

Guests are coming in ten minutes and I'm having another Bing! Moment: I am completely fear driven, every minute of the day. And not just about negative things. Even in the midst of happiness I am, like right now. How did fear become my driving force?

As stressful as the fiasco at Morava was, I felt so alive there. The crisis forced me to be in the moment, to experience myself firing on all cylinders for the first time since I was in film school with Mia and battling Nick in court. I'm setting out the silver on the buffet and thinking this: if crisis makes me feel so alive, then to have that feeling when there isn't an actual crisis, I create *potential* crises, up in the penthouse suite. *That's* what fear does for me. Keeps the adrenaline going; it makes me feel alive.

I share this with Mia when she comes to help me with last-minute preparations.

"Mom, please, you're a total adrenaline junkie. All drama queens are," she says matter-of-factly, eating cherry tomatoes out of the salad. "Don't tell me you just got that."

"Well, yeah, I did. Stop picking out the tomatoes."

"You're usually the last one to know anything about yourself. I knew you would be Morticia before you even took Focus. So did Sunny when she saw you at Morava."

"No way."

"Come *on*, Mom, everything in our house is black, it's all you wear, all your stories were depressing, it felt like *The Addams Family* here sometimes."

She gives me a kiss as she takes the salad out. "Don't worry, *The Addams Family* was a cool show."

I open the door and we both scream. It's Hilary, but she looks so different! So . . . cool. Her hair is no longer the long frizzy halo I remember but a very chic, short bob which she's gelled into place. A leopard print purse dangles from her shoulder and she looks great in a black miniskirt and top. I have just enough time to give her a hug when my two other friends come running up the driveway.

We do the girly oh-my-God-look-at-you screaming session before moving inside. The conversation starts as small talk, which is funny to be doing with the same girls I used to stay up late with talking about the gross things adults do to each other. A lot's changed since slumber parties when we were fourteen.

I keep making excuses to leave. It's not their fault, they're not trying to leave me out, but I can't relate to anything they're saying—boys, hair products, music.

"Mia, go back out there, you're being rude," my mom whispers.

"But it's so awkward! They keep bringing up movies or songs I've never heard of! It's my birthday and I don't want to feel like an outsider on it. There'll be plenty of time for that once I'm home," I add as I huff back into the room.

I listen to my friends gossip some more. Finally, Jenna asks the *question.*

"So, what's it like in there?"

"Yeah, your mom told us about it, but, to be honest, it sounded kind of weird," Leila whispers.

I try to explain to them how different it is, how open, how real, how much you learn about yourself even though there are months where all I want to do is murder everyone, but I don't think I'm doing much better than my mom did. They say oh and nod politely, but I know how it sounded to me when I first heard it. Leila's right, to an outsider it is weird. I'd need a whole book to explain it.

I think Hilary can tell I'm uncomfortable because she brings up her recent trip to Europe to change the subject, which doesn't much help because then they all start talking about places they've visited, road trips they went on. I'd love to have something of my own to add but somehow I don't think being driven into town in a locked van to see a doctor is much of a road trip. I feel so different from them, on the one hand older and on the other so far behind. It's not a good feeling.

* * *

Paul and I eavesdrop shamelessly from the kitchen. The girls are so excited to see Mia, and I can see that she feels it both as special and as a burden. They're ahead of her socially; Mia's ahead of them psychologically.

We can hear in Mia's voice that she's nervous, trying to fit in and ask the right questions. But when Hilary complains about her parents wanting her to spend New Year's Eve with them in Paris, Mia's nervousness vanishes and she says soberly, "You wouldn't say that if you hadn't seen them for a long time." There's an embarrassed silence, as if Mia's inadvertently chastised them.

At one point the girls are talking about where they're applying to colleges, rattling off Ivy League schools, elite private colleges. Other than Harvard or Yale, Mia's not familiar with most of them. She's been out of the academic world since the tenth grade, though she doesn't want to show it.

"Yeah," Mia chimes in spiritedly, "after a year at Santa Monica, I'm thinking of transferring to Chico State!"

Bam! It's a fist to my chest. We can see her smiling, excited to be part of the discussion—and that she has no idea that it's a school that's the butt of jokes. God bless these girls, because they pretend to be excited with her. Tears well in Paul's eyes, and it's one of those moments when you just die for your child.

How much she's lost is all I can think. All the excitement these girls share, over first dates, senior trip, bright futures, and what to wear to prom. Most of the kids Mia's with at Spring Creek just hope to stay away from drugs, jail, or abusive boyfriends. I'm afraid Mia isn't going to fit in either group.

Here I am again, picturing her future based on my fear that she'll be an outsider. Mia will either find other creative, energetic young people like herself at the college or she won't. The big question for me is this: can I be with her wherever she's at? Can I be a conscious and loving presence even when I don't support her choices? Can I let go of fear and anger and hold in my mind an image of Mia as strong and healthy even when she doesn't hold that for herself? This is the mother Mia will need when she comes home.

One aspect of our relationship has never needed to change, however, and never will. Every night after Paul kisses her goodnight, I still sit beside her and sing lullabies. She still holds my hand and falls asleep smiling.

We've noticed that Mia is more conscious of her femininity. She takes longer to dress and doesn't hide in big clothing. She puts on a bit of mascara and comes out of the bathroom with a new shade of lipstick every day. When I ask what color it is, she replies mysteriously, "It's a blend." I think she likes having something all to herself, something that I can't know.

I find all of this so endearing that when we leave to go to dinner, Mia carefully balancing herself in my heels, in a new dress and blended lipstick, I get that big sigh feeling. Paul smiles and squeezes my hand as we follow her to the car.

She knows it, too, how she's blooming. As she walks a little ahead of us through Century City, she looks at her reflection in a store window and turns back to us, smiling from ear to ear and raising her shoulders up to say, can you believe it, it's really me!

The morning before Mia leaves is the actual day of her birthday. Paul and I are taking her to the beach. We have a tradition of coming to the beach on birthdays to write our wishes in the sand and watch the ocean carry them out to the universe. I can still see her scrawly six-year-old printing our first year here:

nuw frends   dog   no old dad

When we return home the phone rings.

"There's been a verdict in your case this morning, Claire," my attorney says. "I'm conferencing in the judge to read the final judgment to you."

Fourteen years after the fact, on her seventeenth birthday, the court finally held Nick accountable for what he did to Mia. And for more than a dollar a month. The same week of our trial, a precedent was set in another trial where a man with a nice retirement account claimed he was too poor to pay what he was ordered. Giving the family of Ron Goldman access to O.J. Simpson's retirement nest egg.

Our judge cleaned out Nick's pension.

35.

For Hilary—my purple wand. I know it's kinda dumb but I've had it since
I was three . . . it's managed to keep away most of the bad guys.

    For Leila—my pink pig.

This note falls from the pages of one of Mia's books, telling us what to
give to her friends after she ran away. As if she was never coming back.
Two years ago, I went through the things in Mia's room so I could feel
something of her in my arms after she'd left home. Today, I am going
through them because she is coming back. Setting everything out for her
to put into new bookshelves and furniture. And to hold something of
herself in her own arms, to remember.

    It seems severed, her childhood. Another Mia and me in another life-
time. I used to think of it as the magical time *Before*. But, what has till
now been the painful time *After* is becoming a new kind of before. I'm
rushing about, getting my home ready with the same excitement I did
when I was pregnant with her.

    Sometimes, we have to give birth to our children twice.

*I walk down the path I could now follow in my sleep. Mike's little cabin is half-
buried in the snow. As always, there are kids waiting; today, it's three lower-
level girls. It was always hard for me to accept that I was just another client. He's
been such an integral part of my life the past year-and-a-half, it hurts to think
that his life will continue exactly as it did before I came. It sounds childish, but I
always told myself that I was his favorite patient. I'm sure all the kids do.*

    *I walk up his cabin steps, smiling at the girls because they're on silence. I can
see them eyeing my makeup and earrings with envy. I peer in Mike's window.*

He's on a call but he motions for me to come in. I'm sure this makes them jealous, too. I don't tell the girls this is the last time I'll walk through this door. I don't tell them that I'd gladly trade all my makeup and jewelry for more time with Mike, that I envy them as much as they envy me.

Mike's trying to reassure a parent whose child just dropped from Level 5 for cheeking his meds. I grab a handful of Tootsie Rolls and sit down.

"No, this doesn't mean Justin's going to come home and fall back into drugs, it just means he has more work to do with himself than we anticipated. And that's okay."

Mike's always in the middle of a crisis. He finally hangs up, picks up his now cold cup of coffee and exhales.

"Long day?" I ask.

"Long year!"

Mike's everyone's miracle maker, Spring Creek's own Teen Whisperer. I'm suddenly aware of the fine lines around his eyes, the tension in his forehead. Maybe he's always looked this way, maybe because it's our last session I'm allowing myself to see this, that however much he loves his work, it takes a toll.

"Do you ever get sick of hearing about people's problems?"

He looks down a minute, thinking. "No," he responds. "There are times I want earplugs when people don't want to deal, just whine and blame. But those moments when I really connect with a kid, when I witness a breakthrough, honest to God, I wake up every morning excited to come here because of them."

"Yeah, but there's got to be days when you want to kill us, and you don't have anyone to go and bitch at."

"You mean even the go-to guy has to have someplace to go to?" He smiles a second, appreciative and amused. "I talk to my cows."

"Somehow I think you're actually serious."

"Dead serious. When I've had a long day or I'm feeling blue, I just blow through the house, grab some feed, and spill my guts."

"I guess you couldn't get better listeners."

"No, you can't—and they moo in all the right places. One night a while back I needed to blow off some steam, personal difficulties, a bunch of stuff. It was ice cold out, but the stars were just beautiful. I sat up on the bale feeder watching the stars and suddenly about eight of my cows came up. Just stood there with me. But then my bull—and this is a two-thousand-pound, big-ass bull—comes up to me and bends his big old head down before me. I scratched behind his ears,

looked around at what I had. Made me remember all over again that I am one lucky son of a gun."

He smiles at me. "So, how ya' feeling, kid?"

"Good, actually. I'm nervous, but more about little things, like learning how to drive, making friends. It might sound cocky or unrealistic, but I'm not that worried about drugs. I don't have the desire. I'm a different person now, I guess."

"Or you're back to being the same, depending on how you look at it. To tell the truth, I'm not too worried either. I think your biggest struggles will be with your mom, the whole control thing, and with your own mind. You've always been your own worst enemy. And your own best friend. Just make sure you stick with the latter."

It's silent for a minute. He could give me all sorts of last-minute advice, I could list every fear, but we both know there's no way, really, to sum up how we feel.

I jump up and hug him as hard as I can.

"I love ya,' kiddo."

"I love you too, Mike."

I turn and walk out quickly. This is hard enough without saying the actual words good-bye. I know he understands. I think Mike understood me from the first time I saw him.

"How can you be so selfish?" Brooke demands, appalled and confused.

We came to say good-bye to Sonia, who dropped three days after seminar for passing notes to a boy and biting a staff member when confronted. She's been in the Hobbit ever since, alternately screaming, crying, and sleeping. With Discovery, the pendulum swung too far in one direction and now she's swinging back as hard as she can.

She talks about missing heroin, how one night of stripping pays for a week's supply. She taunts the male staff, flirting with them one minute and saying fuck off you disgusting pig the next. Brooke's been trying to instill some last-minute sense in her before going home.

"Me? Selfish?" Sonia smiles coyly.

Brooke is fighting tears, and I have the urge to shake into Sonia the knowledge that she'll only end up killing herself, either quickly in an overdose or more slowly, probably AIDS.

"I'll meet you at the bonfire, Mia," Brooke says, turning and quickly leaving.

I sigh. I understand Brooke's reaction, Sonia's going back to her old lifestyle is selfish, a fuck you to her parents and friends. But, it's more than that.

The first time I ran away I knew it would hurt my parents, but I truly thought they'd get over it. I convinced myself that their being sad for six months (or whatever the standard time is for getting over your child) was worth my happiness and that once they stopped missing me, they'd be happy I found a life that made me happy. Ridiculous, I know.

But, in trying to better understand my mom and build a relationship, I'm beginning to understand the ability of love to both create and destroy. I'd never been in love, never had a child, I'd never loved unselfishly. So I couldn't fathom how someone's love for me could also be their undoing, make life unbearable. I wasn't capable then of understanding the pain I caused, just as Sonia isn't now.

Nor did I grasp the capacity of love's absence to destroy, that my lack of love for myself made my own life unbearable. You take someone whose life experiences have taught them they're worthless, string them out on drugs, and you have one miserable person. How could I have given what I didn't have? It's hard to value another life when you view your own as dispensable, hard to understand how you can have so great an effect on someone else when you don't think you matter.

I want to tell Sonia this, but she's in no frame of mind to hear it.

"Sonia, I was on Level 1 when Roxanne said good-bye to me. I'd been in the program only a month less than her, but she was going home. I know you hate me for finally getting out of here and leaving you behind. But I also know you want to hug me good-bye.

"There's a lot I want to say to you but you've either heard it already or aren't yet ready to. I guess I just want you to remember. I'll never forget how peaceful you looked after that one process and wherever you go after this, I want you to remember that there are people who've seen you happy. That you know how to create that for yourself whenever you choose to. And that I love you."

Sonia stares at me in silence. I lean in to hug her, but she stiffens and turns away.

I walk out of the Hobbit and get about twenty feet away when I hear a pounding. It's Sonia, one hand pressed against the window, the other clenched in a fist pounding it. Tears stream down her face and she stares at me like a caged animal. One that doesn't realize it holds its own key.

* * *

"The girl is trouble, she's garbage." Malka frowns as she scissors off chunks of my hair. My hairdresser has a daughter who's begun hanging out with a troubled girl. She doesn't know about what happened with Mia.

"Her mom's gone, her dad drinks. I know she does drugs, she dresses like a slut."

"Do you think your daughter is doing drugs?" I ask.

"No, that's the thing, she thinks she's gonna help this girl. It's not her responsibility!"

"You're right, it's not. But the girl isn't garbage. She's hurting and scared."

Malka stops cutting a moment, then starts again. I look at my reflection in the mirror and I see a very different woman than the last time I was here. Once your child becomes the "garbage" other parents are afraid of, you never look at any teen, or yourself, the same again. All you see is the child they once were. And their miserable parents.

"She's just lost, Malka. She's lost and let's hope that somehow she finds her way."

I was once Malka. I blamed Talia for "corrupting" Mia, I hated the "garbage" at the Promenade fountain who sold Mia drugs. I couldn't even bring myself to go there until a few months ago, on the last day of the Focus seminar. Lou gave us a challenge: we had to go out on our own and break bread with a stranger. I knew immediately where to go.

There were two smoking, jittery girls at the fountain who looked like they slept on the concrete beside it. They were rail thin, coarse-mouthed. One looked at me with suspicion, the other with delight.

"You mean, just for breakfast, no bibles or lectures?" She grinned and stood quickly, as if I might retract my offer of lunch. She was short, her oily, blonde hair clung to her head, and her clothes and skin had the ground-in grime of being on the street a long time.

She ate very little but she did drink two huge lattes. She poured nearly a cup of sugar into each and seemed glad I didn't say anything. Only an addict eats sugar like that.

She couldn't sit still, picking, scratching, wiping her nose. She avoided my eyes. It was as if she'd forgotten how to look at someone being kind to her. She talked about her boyfriend, about the place they were going to get where she could sleep a whole night through.

"I'll sleep on the floor, as long there's a door I can lock."

"Is there a shelter you can sleep at where you feel safe?"

"Yeah, but they've got a lotta rules. I like my freedom."

Her freedom to use. Shelters don't allow drugs.

"When was the last time you slept at home?"

"Two years ago. It was worse than the street. I used to worry about my little sister, but she's gone now, too. When I have my own place, I'm gonna find her."

She smiled as if she really believed it. She has to. How else does a sixteen-year-old girl who lives like this survive? She stashed the leftovers in her pockets along with two handfuls of sugar packets. I gave her money I knew would go for drugs, but at least she wouldn't have to beg for it, or worse.

I've gone back there several times, but I've never seen her again. I hope she found a place to sleep with a door she could lock.

Mia will be home in a few days and I sign onto the Link to share the news. I haven't spent as much time on it as I used to. Tonight, I'm reading about the challenges of a kid's coming home. Parents often post their home contracts, which I always print out to study for what might work when we create our own.

The last seminar is one parents and teens take together, creating a Value Frame and Home Contract that students take back to fine-tune during their final phase at the school. Issues that come up as the contract goes back and forth usually mirror what went on in the home before, and will when they come home. It has consequences, rewards, and levels linked to family, school, friends. It requires great commitment, because during Level 1, your kid is with you every minute they're not in school. Which often means they go to work with you. Kids usually finish the contract in six months to a year.

The most important vocabulary word David teaches in this seminar is "bummer." It's the word parents learn to use when their teen starts manipulating and whining because you're holding them to the contract, one *they* helped create.

"But Tiffany's parents don't care if she's in by two!"

"Bummer."

"Don't you realize how much easier your own life would be if you let me drive myself to school? You guys are so program, it's fucking ridiculous!"

"Bummer."

"This is so unfair!"

"Bummer."

A highlight of the seminar is the look on the kids' faces when David tells them that turning eighteen is Independence Day . . . For Your *Parents*.

Thus, the Exit Plan. It's for kids eighteen and over who are out of alignment with the contract or the family's values. For most it means they get a few hundred dollars, their bed, desk, and see you for Sunday dinner. It is a loving send-off—we love you but we don't support your actions. For some kids, the real world gets them back on track. They have no idea that that little ringing thing in your home comes with something called a phone bill.

This final seminar is where you can really see the difference between parents who took the seminars and those who didn't. You see the latter's ineffective way of interacting with their kids and you see your old self. You also see the sadness and disappointment on their kids' faces. They know they're going home to deal with parents who are like Level 1 kids, who blame, control, and manipulate; who don't see the countless subtle ways they don't keep their word; parents who think getting honest feedback means being made wrong.

I saw a few of my fellow Focus attendees at our Parent/Child seminar. Two were ballerinas who were so tightly wound, one Focus staffer actually told them to unclench their buttocks. They've become different men, hugging their kids openly, crying without embarrassment when appropriate. Amazing what a pink tutu can do to a man. And it's not until it's pointed out to me that I realize I'm not wearing black.

One grad who was very popular on the Link has just relapsed, which is discouraging to everyone. It started when he began hanging out with his old friends. That and dating are usually the trigger. The parents got that sinking feeling when he got a pierce, then a tattoo—minor things for most teens but red flags for ours. They did a random drug test that came up positive. He's young enough that they stuck him back in Spring Creek. The kids were shaken by his return; he had been a role model and mentor.

I'll be signing off the Link once Mia is home. I'm ready to focus on my own family for a while. I treasure the parents I've come to know and will stay in touch with several. Together, we struggled through a process of self-examination and transformation that will always be one of the biggest blessings in my life. I have learned so much from them about integrity, commitment, courage, and love. About possibility and staying connected to your heart. They will remain in mine always.

One of the most remarkable things I've witnessed in these families is the power of our words, the power of declaration to create reality. We really do speak our lives into being; it's one reason "languaging" is stressed in the program and seminars.

Trish, the mother I called for a Morava referral, left a kids' seminar at Spring Creek with a declaration to make a difference in the lives of children less fortunate than her own. She's opened Starshine Academy in Phoenix, a charter K-12 school that uses the program's principles of accountability, integrity, and self-discovery, along with financial literacy. It's already been selected by the UN to host their international art contest for kids and Thunderbird, The Garvin School of International Management has chosen to promote the school's mission internationally as a means of economic development.

Karin recently finished another seminar on finding purpose and vision, where she made a declaration that resulted in her starting two successful ventures within a year.

"Oh, is Barbara going to have a field day with you, Claire," Karin says of the facilitator. What would have been a warning in the past is now an enticement.

But nothing drives this principle home more than a declaration Mia herself made, when she was only seven. I'd recently gone through some of my old journals and found a page on which Mia had drawn flowers. This was highly unusual as I kept my journals private, it would have been quite out of the ordinary for it to have been left open for her to draw on. The flowers drew my attention to the entry on that page:

> December 1990. I finally had it with the hair battle every morning and vowed to cut her hair. She vowed to run away. I asked her where she'd go, who would take care of her, she was only seven. "Well," she said, "I'm running away when I'm fifteen! And I'm going to write it down so I won't forget it!

"How are you going to hold up when you're being dangled off the edge of a cliff? Are you gonna start crying when you're lost and freezing?"

Gravel Pit sounds like a picnic compared to this. Sunny, Brooke, and I were rounded up an hour ago, along with the rest of the people graduating, for a process known as Trail of Lights. Processes are confidential, so I don't know why Max is telling us about it, other than to scare us to death.

I haven't seen much of Max lately, but he hasn't changed. He's as cocky and aggravating as ever, though I now find it more endearing than annoying.

"There'll be lots of staff around to help because you'll be blindfolded. How will you treat them? Will you depend entirely on them, will you push them away, attack them because you're cold and tired? This process will bring out your weaknesses. If you're lazy, you'll want to give up, if you're stubborn, you'll take on too much by yourself. It's a very physical process, reacting from pride or anger or fear could be dangerous."

We try to look calm, but we're so tense we could shit stone, and Max knows it. Everyone jumps at the sound of a gunning engine. Chaffin walks in, all business, and nods at Max to wrap up.

"By the same token, this process will bring out your strengths. You'll find traits within yourself you underestimated or didn't realize were there. Use them, they're what will carry you through."

Well, that was one hell of a pep talk.

"Okay, kids, let's go!" Chaffin announces.

A blindfold is placed over my eyes and I'm led outside and into a vehicle. After the first few turns I have no clue where we are. I feel the van stop and hear the door open. We're ushered outside and someone takes my hand and we walk a ways on what feels like concrete.

Suddenly, the ground changes to softer footing. We must be in the woods. I automatically lift my free arm out in front of me, I know how dense these woods are. Still holding someone's hand, I walk unsteadily for about thirty minutes.

"Follow the music!" I hear Chaffin's voice call out from far away. What music? Then I hear a light, twinkling sound, like glasses being played or wind chimes. It's too far to tell which direction it comes from and the blowing wind doesn't help.

"Follow it! Come on! Don't lose it, you'll be left behind!" he calls.

I think it's coming from my left. I drop my guide's hand and spin toward the music. Arms outstretched, I move toward it, my hands clutching at the air to make sure I'm not about to hit a tree and moving my feet as fast as I can without falling.

Wait, I lost it! I stay still a moment, straining to hear. There it is again! It's *somewhere directly in front of me. I break into a run, but the ground changes and I trip and fall. I feel the ground to get a sense of the terrain—snow, roots, and rocks. Then I realize the ground I'm patting is practically vertical.*

"Staff . . ." I call out. "Can someone help me?"

From the darkness, someone takes my hand and helps pull me up, then guides me along by placing branches in my hand to pull myself up the slope with, warning me in advance of the root or rock in my path.

It feels like I've been hiking and listening for the music for hours. My fingers and face are numb. When I finally hear voices and feel heat from what can only be a fire, I nearly cry from relief.

"Sit here," someone says to me as they guide me backward.

I feel a log behind me and sit, palms pointed toward the fire in an attempt to thaw them out. I hear Miss Kim's voice. I didn't know she was here!

"What came up for you guys tonight?" she asks. "What held you back, what'd you realize about yourself that can potentially hurt you?"

People start calling out, I get too angry too easily, I give up too easily, I rely on other people too much, I think of everything as a joke.

I hear Sunny call out, "I realized I whine waaay too much. I got really annoyed with myself because I wouldn't shut up!"

If Ruza could hear her now, our little lesbian who cried when the kakao ran out.

"I should have asked for help earlier," I say.

"What's that about for you, Mia?"

I can feel Miss Kim smiling, she already knows the answer. Who knew that warm, little hand in mine was hers?

"Trust. I'd rather hurt myself than trust someone and be let down."

Someone removes my blindfold. On logs around a roaring fire are the same fifteen people I was with back in the cabin, except we all look different. Faces and hands are marked with dirt, small cuts from branches, clothing is ripped and dirty, hair is wet from the snow. Behind us stand staff, the flames casting mysterious shadows on familiar faces. They're all there, Miss Kim, Mr. Greg, Miss Marcy, Cameron, Chaffin.

"At your feet you'll find ten note cards and a pen," Chaffin addresses us. "On them, write the five most important people and five most important values to you."

Eric Clapton's "Tears in Heaven" starts playing in the background.

"At the end of this song you'll burn one card. What do you want to hold onto, what will you give up?"

The song ends. I look down at my cards. My five values are trust, love, happiness, peace, and respect. My five people are my mom, Paul, my cousin Rosie, Bubbie, and myself. I start with my grandma, taking the card with her name on it and casting it into the fire. I threw her away the first time I found out Brian was a skinhead and remained silent.

After each card we throw into the fire, a new song comes on for us to listen to while deciding what card to burn next. When it comes time for that final card, everyone tenses up. People don't want to let go of this one. As we all burn the most important person to us, we shout out who. My mom, my dad, myself, my best friend, they all go up in flames.

I watch my last card's edges catch fire. I want to jump in and grab it out of the flames. It's unbearable to watch the word "Mom" burn until it disintegrates into ashes.

"I won't throw her away, I won't!" Brooke cries.

I look through blurry eyes at Brooke curling herself around the card clenched in her fist. It reads, "My baby," the one she aborted.

"You already did, Brooke," Chaffin proclaims. "You all did! It's so hard for you to burn a little piece of paper but you had no trouble doing it to the real thing back home! What's going to keep you from doing it again?"

We're all silent, staring into the fire.

"Come on, what will keep you from doing it again?" he asks gently. "What did you learn about yourself tonight? What qualities do each of you possess that will keep you strong, help you follow your path?"

A petite girl stands. Something about the short, dark hair and the slight slouch reminds me of Samantha. I think about the night she danced around to Bananarama and send out a silent kiss to her, wherever she is.

"I realized I can endure a lot more than I tell myself I can."

As I think about Chaffin's question, I realize that for once, I didn't argue with myself. Normally, my inner voice is a running angel/devil debate. In the past, my instincts would have been to get angry and impatient. As soon as I got frustrated, I would have quit and called the process stupid. Tonight, my instincts were to be patient, to listen, to ask for help when I needed it. I listened to the voice that said I could do this.

I raise my hand.

"I realized that I trust myself not to be a fuck-up anymore."

Chaffin nods. He holds out his hand to grab a red-hot piece of ash flying from the fire.

"This fire's filled with your friends, your family, your values. It's a ruined pile of everything you threw away. But beneath it all, beneath the ash, beneath yesterday's choices, is a gift that's yours to rediscover."

We listen to him in wonder. Buried treasure?

"Well, don't just sit there, dig!"

In a frenzy, we dig where he points at the edge of the firepit, with anything we can find, sticks, rocks, our shoes.

"I hit something!" a boy's voice yells.

We crowd around him and work together until out of the smoldering embers we clear away a metal chest. We pull open the lid and find labeled packets. I spy the one with my name and snatch it out.

"Before you open these, grab a candle and light it, then take your packet somewhere private to read."

I light mine and find a spot with the fire to my back and the lights of our cabins far, far below me. I recognize my mother's handwriting on the first envelope I pull out.

Dear Mia,

This past year you have tested our strength, our will, our faith in ourselves, but never our love. That was, and always will be, unconditional. It is what has given us courage through the darkest times, it has been our light. You've shown us the light that love can be, and what true courage is. You've always had more of both than you realize. Do you remember the trip we took to Williamsburg when you were eight? I've always loved walking in the woods at night and one night I decided to walk back rather than take the bus with you and Paul. You were terrified and told Paul, "Don't let Mommy go!" The forest was pitch black and I could hear you hollering and begging Paul to go save me. He was angry with me for going and wanted to wait with you by the bus stop, which was brightly lit. So, you did something almost no child would do. Your love for me was greater than your fear, which was HUGE, and you left Paul and ran down the street into the woods to save me from whatever demons you thought were lurking there to get me. You grabbed my hand and said, "I'm here, Mommy! I don't want you to be alone." And so we learned from you, Mia, how much strength and courage love gives us, how it can light our way

through the darkness. And now you must do that for yourself, be your
own beacon.

> With all my love and support, your biggest fan—Mommy

*Through everything, I was still her little monkey, her little girl. I have always
thought of my mother as my hero, and here she is making me feel like one!*

*We return to the fire red-eyed and blissful. The process makes complete sense
now, and it's so powerful in its simple metaphor. We blundered our way
through the darkness to rediscover what was always within us. I think of my
brave little self running into the dark to save my mom, much like she ventured
into the darkness to save me, and feel happier than I think I ever have.*

*Chaffin makes eye contact with each one of us before speaking. The love that
radiates from him is amazing. Here's a man that at one point or another we
spit on, swore at, or punched, commemorating each of us before we leave.*

*"You graduate from here feeling ready to conquer the world. And you are.
But there'll come that inevitable moment where the world conquers you, and it's
then that you'll choose. We live by two things—love and fear. Every choice,
every thought, every action, stems from one of these, and when your time comes,
when you reach out—if you reach out—it's love that will save you. Love will
get you through everything."*

36.

"You know, I ran away once, too, before the war," my mother mentions to me casually. I nearly drop the phone.

"You did? Why? How old were you?" This is so typical, doling her life out piecemeal, dropping a bomb every five years or so.

"I was about eight. My mother wouldn't let me borrow her new shawl, so I got mad and left."

"Just like that, at eight?"

"Oh, if I was mad, off I went. I climbed out the bathroom window at school when the teacher made me stay after."

"You were in detention? What for?"

"Probably because I tried to drown his cat."

"You did what?" No wonder she knew Mia'd get arrested, she knows how the criminal mind works.

"Well, not actually drown it, just give it a little scare; I hated that teacher. Boy, did my moth—see why I don't like telling you anything!" she interrupts herself. "You turn everything into a history lesson! Let me finish my story. So, I left our village and kept walking and it started raining and getting dark and I got scared. I kept going until I saw a little house with a light on. So, I knocked on the door. In those days, I wasn't such a chicken."

"No, just a cat drowner."

"Very funny. Anyway, a little midget answered the door. She was about sixteen, very cute except she was tiny. She said, 'Oh, come in! I'm so happy to see someone!' Her parents were gone and she was scared, too. She was very chatty, poor little thing. So, as we're talking, it turns out that we were cousins. And that's all I'm telling you. How is Mia? It's about time you let her take the bus to the college. You can't control her every move, you know, she's almost a grown woman."

Yes, she is, and apparently, one even more like my mother than I thought—escaping out windows and taking off young. They both even found themselves hiding in plain sight from Nazis in one form or another. My mother was just thirteen when she left home. Her mother had died and she always wanted to see the big city. So, she packed her bag, got on a train, and, in doing so, saved her own life.

I remember the first, and only, time I saw the little girl that climbed out of her village school window. She and I were in the Caesar's Palace shopping mall in Las Vegas, which is eye-popping. I had gotten separated from my mother and caught sight of her from a distance. She was standing in the middle of all the glitz and glamour, gazing around with big eyes, smiling, and at that moment all I could see was a girl from a little village gazing with excitement and wonder at the cosmopolitan city that was Budapest in 1942. I saw past the survivor's face, the skeptic's face, the bitter face. I saw a precious, innocent girl for whom the world was still safe.

I saw my mother as she *really* was, if only she would remember. This is who I want Mia to see, when she sees her mother, who I really am. It is how I have always seen her and always will, my One True Child.

This is how all mothers see their children, as they were when they still believed they were kings and queens with magic powers. They are that precious little being to us no matter how old they are, no matter what they've done or who they've done it with, no matter how much pain they, in their own pain, inflict.

Mia plunged us into a darkness that felt at times as if it would consume us both. But there is darkness in the womb as well; inside a cocoon only blackness is visible. Yet, the creature inside is exactly where it needs to be in order to transform itself. And there's only room for one. I could put Mia into a cocoon called Morava or Spring Creek, but only she could put her broken pieces back together and emerge the winged girl she is. Mia was never really mine all mine, as I had once thought. Mia only ever belonged to herself.

And this, perhaps, has been one of the greatest gifts being Mia's mother has given me. It has returned me to myself as well, allowed me to reclaim my own spirit. I think no mother is prepared for what happens to her when she brings a child into the world. When our bodies open to release our children, what spills out behind them is light. Our children illuminate us.

Mia came home on Valentine's Day, a little over two years after she climbed out her bedroom window. She's been home now several weeks, and it feels like we're in the happily-ever-after part of a fairy tale. Though she's absurdly happy, the transition home has been gradual. She's gone from one world to another and she's still both wondrous and wary. The produce section and a hot bath still delight her and crowds and freeways still unnerve her. She adores traffic jams, "because then everybody has to go really slow."

She still speaks with Mike about once a week and it's obvious that they'll continue to stay in touch. He's been like an angel who appeared in her life when she needed him. An angel in cowboy boots.

Mia's not yet made friends at school, which doesn't seem to bother her. She's happily thrown herself in her studies and is the pride and joy of the French department.

Paul and I had been worried that the drugs made a dent in her IQ, but I had no idea Mia was worried, too. One afternoon as she was editing her paper on the various depictions of "Judith and the Head of Holofernes," she suddenly shouted, "I can't believe I'm thinking these things! It's amazing, my brain! I have a good brain, Mother!"

We normally spend years accumulating experiences before we gain wisdom. Mia's done it in reverse, gaining wisdom before accumulating most of her experiences. She watches Dr. Phil and shakes her head. "He's letting them off way too easy."

There is a vulnerability and honesty between Mia and I now that has transformed our relationship. People often marvel at how open we both are to giving and receiving the kind of feedback and coaching most people pay a professional a lot of money for. Still, the relationship between any mother and daughter is both primal and complex. The same intimacy and intensity that brings such joy to our relationship will also bring the inevitable storms; what we've learned is how to stay connected and communicating through them.

We know how lucky we are, how close we came to losing each other.

Mia takes nothing for granted. And neither do I. And Paul's just happy everyone's getting along.

I came across my old passport photo today, the one taken in Utah before running away. Maybe it's the program, maybe it's being two years older, but I haven't felt the way I looked in that photo for so long it was almost like seeing a stranger. I felt tender seeing how falsely cocky this girl was, how scared.

It's funny how things come full circle. Morava and Spring Creek's philosophy is based primarily on accountability, of being aware of your choices so you don't wake up one morning miserable and wonder how you got there. But, it's ironic that the most powerful lesson I learned, the awareness that you alone create your reality, is one that children instinctively know. It never occurs to them that there isn't anything they can't do or be. And it shouldn't occur to adults either; we've just grown accustomed to living with limitation.

The program takes you back to where those limitations originated, to those first moments you were told, by someone's words or actions, that you weren't good enough, that you're different, stupid, bad. Or invisible. To an abuser, you hardly exist; you're right there while they're doing it, but they don't see you, not really. The very nature of the act erases identity. And it's a double whammy because you're not just punished by being abused but because you were abused—as a society we don't know how to listen or talk about it. So you're told you don't matter twice, first by your perpetrator, then by everyone else.

No one says this louder than our legal system. In many states, all it takes to be a successful pedophile is to rape your own kid instead of the neighbor's. It seems the concept that "all citizens are equal before the law" applies to adults only.

Perhaps that's why abused kids so often act out, to force acknowledgment of their existence. The vast majority of addicts, street kids and people in prison were abused. I don't find that coincidental.

Abuse of any sort forces you to grow up prematurely because you're always aware that you know something about the world, about people, that most kids your age don't. Perhaps at some point, you decide to reverse the clock, to reclaim what was taken and what easier way to do this than drugs, than running away, than escaping reality any way possible?

I often wonder if what I did at fourteen and fifteen was my way of pulling the emergency brake, of bringing impending adulthood to a screeching stop. The "streets," drugs, are as close as teens can get to never-never land, to a life free of both responsibility and supervision. Being high often feels similar to being a kid—spontaneous, happy, energetic, powerful, imaginative.

But drugs are also where the fantasy dissolves because the reality is brutal. Kids prostitute themselves or steal from those they love for a fix, some overdose, some commit suicide, some get murdered. First adults take their innocence, then they take their own to maintain its illusion.

I count my blessings that I was pulled from this cycle and placed in an alternate reality carefully constructed to elicit my best self. A self that has learned to operate from love and faith rather than fear and mistrust, and that no longer wants to run from the world. Now, I want to run toward it, and all the gifts it holds.

I used to hate how much my mother loved me. Every time I did something that hurt her, that angered or disappointed her, there was that unshakable knowledge that she still loved me. How she could love someone who, at the time, I couldn't stand was incomprehensible to me.

But in struggling through the last two years together, I've gone from bafflement and hostility to gratitude and appreciation. My mother taught me something I didn't have to travel anywhere to learn. How to love, and let myself be loved, unconditionally.

Growing up, I wanted a mom like all the other moms. One who cooked casseroles and apple pie, who made a cozy house. I wanted a mother who was soft and cuddly. What I got was a mother who accidentally incinerated my stuffed animals in a misguided attempt to kill dust mites and who gave entire art history lessons every time she dragged my seven-year-old self to a museum. I knew who Susan Sontag and Camille Claudel were before I'd ever heard of Mariah Carey or Julia Roberts. But now that I have the maturity to recognize it, those same traits I was embarrassed by growing up have helped shape me into the young woman I am becoming.

My mother is many things—a writer, a wife, a warrior. But, she was always, first and foremost, a mother. My mother, mine. I didn't find true peace or happiness until I returned to the love that I came from. It gave me life and, ultimately, saved it.

* * *

Jan was right, this journey has been a blessing in disguise, and our lives did change in ways we couldn't possibly have imagined then. How could we know, when this journey began, that the path would lead us not to somewhere new, but back to the beginning? To who we have always been, two little girls who galloped out of the woods together and flew.

epilogue

Mia finished her year at Santa Monica College with a 4.0 average and was accepted into several universities. Suffice it to say, her application essay was unique. She went on to graduate from one of our nation's most prestigious universities in December 2004, with a major in English and a minor in both French and Culture & Politics. While there, she tutored inner city kids in reading and interned at both the Smithsonian Institute and *National Geographic* magazine. She is currently pursuing a career in publishing.

Claire spent a few years assisting other parents as one of the note-takers at the back table in seminars. She returned to France, but only after learning enough French to level the playing field. She lives in Los Angeles and continues to write. She blogs at Clairedujour.com and leads memoir-writing workshops.

Cameron and Chaffin continue to dedicate their lives to reparenting our kids.

Mike is still birthing calves and teenagers.

Sunny is getting her degree in, what else, botany. Roxanne is pursuing her master's in Chinese medicine. Sasha's embarked on a successful career in home furnishing sales and design.

The girls who comprised the composite characters of Brooke, Katrina, Lupe, and Samantha went on to become artists, graduate students, and happily married mothers.

Glenn and Steve Roach returned to the United States and were cleared of all charges. Peter and Zuza were cleared as well and went on to find work in other fields. A year after he shut down Morava, Karel was sentenced to ten years in prison for planting evidence in another case.

Debbie Norum followed Lou and became a facilitator. She has changed the lives of thousands of kids and families for the last four years. John Dean hasn't scowled once since he left Focus. Aging Barbie threw out her bathroom scale, left her corporate career, and is now a successful life coach known as Deana Riley.

Karin Anderson made a few more declarations—to sail around Madagascar, find a husband online, then write a book about telling other women how to do it. She did all three. She reams me regularly.

Although this journey was often dark and difficult, it was also filled with blessings, often with miracles. Countless people—social workers, police officers, teachers, family, friends, strangers—were in the right place at the right time. My brother turning that corner at that moment, a Utah state trooper at that exact stretch of the I-15 that night. All of you played a critical role and we are so very grateful. Without you, this story might have turned out very differently.

WE ARE DEEPLY INDEBTED TO:

Judith Regan for letting us tell our story. Our editor, Cassie Jones, for her brilliance, patience, delightful sense of humor, and for being available for nearly anything, anytime. Tammi Guthrie and Sabrina Faludi for their kind assistance, diligence, and insightful suggestions. Kyran Cassidy, for his meticulous care and wise counsel. Our talented and dedicated publicists, Noelle Murrain and Chase Bodine, and the entire staff at HarperCollins, our heartfelt thanks for all your efforts.

Our agent, Stacey Glick, for her belief in our book and tireless efforts on our behalf. Jane Dystel and Miriam Goderich, for their knowledge and sound judgment.

Our legal crusaders, would that all children had you in their corner. Salome, Julio, and Henry, who helped us to know laughter again. Mia's therapists, "Ella" and "Colleen," for caring so deeply.

Chaffin Pullan, Cameron Pullan, and Glenn Roach, for having the courage to do it differently and for creating a world where kids can return to themselves. Kim Sparks, for your wisdom and generous spirit. "Mr. Greg" and the entire staff at Spring Creek Lodge for your hard work and support. Charlie Denson, for technical wizardry. Dallas Wilder and John Bundy, for your dedication and compassion.

"Zuza" and "Peter," for your devotion and courage; you maintained your dignity and integrity through everything. The Czech staff at the former Morava Academy, in particular, "Dusana" and "Olga."

Mike, Elaine, and Jonathan Broida, for your love, advice, and support.

Cally, wise soul, gentle spirit, storybook Grandma. Richard, for giving Paul a blueprint for being a great father.

Attorney and author Andrew Vachss has been an inspiration. Few have fought more passionately, creatively, and tirelessly for America's children.

PROTECT, our nation's first lobby dedicated solely to fighting child abuse, for their courage and vision. We urge readers to become members (PROTECT.org) and, for the first time in history, give our children—our most precious resource—the same clout in Washington we give whales, guns, and clean air.

Darkness to Light (d2l.org), for their efforts to prevent child sexual abuse. Dr. Kathleen Brooks, for enlightening listeners nationwide with her Internet radio talk show "Darkness to Light: Breaking the Conspiracy of Silence."

Samantha Dunne, Patti Felker, Linda Gornick, Leah Komaiko, Michele Kort, Joan Jaffe, Gina Robbins, for your support and generosity.

Claire would like to thank:

Nancy Marsden and Karin Anderson, because one can never have enough sisters. Jordana Glick-Franzheim, and Cristina Colissimo, for friendship, France, and everything in between. Susan Oldfield and Erin Martin, for your friendship and kindness. Susan Franzheim, a mountain worth climbing.

The inimitable Christine Witebsky, I thank you for my daughter.

Paul Nagel, for being the kind of teacher who changes lives. I'm sure you didn't think being my adviser would become a lifetime job. And Marge Nagel, for your wit and wise words. Your encouragement, care, and keen editing skills have been invaluable. I love you both.

Susan Forward, PhD, for your treasured friendship and for having the courage to write *Betrayal of Innocence: Incest and Its Devastation* before the media would touch the subject. Wendy Forward, for your spark and your smarts. Your mother-daughter relationship has been an inspiration.

David Gilcrease, Duane Smotherman, Lou Dozier, Jan Presley, and all the folks at Resource Realizations, Inc., masters of transformation. Wendy Greene, laser sharp and loving. Link sages Dr. David Stoker and Laura Murphy. All the parents who were part of this journey, in particular Celeste, Judy, Lynn, Nancy K., and Wayne.

Trish Adams, for her commitment to healing the planet, one child at a time.

Barbara Fagan, for empowering me to write the proposal for this book. Your skills are peerless, your heart grand.

My sisters, who were always there for us. My brother, for bringing Mia back to me. My father, who urged me to know that the Light Within is *always* on, even when we feel only darkness. It just took me thirty years to listen. My mother, for her love, her honesty, and her prophetic wisdom.

Mike Linderman, the Teen Whisperer, for your extraordinary gift.

And to Paul, for everything.

Mia would like to thank:

To the man who taught me how to throw like a boy—I couldn't have asked for a better dad. You've loved me as your own from the beginning and given me the priceless knowledge that when I wake up, I have not one, but two parents who love me.

Bubbie, for your quiet understanding of me, your courage, intellect, and humor. Thank you for giving me my mother.

Danielle Rose, for sharing my childhood; I love you and am deeply proud of you.

My aunts and uncles, for your unconditional love and support.

Nancy, because sometimes we need more than one mother. You've been there for me both whenever I asked and when you simply knew.

Karin, you've made enormous sacrifices generously and unhesitatingly and your humor, determination, and strength have always been an inspiration.

To all of my "Aunties," Jordana, Cristina, Susan, Michele, and Miriam, thank you for helping to make my childhood magical.

Abel, for loving me as I am, for supporting me and laughing me through all the rough parts.

My college friends, Alex, Alexandria, David, Sean, Seleba, Simone, Soraya, and Yoomie. It's been incredibly fun growing each other up.

Gerard, for seeing me through a different kind of transformation.

Lauren, for who we were and what we had. Hurting you has always been one of my biggest regrets.

My teachers at Santa Monica College, Dr. Diana Engleman, Dr. Christine Schultz, Dr. Karin Breedlove, Dr. Miguel Aparicio—for your encouragement and support.

Sunny, for being the most faaabulous friend a girl can have.

My Morava girls, for sharing something with me that neither time nor distance can diminish. I love you all.

Mike, for having the patience and insight to see both who I was and who I could become, and for helping me see that in myself. For putting up with all the attitude and defenses, for kicking me out and loving me back in.